Guiding the
Invisible
Hand

Guiding the Invisible Hand

ECONOMIC LIBERALISM AND THE STATE IN LATIN AMERICAN HISTORY

Edited by
JOSEPH L. LOVE
and
NILS JACOBSEN

PRAEGER

New York
Westport, Connecticut
London

Library of Congress Cataloging-in-Publication Data

Guiding the invisible hand : economic liberalism and the state in
   Latin American history / edited by Joseph L. Love and Nils Jacobsen.
      p. cm.
    Bibliography: p.
    Includes index.
    ISBN 0–275–92945–0 (alk. paper)
     1. Latin American—Economic policy. 2. Laissez-faire. I. Love,
  Joseph LeRoy. II. Jacobsen, Nils, 1948– .
  HC125.G816   1988
  338.98—dc19   88–11985

Library of Congress Catalog Card Number: 88–11985
ISBN: 0–275–92945–0

First published in 1988

Praeger Publishers, One Madison Avenue, New York, NY 10010
A division of Greenwood Press, Inc.

Printed in the United States of America

The paper used in this book complies with the Permanent
Paper Standard issued by the National Information Standards
Organization (Z39.48—1984).

10 9 8 7 6 5 4 3 2 1

CONTENTS

PREFACE

Economic liberalism was that corpus of ideology, theory, and policy prescription that sought to free economic activity from all constraints on the market and to promote the international division of labor through the alleged complementarity of parts of the world economy. The doctrine appeared earlier and lasted longer in Latin America than in any other area of the Third World, and was at the center of the strife-ridden passage from "status" to "contract" society. Today its policy prescriptions are far from dead in the continent, and indeed, they have shown vigorous signs of resurgence in recent years. This fact is illustrated by government stimulation of traditional and nontraditional exports, crucial in current struggles to mitigate Latin America's crushing debt burden; by attempts to privatize state-owned enterprises; and, more broadly, by efforts to limit the role of the state in the economy. While the espousal of neoliberal policies in part coincides with worldwide political shifts and in part is forced upon the Latin American nations by international banks, monetary organizations, and Western governments in response to the debt crisis, it also owes much to internal trends in the wake of a rapidly shifting kaleidoscope of economic policies implemented in the region since 1930. Neoliberalism, though currently regnant, is itself under attack for contributing to the debt crisis, though no contrary trends have clearly emerged.

The study of economic liberalism in Latin America is not only timely for reasons having to do with pressing political choices, but also because it addresses questions that recently have moved to the center of historiographical debate. During the last two decades historians of Latin America have increasingly emphasized social and economic structures. Many of those studies were inspired by structuralism, Marxism, or the dependency school, which often outlined social stratification and the functioning of an economy for a given point in time and then drew an abstract or mechanistic picture of the transformation of that structure into a new slice of history, another synchronic structure. But how this transformation was accomplished remained unclear or vague, because explanations concentrated on rather abstract and impersonal forces—for example, "the extension of the capitalist world market," or "the consolidation of the national oligarchy," or "the disintegration of the colonial *sociedad de castas.*" These structural or Marxist approaches, having rendered the invaluable service of bringing to history a central concern for social and economic phenomena, simultaneously tended to throw out human agency, and such an omission also implied that of the political and ideological processes of change.

For Latin America from the late eighteenth to the mid-twentieth century, the study of economic liberalism is crucial for understanding historical processes and, more particularly, the actions specific groups of people, or individuals, took to realize their visions of society. During that long period the theorizing, policy making, and practical notions about the economy, society, and polity can be understood in good measure as the struggle over rejection or acceptance of liberal precepts imported from Europe and, even more, as the struggle over their interpretation and adaptation by diverse interest groups, regional coalitions, and intellectual circles.

Since the 1930s liberalism has been the subject of historiographical as well as political censure. The dependency school of the last decade is but one of several to pronounce the liberal era a failure—or worse, a series of crippling distortions of Latin American economy and society. As the epoch during which policies and doctrines were explicitly aimed at correcting and overcoming those liberal failures has now apparently come to a close, we may assess Latin America's experience with liberalism from a new vantage point. The broad question that concerns the contributors to this volume, then, can be put in the phrase that John Coatsworth has suggested for the Mexican case: "Was liberalism the path from backwardness to underdevelopment?"

Economic liberalism was so central to the economic and social life of Latin America for the century after the wars of independence that it is not surprising to find most historians holding a firm position on the issue: Until recently liberalism has mostly been portrayed either as the doctrine that helped to modernize the region and that facilitated economic progress or, as noted, as the embodiment of neocolonial distortions and impoverishing underdevelopment. The direction in which this volume moves that debate and the question "Where do we go from here?" are skillfully explored in Florencia Mallon's concluding essay.

The reader will easily gather an appreciation for the varieties of liberalism, for its adaptation across a wide spectrum of local conditions, and for its flexibility to serve first as a revolutionary doctrine and then as one of a conservative, outward-oriented economic order—with the necessary tacking and trimming in between, sometimes even articulated by individuals whose careers spanned both phases, such as Domingo Faustino Sarmiento. Had economic liberalism not been so adaptable to changing circumstances and diverse visions, one can well imagine the triumph of a later European ideology—to speculate, let us say, for example, Léon Bourgeois's solidarism—in the two decades before the arrival of corporatism and communism. Nonetheless, distinctly anti- or preliberal strands of social and economic thought (of colonial Hispanic or even pre-Columbian origin) do seem to have had a greater staying power than one might have anticipated. This volume offers insights into the symbiotic relationship between liberalism and its ancient adversaries.

The essays offered here encompass the whole liberal era, from the protoliberal speculations and experiments of the late colonial regime to the Great Depression of our own century and its ideological and practical consequences. Although the opening and closing decades of this long era receive less attention in this book than the middle century after independence, the main contours of liberalism even in the end periods should be evident. The geographical scope of the chapters ranges from continentwide to region-specific within countries, and explicitly treats Mexico, Brazil, Argentina, and Andean nations. The authors demonstrate that liberalism was woven into the fabric of ideological discourse at all levels of economic activity.

The book does not offer a systematic treatment of this immense subject, in the style of a handbook or an exhaustive monograph. The relatively well studied problem of the alienation of the corporate property of the Catholic church and of indigenous communities receives little direct attention here. Some other issues, for example, the uses of liberalism as an ideology of social control and its role in battering down internal barriers to trade, await fuller treatment. The following studies do, however, address a range of salient issues in the current historiographic debate and provide new interpretations, based on a reexamination of contemporary documentation, recent monographs, and, in most cases, archival research.[1] The role of the state, for example, in achieving liberal ends is a central theme of the book. As a rule, Adam Smith's "invisible hand"—the doctrine that pursuit of private interest would benefit the whole community—was tempered by state oversight or direct intervention in the economy. To "bring the state back in," as Theda Skopcol exhorts us, is patently necessary to make sense of the fate of the liberal experiment in Latin America.[2] Argentina provides the exception, and the contrast between its experience and the "statist liberalism" (as Tulio Halperín Donghi calls it) of other Spanish American countries is striking. In general, given the weakness of local bourgeoisies, the problem of whether the state could create them had to be faced. And the issue whether such experiments were successful is still with us.[3]

The chapters in this volume are revised versions of papers presented at a seminar convened at the University of Illinois, Urbana-Champaign, in April 1987. In addition to the authors, participants included Werner Baer, of the University of Illinois at Urbana-Champaign; Jonathan C. Brown, of the Uni versity of Texas at Austin; John K. Chance, of Arizona State University; John H. Coatsworth, of the University of Chicago; Charles A. Hale, of the University of Iowa; and Enrique Mayer, of the University of Illinois at Urbana-Champaign. Their presentations and contributions to debates at the seminar helped signally in identifying and clarifying the issues addressed here.

Financial assistance to hold the seminar, which we gratefully acknowledge, was provided by the Center for Latin American and Caribbean Studies, the Department of History, and International Programs and Studies, all at the University of Illinois. We especially wish to thank Enrique Mayer, director of the Center; Peggy Cook; Thomas Kruggeler; Lisa Offutt; and Pam Patton for their kind assistance.

J.L.L. and N.J.
Urbana, Illinois
November, 1987

NOTES

1. See the bibliography at the end of the book.
2. Skopcol, "Introduction," pp. 1–37.
3. Not to mention the vexing matter of whether to categorize local oligarchies as bourgeoisies or something else.

Guiding the Invisible Hand

1

STRUCTURAL CHANGE AND CONCEPTUAL RESPONSE IN LATIN AMERICA AND ROMANIA, 1860–1950

Joseph L. Love

The relationship between shifts in the world market and ideas on economic development in Latin America contrasted sharply with that in Romania before World War II. In the latter country, market failure, social upheaval, and access to the continuing Russian debate led to new theoretical responses, in both Marxist and non-Marxist discourses. In Latin America, the perceived success of the export-driven economy, combined with institutional factors and the absence or feebleness of certain critical traditions known in Romania, resulted in a prolonged inability to mount a theoretical attack on the "outward-directed development" prescribed by the Ricardian thesis of comparative advantage. Thus in Latin America, with which this essay is principally concerned, both Marxist and non-Marxist challenges to the region's place in the international division of labor were relatively ineffective before the war's end. Industrial development was well underway in some countries before government policy pushed in the same direction, and a theoretical justification of industrialization came last—even if it was the first important Third World contribution to development economics.

This chapter first considers the economic experience of four major countries in the region—Argentina, Brazil, Chile, and Mexico—and then turns to the social situation of Latin American intellectuals and their ideological responses in these and other nations to the shifts wrought within their countries by the international economy. The larger part of the chapter deals with intellectuals and their ideas and includes explicit comparisons with Romania, the Eastern European country with some important similarities to, and instructive differences from,

Latin America; it was also the one whose intellectual traditions had a direct impact on Latin America, through the works of Mihail Manoilescu.

ECONOMIC TRANSFORMATION

In the years from independence down to the Great Depression, Latin America was subject to three Kondratieff waves. The first was unfortunately timed, because the London stockmarket crash occurred in 1825, just as Latin American governments were seeking foreign loans to rebuild their shattered mercantilist economies.[1] States such as Argentina, however, had already contracted loans and were now defaulting. In fact, except for the years 1823–24, Spanish and Portuguese America received very modest amounts of European investment during the whole first half of the nineteenth century. The period 1825–50, when such investment might have occurred, roughly corresponds to the "B" (downswing) phase of the Kondratieff wave. For a variety of reasons, of which the lack of foreign funding was probably second only to political disorder, Latin America experienced little economic growth in those years.[2]

Chile established a stable constitutional regime in 1833 and was widely admired in Spanish America for its stability. Brazil had done so earlier (1824), but only overcame the fissiparous tendencies of its agrarian elites after 1848. Mexico and Argentina would not know stable regimes until the 1860s. Many exports that helped make stable polities possible had their origins in the colonial period, but new ones developed in the middle decades of the nineteenth century in response to Europe's industrial and consumer needs.

Yet it was the last quarter of the century that witnessed a real transformation of the region's export economies. The so-called Second Industrial Revolution, associated with technological change in the production of capital goods and with the application of science to industry, brought unprecedented investment, technological innovations (steamships driven by screw propellers, railroads made of Bessemer steel, refrigeration, barbed-wire fencing), and above all a huge new demand for capital goods inputs (for example, copper, rubber) and consumer goods (sugar, wheat, beef, coffee).

In terms of sheer growth, the region benefited immensely more from the second Kondratieff cycle, peaking in 1870–73, than from the first; in fact, Latin America continued to receive significant amounts of foreign investment through the long depression of 1873–96. The area received its largest investment by decade in the 1880s, partly as a result of a strong expansion of tropical trade.[3] Yet the region was geared into the European economy at the price of consolidation of the latifundium and monocultural dependence on the world market.[4]

The transformation and dynamization of the Latin American economies occurred at different moments in the national histories, depending on the export commodities involved and the relative success of state building. Chile was affected by overseas demand as early as the 1850s (copper exports to Europe, wheat to California), and Argentina and Brazil followed in the 1860s. But the period 1870–90 provided a much more rapid ascent. These countries, plus Mexico, now felt the full impact of the combined effects of the European economic expansion, which, in the Argentine and Brazilian cases, brought in its train unprecedented levels of European immigration.

Argentina is the best exemplar of these processes; it was created as a nation— in the sense of definitively bringing the national territory under a single regime— in the third quarter of the nineteenth century. Formal political unity was achieved in 1859–61, with the accession of Buenos Aires province to the Argentine Federation. But the governance issue was only resolved in the following two decades, with the closing of the Indian frontier in Patagonia, the suppression of the last regional revolt and the creation of a federal district separating the city of Buenos Aires from the province of the same name (1880).

Argentina's economic growth was spectacular. On the average, exports increased 5 percent yearly between 1875 and 1914, both by quantum and by value. From 1.6 million kilos of wool in 1840, Argentina was exporting 211 million kilos per annum by the latter 1890s (peak years). Profiting from the invention of refrigerated shipping, Argentina began to export frozen beef in 1885, sending abroad 328,000 tons in 1914, in which year chilled beef (a higher-grade commodity not produced in 1885) accounted for 41,000 tons. Overseas sales of canned meat in the same interval expanded ten times. Meanwhile wheat exports increased twenty-three times in value from 1880–84 to 1890–94. Transatlantic sales of both wheat and maize rose so rapidly that they had replaced beef as the chief exports by value on the eve of World War I.[5] In the words of Carlos Díaz-Alejandro, "From 1860 to 1930 Argentina grew at a rate that has few parallels in economic history, perhaps comparable only to the performance during the same period of other countries of recent settlement."[6]

Other countries were less completely transformed than was Argentina, with the debatable exception of its small neighbor, Uruguay, but the three others treated here—Brazil, Chile, and Mexico—were all profoundly affected by the forces we associate with the Second Industrial Revolution and the Age of Imperialism. Brazil's gross domestic product, for example, grew at a faster annual rate (2.5 percent) than did those of developed countries between 1920 and 1929.[7]

Land tenure patterns changed in response to international demand, and it is abundantly clear that estate owners were generally responsive to price signals.[8] The first victim of estate owners' land hunger after 1850 was the Catholic church, which controlled as much as a third of the rural real estate in early nineteenth-century Mexico. One historian has remarked in this regard that the greatest service of the state to the landowning class was the forced sale of church property—though this was much more important in Mexico than in the other countries considered here.[9] Yet peasants suffered too. Even in remote Andean villages, peasants began to lose their land as high prices for sheep and alpaca wool brought about a diminution of peasant holdings.[10] Estate owners in Chile began to engross peasant lands in the 1850s and 1860s.[11] In Argentina, the latifundium arose in the nineteenth century, despite an open frontier stretching southward by the 1880s to Patagonia; likewise, the rise of the large plantation in São Paulo, Brazil, was a product of the nineteenth and even the twentieth centuries. In Brazil's census of 1920, only 3 percent of the rural population owned land, and of that group, 10 percent owned three-fourths of the rural property.[12] In Mexico, the hacienda had its origins in the seventeenth century, but the Mexican Revolution of 1910 had as one principal source the vast and unprecedented alienation of community lands by *latifundistas* during the dictatorship of Porfirio Díaz (1876–1911). For Spanish America as a whole, Arnold Bauer remarks that the rural population "probably underwent a greater change [in 1870–1930] than at any previous time . . . except for the conquest."[13]

Labor systems associated with the export boom varied widely, but often involved coercive elements. In the case of Brazil (led by the dynamic province of São Paulo), the coffee economy bid away thousands of slaves from other provinces in the 1860s and 1870s; in the 1880s slavery gave way to European immigrant labor based on a unique mix of wages, free housing, and usufruct. In Argentina, when the Mesopotamian region north of Buenos Aires became one of the world's great wheat granaries, the land was subdivided and leased to Italian tenant farmers. In the Argentine case, and to a lesser extent in southern Brazil, there was a low labor-to-land ratio that resulted in relatively high rural wages. Elsewhere in Brazil the condition of rural labor was considerably worse, and a kind of debt slavery was associated with the rubber boom in the upper half of the Amazon Valley.

In Chile, a rising demand for labor in the wheat farming area of the Central Valley, coupled with expansion of the large estates, led to a worsening of the peasants' lot in tenancy arrangements (*inquilinaje*) and to an increasing proletarianization of the *inquilinos* and other peasants.[14] Mexico had perhaps the largest variety of labor systems by the turn of the century, including illegal but de facto slavery for the Yaqui and Maya Indians, instances of debt servitude, sharecropping, and in some places rural wage labor and tenancy.[15] Vagrancy laws forced the proletarianization of Indians and mestizo peasants in Central America and parts of Mexico. In Argentina such laws were important in remote Tucumán but also on the pampa, where the vanishing gaucho encountered similar legislation.[16]

Thus Latin American rural labor systems became much more highly differentiated as a result of the transformations after 1870. Whereas "parts of Latin America, like Eastern Europe, experienced a sort of second enfeudation with the spread of a capitalist market,"[17] the immigrant-populated wheat regions of Argentina and the coffee regions of Brazil had modern labor and tenancy systems. A great contrast existed between the rural labor systems of Chile and Argentina, despite their common export booms in wheat (though the timing and markets were different) and despite Chile's impressive advances in manufacturing (see below). In Chile, the man-land ratio was considerably higher than in Argentina, the latifundist elite were probably more unified, and land rents were less differentiated. The last-named element was related to the striking differences between the relative independence of southern European immigrants (many of whom were literate) in Argentina and the dependent *inquilinos* in Chile, where deference to the landlords was demanded and rendered. In the view of one student, Chile followed the "Junker route" to agricultural capitalism in the nineteenth century. Chile's rural society, it is argued, was close to *Gutswirtschaft*, while Argentina approximated *Grundherrschaft*, with its widespread rural leasing, despite a relative concentration of rural property ownership.[18]

The nature of the process of production during and after this period is the subject of much controversy today; those who defend a feudal interpretation of the production system usually have in mind manorialism, which, as Marc Bloch pointed out, antedated feudalism and survived its demise.[19] The hacienda of this period is sometimes seen as poised between two worlds—the inner one of dependency and even extraeconomic coercion of the labor force, while the outer one is recognizably capitalistic in its response to world markets.[20] A similar pattern has been observed in Eastern Europe, as we shall see in the Romanian case.

Yet Latin America before 1930, like some regions of Eastern Europe, was not simply an exporter of primary commodities with variegated labor systems. Recent research has established that manufacturing in Chile, Argentina, Mexico, and Brazil was well established before World War I; thus, contrary to received wisdom, the war did not create Latin America industry ex nihilo. Rather, it provided the opportunity for the full use of existing capacity, involving in some plants three shifts a day, as the hulls of North Atlantic suppliers failed to ply Latin American waters over a five-year period. Yet the war may have on balance inhibited industrialization (as opposed to raising industrial output) because of the inability of industrialists to import capital goods during the conflict. Output and capital investment had different rhythms until the late 1930s, when the larger Latin American countries began to produce capital goods in significant quantities for the first time.[21]

Perhaps the most advanced country in terms of the structural transformation of its economy in the prewar era was Chile, where José Gabriel Palma has shown that industrial development was extensive between 1875 and 1900, despite a literature that emphasizes lost opportunities for modernization under the regime of a traditional landed oligarchy. True enough, these were the halcyon years of "outward-directed growth," based on Chile's fabulous nitrate fields, many of them wrested from Bolivia and Peru in the War of the Pacific (1879–83). In the succeeding years the elite introduced a fiscal system that was heavily dependent on export taxes, and government services were tailored to the needs of *latifundistas* and mineral exporters. Nonetheless, Palma found that import substitution industrialization—prescribed by the U.N. Economic Commission for Latin America after 1949—was already well underway in Chile by 1914 and was reaching its limits by 1934, much earlier than in other countries. He also found a correlation between export growth and the growth of manufacturing before World War I, but not later. Palma for Chile, like Warren Dean for Brazil, argues that export expansion was a precondition for industrialization.[22] Later than Romania by five years, Chile was nonetheless the first Latin American country in which the state extended credits to manufacturers, beginning in 1928. But more meaningful aid only came after 1939 (see below).

The First World War caused serious disruptions in the Latin American export economy, and grave problems followed the war in certain commodity markets, but the export boom continued in phase with the third Kondratieff wave. A major structural shift in the postwar era was the growing displacement of Britain by the United States as chief lender and investor. For instance, the United States sent three and one-half times as many exports (by value) to Mexico as the British did in 1913, and the ratio was ten to one by 1927. Great Britain led the United States in the other three countries considered here in 1913, but by 1927 the latter had dislodged Britain as the leading trading partner in Chile and Brazil, and in Argentina, Britain clung to its lead by a single percentage point.[23]

Though Great Britain's overall capital investments in the region were still larger in 1929, the United States had far outstripped Britain in its postwar lending, both direct and indirect. Unfortunately for Latin America, U.S. policies were not as geared to maintaining the international trading system as Britain's had been. The United States remained highly protectionist, while North American banks "pressed loans on unwary governments" in Latin America.[24] The problem was insufficient means for repayment, since the United States raised barriers to trade that affected third countries in the trading system as well as the countries of this hemisphere. Argentina especially found itself in straits, since it sought both U.S. investment and industrial goods (notably motor vehicles) but could not sell to the United States, partly because of lack of complementarity between the two countries' rural economies.

If the displacement of Britain was one structural change after the war, another was increasing commodity export instability. This problem was no less than a disaster in the case of rubber, which briefly rivaled coffee as Brazil's leading foreign-exchange earner in the prewar era. Brazil not only lost its place as the world's leading supplier, but ceased even to be a *consequential* supplier between 1912 and 1920, when Southeast Asian plantations went into high gear.[25] Another problem—technological innovation—beset the exporters of Chilean nitrates, as a result of ingenuity in the German chemical industry during World War I. Violent price fluctuations on world markets also afflicted Argentine wheat and wool.

The diffusion of new agricultural technology in the 1920s—most dramatically the tractor—greatly increased the productive capacity of wheat farms in Argentina and elsewhere in the world and thus helped bring down prices. Another agricultural problem was self-inflicted: Brazil's coffee stockpiling—the valorization program—was promoting ever-greater production of that commodity, whose prices would collapse in 1929, a few weeks *before* Black Thursday on the New York Stock Exchange.

On top of these problems came deteriorating terms of trade after the war. On the average the terms of trade for all primary products in 1926–29 had significantly dropped below their levels in 1913.[26]

The impact of the Great Depression was severe. Already in 1929, unsold and unsalable coffee stocks in São Paulo were valued at 10 percent of Brazil's gross domestic product, and the situation would worsen over the next four years, as new trees began to produce.[27] In Argentina, the dollar value of exports in 1933 was one-third the 1929 figure, and Chile's export performance, if anything, was worse. The depression unseated governments in all three countries. Mexico was spared political upheaval, perhaps because of the growing consolidation of the revolutionary regime after the founding of the official party in 1929.

The 1930s was a period of significant structural change for the larger Latin American economies: convertibility and the gold standard were abandoned early in the depression in Argentina, Brazil, Chile, and Mexico. In those countries, the rise in prices of importables, because of a fall in the terms of trade and exchange devaluation, encouraged the substitution of domestic manufactures for imported goods, as did expansionary fiscal and monetary policies.[28]

Argentina, Brazil, and Chile made rapid advance in industrial production during the early depression years, so that by 1935 a North American economist would hazard, "There is probably no major section of the world in which there is greater industrial activity relative to predepression years than in temperate South America" (i.e., Argentina, southern Brazil, and Chile).[29] When war came in 1939, manufactures in international trade became scarce again, permitting industrial advances to the extent that capital goods, fuel, and raw materials were available.

THE *PENSADOR* TRADITION

The preceding survey of economic transformation, however brief, provides a foundation for understanding the ways in which Latin American social thinkers and statesmen of the era conceptualized their nations' place in the order of things. The perceived success of the open economy strategy, beginning in the midnineteenth century with rising levels of exports in Chile, Argentina, and Brazil, it will be argued, shaped the terms of ideological discourse even into the 1940s. However, before proceeding to the ideologies that attracted Latin Americans and that were in turn adapted by them to local conditions, it is necessary to consider the sociological situation of the intellectuals who were the bearers of such ideas and values.

The intellectual traditions of Latin America revolved around the *pensador* (thinker), a man who prided himself on his broad culture and who eschewed specialization: he often wrote as readily about contemporary sociology and politics as he did about literature, and his studies frequently crossed disciplinary lines. The *pensador*'s vehicle was the essay, a literary form that in Latin America retains the prestige that it has all but lost in the English-speaking world.[30] The style perhaps was appropriate to highly stratified, preindustrial societies; in any case the *pensador* often wrote without reference to monographic studies. His judgments tended to be definitive; his treatment, historical. Before 1900, and even later, few Latin American essayists were academics, and fewer still had studied in Europe. If they had, they almost never took research degrees.

One feature distinguishing Latin American society from that of Eastern Europe in this period is a relative lack of an intelligentsia, in the classical sense of an underemployed intellectual community radically at odds with prevailing power structures. This fact owes chiefly to the limited number of university students, compared with employment opportunities in law, journalism, and civil service. Furthermore, intellectuals frequently held important political posts. In any event, seldom could the *pensador* be Antonio Gramsci's "organic intellectual," a spokesman for well-defined class interests, since social classes were still relatively inchoate.

A sociological reason for the persistence of the *pensador* tradition is that academic institutions were seldom oriented toward research. In addition, Latin America suffered from a relative dearth of social research institutions as such. There was nothing comparable to Dimitri Gusti's Romanian Institute of Social Science, founded in 1918. Romania also boasted an Economics Institute (established in 1921) and a Business Cycles Institute, modeled in 1933 on those at Harvard and the University of Berlin. The only analogous institute anywhere in Latin America in the 1920s and 1930s was the research division of the Argentine Central Bank, which Raúl Prebisch had organized in 1928.

In Charles Hale's survey of Latin American social and political thought over the half century ending in 1930, only one intellectual of some ninety treated, the Mexican Manuel Gamio, held a Ph.D.[31] Such a fact might serve as a proxy for the weakness of a research tradition, as opposed to the abstract theorizing and indifference to the systematic collection of data so characteristic of the *pensador* style. There was, for example, nothing to compare with the Romanian community studies of the 1920s and 1930s carried out by Gusti and his students, based on the theories and methods of Frédéric Le Play and A. V. Chayanov. The partial exception was provided by Mexico, where Gamio and other anthropologists had begun to map out local village ethnography.

THE ADAPTATION OF LIBERALISM

The *pensadores* at issue lived in an age of triumphant liberalism, with manifold subthemes and arabesques. In Latin America, as elsewhere, liberalism implied the diffusion of materialism, rationalism, and pluralism (the latter used by reformist states against the church). Liberalism gained strength in the middle decades of the nineteenth century, as economic advances improved the climate for the reception of liberal economic ideas.[32] Following the European lead, Latin American liberalism changed over the course of the century, and in the early years of independence its paladins focused on opening international trade, secularization, and securing equality before the law in a society still dominated by estates and corporations. Late in the century, when liberal politicians reigned supreme, there was much less concern with individual rights: "English liberties" were frequently seen as less important than economic growth and the orderly development of the social organism. Thus liberalism, in Hale's words, was transformed over the course of the nineteenth century from an "ideology in conflict with the inherited colonial order" into a "unifying [establishment] myth."[33] It also offered a rationale for social control within the new order.

In general, Latin American statesmen and intellectuals welcomed the economic transformation of their region accompanying the Second Industrial Revolution and the expansion of European trade. Thus there was little debate about the desirability of integration into the dynamic North Atlantic center as an agricultural and mineral periphery, in contrast to the Eastern European response by the 1880s. Latin Americans embraced the doctrine of comparative advantage, though few were aware of David Ricardo's formal demonstration that a comparative (relative) advantage in the production of two goods in two countries implied mutual benefit to both trading partners. The vast majority of Latin American "economists" simply argued from the perception of absolute advantage, that is, they saw world commerce as a mutually beneficial process among countries with highly differentiated natural and social endowments.

But the penetration of European trade and investment was, for the Latin American statesmen of the latter half of the nineteenth century, far more than an acceleration of economic growth; they viewed it as part of a transformation from "barbarism" to "civilization," as Domingo Faustino Sarmiento, who would later become president of Argentina, put it in his *Facundo* of 1845.[34] Here there seems to be a parallel with the Balkan countries of the same era, as the Turkish Empire receded. Indeed, some Spanish American statesmen and intellectuals, especially in the second quarter of the century, regarded the culture of the intransigent and irreconcilable Spanish metropolis, where the Inquisition survived until 1820, as the most important cause of Latin America's backwardness. For Francisco Bilbao, a leading figure in Chile's Generation of 1842, "Spain [was] the Middle Ages."

Consequently, Latin American intellectuals tended to view the myriad changes associated with capitalist relations of production and exchange after 1870 as a benign, progressive, and civilizing process. Liberal intellectuals toward the end of the century were in a celebratory mood, eager to create heroic myths, as did the historian and statesman Bartolomé Mitre (president of Argentina, 1862–68). Surviving feudal or archaic elements in local societies were for these men simply the residues of the colonial regime, doomed by the linear march of progress associated with capitalist development. Apart from the pamphlet literature of radical sectors of the labor movement (largely anarchist), there was no "teratological perception" of capitalist transformation, such as Constantin Dobrogeanu-Gherea provided in his analysis of Romanian society in 1910 (see below). All the same, compulsory labor systems and the concentration of land ownership in Mexico were underlying causes of the revolution, which began in the year

Gherea published; to a lesser extent such conditions obtained in some areas of the other three countries under consideration. Where injustice was denounced by bourgeois intellectuals, as in *Los grandes problemas nacionales* (1909), by the Mexican Andrés Molina Enríquez, the fault lay not in the system, but in its local distortions.[35]

Until the twentieth century, liberalism in Latin America, unlike Romania, was strikingly cosmopolitan, as perhaps befitted the open economies of the region.[36] Nationalism began to replace cosmopolitanism gradually—in part because of resentment against the flood of immigrants in Argentina, in part because of the disillusion with cosmopolitanism that Latin Americans experienced in August 1914, and in part because of the disarticulation of the international economy after 1929.

The years of conflict for liberalism to which Hale refers began with independence and continued into the 1870s or even to 1890.[37] Political struggles in the first fifty years of independence, the nonage of liberalism, revolved around human rights (including the emancipation of slaves and Indians); the position of the church in society, economy, and polity; the place of foreign trade; and the organization of the state (centralism versus federalism, taxing powers). After long struggles, these issues were generally resolved in favor of an expansion of the numbers of participating citizens, secularization, an open economy, and a powerful central government, even though three of the four countries considered here finally adopted federal constitutions. The triumph of secularization in some countries had required a powerful state,[38] and partly for that reason liberals in most countries accepted a degree of interventionism alien to classical liberal precepts.

It is remarkable, perhaps, how poorly articulated at an intellectual level the opposition to liberalism was, until the 1920s and 1930s, when corporatism and Marxism became widely diffused. In the nineteenth century, opposition to liberalism tended to be organized around the privileges of the colonial regime, and prelates articulated the dissatisfaction with republicanism, freemasonry, and other modern heresies, ticking off the list of Pius IX's *Syllabus of Errors* (1864). Of course there was nothing approximating a successful bourgeois revolution, to which conservatives might have reacted more inventively. Almost all the leading intellectuals were liberals: only three early statesmen—Lucas Alamán in Mexico, Mariano Egaña in Chile, and José Bonifácio Andrada e Silva in Brazil—perhaps bore some resemblance to Edmund Burke, and there were no systematizing reactionaries in the mold of Joseph de Maistre. Nor was there anything akin to Slavophilism's mystical association of antirationalism and nationalism, partly because Latin American conservatives were not reacting to Hegelianism in the first fifty years after independence. In the early years of nationhood, since conservatism was associated with maintaining or restoring privileges of the old regime, its appeal was limited. For some, however, conservatism was also an outlook attaching fundamental importance to "the existence of a perennial order . . . [for which] change always represents an evil: decadence, perversion, chaos,'' in José Luis Romero's words.[39] Not only was conservatism closely associated with the church, a supranational entity, but in the worst case, Maximilian's Mexico, the church and the Conservative party sold out to the foreign invader, Napoleon III. In most countries, conservatism in the latter years of the century was to be most effectively defended within the various currents of liberalism, especially after liberals consolidated their control of the state.

Liberalism came to Latin America in a variety of forms, beginning with Benthamism in the 1820s and continuing through social Darwinism in the 1890s. A related but distinct ideology was Comtian positivism, influential in all four countries. French philosophy had conquered Latin America with the triumph of eclecticism over a dying scholasticism in the early years of independence, and Comte's all-embracing system attracted intellectuals trained in scholasticism more than did British liberalism. Comte's vision of civilization had the historical process unfolding in three great stages, epistemologically determined—the theological, the metaphysical, and the positive. In the first stage, causation was assigned to supernatural forces; in the second, to abstract forces; and in the third—on the edge of which humanity stood, he believed, in the midnineteenth century—to discoverable scientific laws.

Comte called for the tempering of capitalism by social morality and asserted the need for the state to incorporate the urban proletariat into modern society with social welfare policies. He also supported universal elementary education and the separation of church and state. Naturally, not all of Comte's specific prescriptions had universal appeal, especially those produced after his authoritarian turn in the wake of 1848. The Religion of Humanity of his final years, a grotesque secularization of Catholicism, attracted only a small but vocal sect, especially in Chile and Brazil.

Positivism was attractive to modernizing conservatives, who wanted the benefits of material progress without sacrificing social hierarchy. Comte's philosophy seemed to offer a blueprint for development without social mobilization; the proletariat, as noted, was to be the special concern of a paternalist state. In addition, we may surmise that Comte's emphasis on the *family* as the fundamental unit of social organization—as opposed to the individual, in British liberalism—made his system especially seductive. (Corporatism would make the same assertion in our own century.)

In the 1870s Comtian positivism was closely linked to nation building, and it became the official philosophy of new national normal schools in Chile, Mexico, and Argentina; it played the same role at the national military academy in Brazil. Comte's phrase ''Order and Progress'' seemed to be in tune with new consolidating regimes, and it became the official motto of the new Brazilian Republic.

Yet Herbert Spencer's social Darwinism probably had a wider following by the 1890s; Spencer seemed to represent the interests of a nascent but increasingly self-confident bourgeoisie, at least in Argentina.[40] By the last two decades of the century, Spencer also provided a convenient rationalization for dictatorships, which now had a new staying power, partly because of new revenues resulting from economic growth. Such was the case with the government of Rafael Nuñez, the dictator of Colombia in the 1880s, who used social Darwinism to justify his "scientific peace." In Mexico, where the writings of Comte after 1848 could already be construed as justifying dictatorship, social Darwinism was likewise pressed into service for the Porfiriato. For the *científicos*, who made their debut to justify the fourth term of the dictator Porfirio Díaz in 1892, material progress was a necessary precondition for political liberty. The only liberty for which Mexico was then ready, they averred, was freedom of commerce, which not incidentally legitimated the foreign capital pouring into the country. Díaz's regime was a "social dictatorship," they argued, promoting the interests of the bourgeoisie and those of the nation at large.[41]

Comte and Spencer were simply the most prominent of the French and British thinkers whose ideas were discovered and adapted in Latin America. Of course, as a "fragment" society of Europe,[42] Latin America only imported portions of the European intellectual tradition, and it adapted liberal ideologies to meet a variety of desiderata, such as social control, as the *científicos* perhaps illustrated most starkly. By the 1890s liberalism was an "officialist" ideology, probably accepted most widely in those countries where the export economies performed best.

A ROMANIAN PERSPECTIVE

To better understand the peculiar features of Latin American social thought in succeeding decades—necessarily a truncated and adapted version of European models—a brief excursus on contemporaneous Eastern Europe may be enlightening, on the premise that movements not present in Latin America may reveal something about the history of those that were. One of the traditions so influential in the former region having no reverberations in Latin America was nineteenth-century populism; to most of us this was Russian populism, although the ideology had its roots in reactions to the social processes of the industrial revolution in Western and Central Europe.[43]

Populism was an ideology starting from a vision of local society as backward, even archaic, relative to the developed West. Industrial capitalism, an irresistible force emanating from abroad, was viewed as transforming local agriculture-based societies in undesirable ways: it ruined, then proletarianized, the peasant and artisan classes, partly through a process of unequal exchange between town and hinterland, and between industrial and agricultural societies at the international level. Moreover, capitalism at the local level was seen as degenerate and essentially destined to fail against the superior competition of the West. In its mature phase, populism was an ideology of noncapitalist modernization, akin to socialism.

The best-known and most important variety was doubtless the *narodnik* movement in Russia. Its origins can be traced to the writings and political activity of

Alexander Herzen, the exiled aristocrat who was the first (from 1849) to associate Russia's tradition of communal property, the *obshchina*, and its council, the *mir*, not with a vision of the past, as it was for the Slavophiles, but with a vision of the socialist future. Herzen was thus the first to theorize the possibility of "skipping stages" in moving from "feudalism" to socialism.[44]

In Russia Herzen could build on, and transform, the conservative school of Slavophilism, a reaction to Hegelianism that was irrelevant in both Romania and Latin America. By the 1860s, Russian populism, in its violent form, insisted that action was urgent, since the transition to socialism had to be undertaken before capitalism had triumphed in the countryside, impoverishing the peasantry and destroying the *obshchina*, the basis on which a socialist society could be constructed. The People's Will, viewing the state as the driving force behind Russia's efforts to catch up with the West, assassinated Alexander II in 1881, but czarist reaction easily prevailed.

Clearly, such populist concerns would have seemed alien to Latin American intellectuals of the 1860s and 1870s, for whom state building rather than state destruction was the objective of the era. And many Latin American intellectuals in the liberal era had opportunities to direct the state (witness Sarmiento and Mitre) that Russian intellectuals of integrity simply lacked, even when they spent years in state service, as did Herzen himself.[45]

In Russia, populism and Marxism were movements with strong Hegelian foundations, both dating from the middle years of the century. Populists and Marxists both viewed the penetration of capitalism into Russia and its consequences as *the* social problem, and advocates of the two schools engaged in a modes-of-production debate as it applied to Russia. While the populists strove to overcome capitalism, to pass beyond it, Marxists viewed the triumph of capitalism in that country as a grim necessity—or an accomplished fact, by the time of Lenin's *The Development of Capitalism in Russia* (1899).

It seems clear that however backward were Russia's society and state, Russian intellectuals participated in European social movements and social theorizing in ways not possible for Latin Americans. Herzen and Mikhail Bakunin, for example, were aristocrats with broad European experience. Bakunin was Marx's antagonist in the First International, and Russian revolutionaries, frequently in exile, were continually in contact with Western radicals.

The diffusion of Hegel's philosophy among Russian intellectuals of a variety of social backgrounds was extensive by the 1840s, and Hegel's dialectic was employed by populists like Alexander Chernyshevsky in the 1860s to further develop Herzen's views on stage-skipping to socialism. The fact that Hegel had little influence in Latin America before the 1870s—or later, outside formal philosophy—thus tended to close off the obvious paths to Marxism and populism, both of which ideologies developed in uniquely radical ways in Europe's most reactionary state.

Polarization in Russia was a readily comprehensible process, and hence so were the unique ways in which radical philosophies developed, but it is perhaps more elucidating for the Latin American case to consider social doctrines in Romania. There, as in Latin America, but in constrast to Russia, liberal political institutions prevailed from 1866, when a constitution based on Belgium's was instituted.

Romania, the only country of Eastern Europe where a Romance language is spoken, achieved its formal independence from Turkey in stages between 1859 and 1877. Thus, like Latin America, it emerged from a patrimonial (if non-Western) empire attempting to institute administrative reform. Romania's parliamentary government was controlled by an oligarchy. But like those of some Latin American states, it underwent a crisis and partial transformation in the early twentieth century[46]—in the Romanian case, because of World War I and a subsequent land reform. By the postwar Treaty of Trianon, Romania's leaders managed to double the national territory and population, as a reward for timely declarations of war. Thus, as one of the succession states to the Austrian and Russian empires, "Greater Romania" was even more obviously the locus for a debate about economic development than had been the "Old Kingdom" without Transylvania and Bessarabia.

Romania's Black Sea ports had been opened to Western European trade by the Treaty of Adrianople in 1829, a date often noted as the beginning of the transformation of the country as a grain supplier. Serfdom was abolished in 1864, at a formal level, and exports expanded rapidly.

As in Latin America, the West's influence in Romania was seen as transforming and civilizing, dating from the Napoleonic era, when Romanians began to abandon the caftan and adopt the dress and cultural fashions of the West. As the century advanced, the use of French became mandatory for all those laying claim to general education. Liberal economics was associated with economic development and the civilizing (or Europeanizing) process, and its tenets were taught in the new universities of the early 1860s. In the words of one student, "economic liberties were in harmony with the movement of national rebirth, of passing to a European style of life, of breaking the chains of the regime of Turkish capitulations." Liberal economics was not only seen as a necessary guide for development and a counterpart to liberal political institutions, but was insistently pressed on the Romanians by Britain and France, thus helping to guarantee Romanian independence from Turkey.[47]

The classical era of free trade in Romania was brief, however, spanning only the years 1875 to 1886. The international depression of 1873–96 resulted in the closing of foreign markets for Romania's cereal exports, beginning with Germany's new tariff of 1879. After a customs war with Austria, Romania reactively turned to industrial protection in its own tariff of 1886. Relatively inefficient compared with "overseas" grain exporters to Europe, Romania could not compete in the British market with Argentina and the Dominions.

Nevertheless, Romania's economic growth rate was more than respectable for the last three decades before the First World War, as wheat exports revived and the country began to export petroleum. The value of exports rose from $9 million in 1850 to $136 million in 1914. Between 1880 and 1910, Romania's annual rate of export growth, at 3.3 percent, was higher than that of the periphery of European states as a whole (2.8 percent). And per capita income, at $307 in 1910, was higher than that of Portugal and the other Balkan states, excepting Greece. However, there was a price to pay: 80 percent of all industrial shares were in foreign hands, as were 75 percent of the capital in banking at the time of the war.[48] In addition, there is abundant evidence that the income differential between the peasantry and other sectors of society was widening.

The abolition of serfdom had been an instance of "symbolic modernization," in J. K. Galbraith's phrase, and the peasants' living conditions seriously deteriorated from the 1870s through the early years of the new century: Romanian landlords had been able to compete in the international market by reducing costs, that is, by squeezing more and more labor out of the peasantry.[49] The great peasant revolt of 1907, arising from the evils of latifundist (and often absentee) agriculture, resulted in the army's massacring ten thousand peasants and stimulated the efforts of those who sought to critique the foundations of the so-called liberal economy.

In a country cheek to jowl with Russia, it is hardly surprising that the ideological conflict between Marxists and *narodniki* had powerful repercussions. In Romania, the two leading exponents of both populism and Marxism had spent their formative years in Russia, absorbing the radical ideologies of Russian politics: Constantin Stere, the leading turn-of-the-century populist, was born a scion of boyars in (Russian) Bessarabia, and his Marxist antagonist, Constantin Dobrogeanu-Gherea (born Solomon Katz), spent his youth in the Ukraine. Their debates, and those of their ideological allies in Romanian journals from 1890 to 1920, asked basic questions about the path to capitalist development, including the issue of whether the existing economy of Romania could be defined as capitalist, precapitalist, or some fusion of the two. The Gherea-Stere debate among other things treated the matter whether socialism was an exotic plant in an agricultural country.

Stere deemed socialism irrelevant for a society with eighty-eight peasants for every factory worker. Socialism did not address the problems of the overwhelming majority, he believed, and socialists had no chance of taking power to implement their program.[50] Industrialization, based on high tariffs in 1886 and 1906, had failed, Stere asserted in 1908. The basic conditions were lacking: to become an industrial state, Romania required heavy industry, and the production of capital goods in turn required large markets. Romania had no domestic market of consequence and no realistic chance of competing internationally. Agriculture, Stere contended, citing Karl Kautsky, Germany's leading Marxist theoretician, was not subject to Marx's laws of the concentration and centralization of capital. For Stere, the solution lay in destroying the latifundia and developing agricultural cooperatives and cottage industry.[51] In part because Romania lacked a tradition comparable to the *obshchina*, Stere and his populist allies never advocated stage-skipping to socialism.

Stere's ideological opponent, Dobrogeanu-Gherea, assumed the task of demonstrating the relevance of socialism for a backward peasant society. More important, however, was his Marxist critique of the existing social formation: he was among the first theorists to argue (in 1910) that traditional modes of production in backward countries interacted with capitalism to form a unique amalgam, in fact a new mode, and, in the event, a monstrous one. His novel proposition can be contrasted with the fact that eleven years earlier, Lenin had characterized Russia's economy as one in which capitalism, even in agriculture, was inexorably eliminating its feudal predecessor.[52] For Latin Americanists, it is notable that Gherea's effort to define a mode of production unique to backward countries enveloped by capitalism occurred sixty years before the continentwide debate in which Latin Americans "discovered" modes of production by which capitalism subordinated precapitalist modes in unique patterns.

Reacting to Stere's charges that Romania was overwhelmingly an agrarian nation and that Marxist socialism as a program for the nation was an absurdity, Gherea held that Romania was already a "semicapitalist" country and that the process of capitalist penetration was too far advanced to "skip" capitalism on the route from feudalism to socialism. Though contending that Marxist laws of development were valid for a backward agricultural country like Romania, Gherea conceded that such laws manifested themselves in a much more complex and confused fashion than in the West.[53]

In the same year, 1908, he wrote that Romania had a legal structure appropriate for a capitalist society, but neither a capitalist class nor a proletariat. Backward countries such as Romania were perforce becoming satellites as the capitalist world economy expanded. Gherea now borrowed and reinterpreted an idea—*forma fără fond* (form without substance)—from Romania's Junimia school, whose leaders had been trained in Germany and steeped in Hegelianism. In Gherea's Marxist terms, superstructure had preceded the base, in that Romania had adopted Western institutions without the social and economic conditions requisite for their effective functioning.[54] Commenting on the gap between the formal and the real country, Gherea noted that the situation contrasted sharply with that of absolutist Russia, where the "real" state of development was ahead of that of the legal system. Under the circumstances, thought Gherea, Romanian socialists should strive for the development of an authentic capitalism, which would bring in its train an enforceable modern legal system, instead of the sham which the country then knew.[55]

In "Socialism in Underdeveloped Countries," an essay written in 1912, Gherea elaborated on the theme of the differences between the evolution of the central capitalist countries and their backward dependencies. In the latter, evolution was much faster, and of a different character, since changes in the form or superstructure preceded those in the base. This situation resulted from the fact that the advanced capitalist countries determined the evolution of the whole system. Gherea proceeded to formulate a "law of backward societies," that is, those on the periphery of the capitalist center: "In advanced capitalist countries, social forms follow the social [and economic] base; in underdeveloped countries, the social base comes after the social forms."[56]

For Gherea, backward countries in the capitalist orbit suffered both from capitalism (in Romania, boyar exploitation of peasants to maximize profits in the international market) and the insufficient development of capitalism (its incapacity locally to destroy feudal relations of production).[57] In this regard, Gherea noted that the Romanian bourgeoisie had utterly failed to transform the national economy, as its counterpart and exemplar had done in the advanced capitalist countries. The bourgeoisie of Western Europe had betrayed its defense of the Rights of Man after 1789, but the bourgeoisie of Romania had nothing to betray: while the Western bourgeoisie had to fight for the creation of liberal institutions, they were subsequently imported into Romania by a process in which the local bourgeoisie "played the smallest possible role." Rather, it was the boyars, who, under Western influence, created the liberal state in Romania. The local bourgeoisie, such as it was, took the place of the boyars as a new semifeudal class, keeping intact many feudal social relations.[58]

Dobrogeanu-Gherea's magnum opus had appeared in 1910, addressing the central problem of Romanian society of the era—peasant unrest. The laconic title of Gherea's study, *Neoiobagia* (neoserfdom), epitomized the proposition that a new and monstrous mode of production had reared its head in Romania. Put briefly, the mode was a fusion of precapitalist social and economic relations in the countryside and the economic relations and superstructure of an advancing capitalism at the national and international levels.[59] In the traditional form of *iobagia*, there had been three basic features: the peasant was fixed on the lord's land; he was forced to provide corvée labor for his master; and he had to pay tribute in kind as well as other forms of feudal dues.[60]

Neoiobagia was a hybrid form having the following defining characteristics: (1) Its relations of production were largely feudal. (2) At the ideological and legal level, it was overlaid with a liberal-bourgeois legal system that had the effect of leaving the peasant at the mercy of the landlord.[61] (3) It further included a tutelary legislation that declared the inalienability of peasant land and that regulated relations between the lord and the workers. (4) At the economic level, the system did not provide the small peasant farmer enough land for subsistence, a fact that forced him to become a vassal of the owner of the land he farmed as a laborer or sharecropper.[62]

Neoiobagia came into being as boyars saw opportunities to obtain hard currencies and thereby secure a flow of Western goods. Such wares were especially deemed desirable after the Westernization of the boyar class had begun with the Napoleonic Wars. As a result, wrote Gherea, Romania had entered the "great world division of labor" and now "sends food to the West and receives from it industrial and cultural goods." Concomitant with Romania's growth of trade came a monetized economy, a development that required centuries to consolidate in the West.[63]

Thus for Gherea, as for many others, Western markets had partially revolutionized Romania's national economy. With the appearance of a money economy, Gherea held, the exploitation of the peasantry no longer had any legal limits. An extraeconomic compulsion of the labor force by the rural police (*dorobanți*) to enforce labor contracts, combined with greatly increased periods of corvée labor, further led Gherea to the judgement that Romania had developed "a double agrarian regime . . . [one] both capitalist and serf-based . . . absurd, hateful . . . a monstrous regime."[64] Neoserfdom, as Gherea styled Romania's system, had the advantage for the former boyars of freeing them of all traditional obligations to the peasantry; they could exploit labor without hindrance from the state and without having to deal with free workers (who might organize to resist).[65]

The social regime that Gherea and Stere had condemned was dealt a severe blow by World War I, which resulted in a major land reform, resolving one part of the agrarian problem. Now the tempo of the debate on development quickened, as Romanian intellectuals and statesmen were impressed by two phenomena— the failure of Romanian agriculture to regain the position in wheat exports it had held before the war (falling from fifth to tenth place internationally) and, in the latter 1920s, the massive industrialization drive of the USSR.

In the interwar era, a number of economists—some holding German doctorates—were influenced by social and economic theories then circulating in Europe, including Soviet Marxism, German and Austrian corporatism, the later German historical school of Gustav von Schmoller, and A.V. Chayanov's theories on peasant economics. The influence of Werner Sombart and Rudolf Hilferding was especially notable, and many non-Marxists subscribed to Hilferding's periodization of the history of capitalism into commercial, industrial, and financial phases, to which corresponded the ideologies of mercantilism, liberalism, and imperialism.[66]

In the ferment of the interwar years, the economist whose work was probably most often discussed abroad was Mihail Manoilescu, who had trained as an engineer before educating himself in economics. He was also "furiously ambitious" as a politician, in the words of a British ambassador,[67] and knew triumph and subsequent disgrace in the rough-and-tumble of Balkan politics; in 1940 he ceded half of Romania's newly acquired Transylvania to Hungary under pressure from the Axis foreign ministers, Joachim von Ribbentrop and Galeazzo Ciano. Manoilescu was the only Romanian whose theories were known in Latin America, and his reputation as an economist in the 1930s was probably given a boost in the region by his work as a theorist of corporatism. Both his economic and political works were translated into Spanish and Portuguese in the 1930s and 1940s.

As an economist, Manoilescu's chief concern was with the relationship between the purchasing power of a unit of labor expended in producing a good traded on the world market in terms of the labor of other workers abroad—a concept now called the double factorial terms of trade. Manoilescu held that labor productivity in industry (manufacturing and mining) was inherently superior to that in agriculture, by a ratio of four or more to one. This superiority owed to specific capital, that is, the much higher value of capital per worker in industry than that in agriculture. The Romanian developed a mathematical formula that would array all industrial and agricultural activities by their productivities.[68] Manoilescu, like Marx, Ricardo, and other classical economists, believed in the labor theory of value; since labor could create capital as well as commodities, it should be directed, he believed, toward the activities that would maximize labor productivity. The issue for him was not comparative advantage, as for Ricardo, since this theory prescribed a division of world labor into industrial and agricultural specialists; rather, the issue was whether a given economic endeavor within a country had a labor productivity higher than the national average. If it did, he believed, its development should be encouraged.[69] Specialization in traditional agricultural pursuits required four to ten hours of Romanian labor to purchase the product of a single hour of English labor. Thus international trade was a swindle, and the world market, *un marché de dupes* for raw materials producers. Protection for industry was justifiable, not just in terms of Friedrich List's "infant industry" argument, by which an enterprise would take advantage of economies of scale and external economies over the intermediate run to bring costs down to internationally competitive levels; rather, protection was justified because a sheltered industry that had a labor productivity higher than the national average of economic activities was a boon from its first day of operation. The more the productivity of a given good exceeded the average national productivity, the more the domestic price of that good could justifiably exceed the foreign price.[70]

To engage in agricultural exports, Manoilescu argued, the comparative advantage of domestic agriculture over its foreign counterpart must be greater than the intrinsic superiority in labor productivity of industry over agriculture within the country.[71] Such cases were rare, Manoilescu thought, since agriculture in Romania and other underdeveloped countries with dense populations was primitive in technique and was consequently labor intensive. In sum, by challenging the legitimacy of the international division of labor, he was also attacking international trade theory, and his works quickly drew sharp attacks from leading trade theorists in the United States and Europe.[72]

THE ASSAULT ON LIBERALISM IN LATIN AMERICA

This brief view of social and economic ideas in Romania illustrates the kinds of European intellectual currents adapted by social thinkers in that country. Although the Russian influence in Romania was strong, that of Germany was stronger, of which trend Marxism provides a major example. In comparison with Romania, the dearth of German and Austrian social ideas in Latin America—as distinguished from those in formal philosophy—from the 1870s through World War I is striking.[73] The influence of Russian thought is simply lacking.

In any event, Marxism was anemic in Latin America—as were other traditions of social thought of the German-speaking world, such as the German historical and the Austrian schools of economics. German social science would begin to transform Latin American social thought after the arrival of Spanish exiles fleeing the Franco regime in the late 1930s. Many of these men, of whom José Ortega y Gasset was only the most famous, had studied in Germany and promoted the translation of German works into Spanish.[74]

The Latin Americans' greater familiarity with French, British, and Spanish thought probably tended to limit their knowledge of Marxism, if one can accept Perry Anderson's judgement that there were no significant contributions to Marxist theory in France, Britain, or Spain before the 1930s.[75] Rudolf Hilferding's *Finance Capital* (1910), which was so influential in Stefan Zeletin's *Burghezia Română* (Romanian Bourgeoisie, 1925) and in Romania in general, was not available in Spanish, English, or French until the 1970s.[76]

Another reason for a relatively slow rise of Marxism in Latin America may have been Marx's own indifference toward the region, compared with his interest in Spain, India, Turkey, China, and Russia. He regarded the Latin American political process as the embodiment of Bonapartism and reaction. Furthermore, Marx had a low opinion of the liberator Simón Bolívar, whom he privately compared to Faustin Soulouque, the Haitian dictator whose bragadoccio Marx used to parody Napoleon III. Marx's lack of concern about Latin America has even provoked a study of the reasons for it by the region's leading student of Marxism, José Aricó.[77]

Marxism was thus poorly understood and poorly diffused before the Third International (1919), though the assertion is somewhat less valid for Argentina than for other countries.[78] Latin American radicalism, like its Iberian counterpart, tended to revolve around anarchism more than socialism at least until the 1920s, and in many countries until the 1930s. In addition, most socialist parties were not exclusively or predominantly Marxist-oriented until the Third International forced the issue in the early 1920s. One indication of the thinness of the Marxist tradition is that there were no legal Marxists like Peter Struve or Zeletin in Spanish or Portuguese America; that is, there were no revisionists who argued that capitalism in backward countries would develop through Marxist stages, but that the rise of a local bourgeoisie was both inevitable and beneficial. Ironically, despite earlier twists and turns, the official position of the Communist parties of the region in the 1950s would come very close to Zeletinism, because support for the national bourgeoisie was identified with anti-imperialism and antifeudalism.

The man generally conceded to be the most important Marxist thinker in Latin America before World War II, José Carlos Mariátegui of Peru, was also one of the least orthodox and was heavily influenced by Georges Sorel. Mariátegui's principal contribution to Marxist theory as such was probably his argument that, in the age of imperialism, capitalism had arrived in Latin America too late for local bourgeoisies to emulate the historic roles of their European forebears.[79] Mariátegui would have agreed with Romania's Dobrogeanu-Gherea that underdeveloped countries suffer both from (external) capitalism and the insufficient development of capitalism at the local level.

Mariátegui was also heterodox in another regard. Though his position was ambiguous, Mariátegui hinted that Peru's indigenous *ayllu*, which he understood as an Incaic form of agrarian communism, could be the foundation for the transformation from a semifeudal stage of development directly to socialism in the countryside. Thus Mariátegui would seem to be a "stage-skipper," despite his following Lenin in condemning the *narodniki*. Nor was Mariátegui alone: his view that peasant collectivism could be the basis for passing from feudalism to socialism was shared by a leading Latin American spokesman at the sixth congress of the Communist International in 1928, Ricardo Paredes of Ecuador; Paredes's views were echoed by a Uruguayan delegate.[80]

In any event, Mariátegui's praise of Incaic socialism (a discovery, by the way, of G.V. Plekhanov, a generation earlier) seemed to a Comintern critic in 1941 a reincarnation of the Russian populist tradition.[81] Mariátegui appears to have fallen into populist "error," in part because of the absence of classical populism in Latin America.

The reasons for populism's nonappearance in the region are worth speculating about. In many countries there was no large peasantry, in the sense of freeholders; nor, in most nations, was there a primitive commune in any way comparable to the Russian *obshchina*. Yet neither of these conditions by itself blocked the rise of populism as a major ideological current in Romania. Latin Americans, of course, did not have access to the nineteenth-century Russian debate about capitalism, as did the Romanians, but the late appearance of Hegelianism and then of Marxism in Latin America may also have been causes of the absence of populism. As Andrzej Walicki and Franco Venturi have demonstrated, the rise of populism in Russia was intimately connected with intellectuals' coming to terms with Marxism.[82]

It is nonetheless important to qualify the absence of populism by distinguishing, as Ghiţa Ionescu does, between *populism* and *peasantism*—the latter being a legal political movement based on the newly enfranchised peasant masses, occurring largely after World War I in the cases of Romania and most other countries of Eastern Europe.[83] There is an obvious analog to peasantism in Latin American *indigenismo*, a multifaceted ideology finding its fullest expression in the Mexican Revolution, and encompassing the glorification, "redemption," and study of Amerindian populations. In the 1920s Mexico's minister of education, José Vasconcelos, in a rare commitment to empiricism, sent students into the countryside to observe local conditions. The Revolution's interest in the "real" Indian—as opposed to the old regime's idealization of Cuauhtémoc, the nephew of Moctezuma who resisted Cortés—was necessarily related to peasant land seizures and the peasantry as the foundation of the revolutionary troops that destroyed the Porfirista army. Thus *indigenismo* was linked to agrarianism, officially part of the revolutionary ideology after the approval of the 1917 constitution, which legalized land reform.[84] In the 1920s *indigenismo* also had an impact among intellectuals in Peru, of whom Mariátegui was only one, and *indigenistas* there were able to obtain the institutionalization of the Indian community as a corporate landholder. Yet only in Mexico were Indian peasants widely mobilized—and manipulated—as part of the political process by the 1920s.

This short survey of ideas indicates that Latin Americans were rarely asking the questions posed by Eastern European intellectuals in the years before World War I and more frequently after 1917: Does the capitalist mode of production prevail in this country? Is there a "conquering bourgeoisie," or can one be created? Do there exist unique local modes of production that interact with capitalism? Can a reformist state create a capitalist economy? Communist leaders in the 1920s, it is true, began to pose these questions, but the issues would not be addressed with a sense of urgency and investigated with sophistication in Latin America until after World War II.[85]

Granted, not all the social and economic ideas current in Eastern Europe before the war were applicable to Latin America. Since many countries in the latter region at the time had relatively little surplus agricultural population, most of the post-Chayanov theorizing about dualism, disguised unemployment, and peasant economic rationality—so important in Romania—was not seen as directly relevant. In contrast to their reception in Eastern Europe, the works of Chayanov played no role in Latin American economic thought in the 1920s and 1930s, and the fact that they were only then available in German and Russian was perhaps less important than the fact that they did not seem pertinent to much of Latin American reality, although in retrospect they seem relevant enough to "peasant" countries like Peru and Mexico. Here the technical aspect of Chayanov's formal economics may have constituted a barrier to diffusion in the Latin America of the time.

All the same, the Latin American regimes and the prevailing liberal model that seemed to justify them were being attacked from a variety of quarters by the 1920s, as for example in demands for state intervention in the social sphere and the domestic economy, or in recognition of corporate property. The foreign trade model based on comparative advantage may have been the most durable aspect of liberalism at the ideological level, and its survival probably lessened the impact of "root and branch" critiques of liberalism in general. As noted, many parts of Latin America were profoundly and positively affected by Ricardian prescriptions of export-driven growth. Argentina by 1929 had a per capita income approaching that of Australia, and the real growth rate of its economy had been almost twice that of Australia for 1900–29.[86]

The leader of the Argentine Socialist party and the first translator of *Capital* into Spanish, Juan B. Justo, opposed industrial protectionism as late as the 1920s, because he accepted the role assigned to Argentina in the international division of labor.[87]

Granted, Argentina was the flagship of success before 1930. Those countries where the export model was less successful, such as Peru, may, like Romania, have experienced more intensive efforts to critique the liberal development model before the Great Depression. Radical intellectuals like Peru's Manuel González Prada had denounced "feudal latifundism" in the late nineteenth century. But even in Peru and other countries with corporate peasantries, the liberal model seemed relatively successful to dominant elites; moreover, the indigenous antiliberal discourse was not offered at a theoretical level that found acceptance among Comintern or other European Marxists or, in the case of those who championed national industry, among neoclassically trained economists.

Well into the twentieth century, nonsocialist theorists likewise made little headway against the thesis of comparative advantage. A striking instance concerns a corollary of Ricardo's doctrine, that is, that there are "natural" and "artificial" economic activities based on a country's factor endowments and that artificial industries should be discouraged because they result in a misallocation of resources. In Brazil, for example, Joaquim Murtinho, the Brazilian minister of finance (1898–1902), would do nothing for artificial industries in the financial crisis of 1901–1902, since equal treatment of all economic activities by the state would amount, in his view, to socialism.[88] Such was the policy that governments of the region generally followed until the latter 1930s or later. It was not a laissez-faire policy, however, since such regimes provided direct and indirect support (e.g., through exchange-rate deterioration) for their export industries and the interests behind them.[89]

In Chile, nonetheless, export-led growth, focusing on the nitrate boom before and after the War of the Pacific, laid a foundation for a manufacturing sector, and a Chilean industrialists' association appeared in 1883. This fact was less unusual than that some Chileans favoring industrialization discovered and consistently propagated the ideas of Friedrich List. List found his leading Chilean disciple between 1880 and World War I in the person of Malaquias Concha, who popularized List's infant industry argument.[90]

List was known elsewhere, but seems to have had little influence,[91] and we may say that the central tendency before World War II was that Latin American manufacturers and their ideologues were apologetic, timid, and accommodationist—in sharp contrast, for example, to their Romanian counterparts in this period. In the 1920s, Brazilian industrialists advanced practical arguments—that industry would provide urban employment, that it would save on foreign exchange (through import substitution), that it would help agriculture by consuming local inputs (such as cotton), and that it would provide government with more reliable sources of revenue (through consumption taxes) than the export sector could.[92] Latin American industrialists and their spokesmen sought a place in the sun *alongside* the traditional export activities. This was true of Alejandro Bunge and Luis Colombo in Argentina; Roberto Simonsen, Alexandre Siciliano, Jr., and Otávio Pupo Nogueira in Brazil; it was much less true of Malaquias Concha, the Listian ideologue in Chile.[93]

Almost no one in the 1920s who sought to develop Latin America along capitalist lines viewed export-driven growth as a problem requiring fundamental rethinking, as would the Argentine economist Raúl Prebisch by the early 1940s. Víctor Emilio Estrada, the director of Ecuador's central bank, was among the few who attempted to explain persistently negative balances of payments and deteriorating terms of trade for 1914–21. Estrada anticipated an element in the famous Prebisch thesis of 1949—namely, that Latin America's terms of trade for its traditional exports would deteriorate indefinitely. (That is, for a given quantity of imports, Latin American countries would have to supply ever larger amounts of exports.) Specifically, Estrada, like Prebisch in a more systematic way in the 1940s, attributed the price-scissors problem principally to rising labor costs in manufacturing in the United States (his nation's main trading partner). This fact owed to trade-union activity, a pressure that was lacking in the price formation of Latin American goods, which were chiefly agricultural. But Estrada did not generalize beyond his own country and was only groping for measures to offset the falling prices of cacao, Ecuador's leading export at the time.[94] Estrada apparently had no influence on Prebisch or the structuralist school the Argentine economist founded at the U.N. Economic Commission for Latin America (ECLA).

A more likely candidate for such a role as precursor of ECLA was Manoilescu, the Romanian economist, politician, and ideologue of corporatism, who recommended industrialization à outrance for agricultural-exporting countries. In São Paulo, Brazil, officials of the Center of Industries corresponded with Manoilescu and published Théorie du protectionnisme in Portuguese in 1931. In the early 1930s three important industrial spokesmen in São Paulo—Simonsen, Siciliano, and Pupo Nogueira—took the Romanian's work to be proof of the legitimacy of their interests. Adding a touch of racism, Siciliano neatly adapted Manoilescu's theory by contending in 1931 that Brazil could not continue to rely on traditional exports, because of the lower wages that Africans and Asians would accept in competing agricultural activities, implicitly raising their labor productivities; thus agriculture in Brazil did not possess any intrinsic superiority to industry.[95] Like Manoilescu and others in Romania, the three Brazilians also tried to parry the charge of artificiality by pointing to the apparent legitimacy of the coffee-roasting industry in the United States and the sugar-refining industry in England, for which domestic raw materials did not exist.[96]

Manoilescu's prestige as an economist was complemented by his reputation as a theorist of corporatism. As in the case of Marxism, the literature on corporatism in French had a much larger impact than did that in German. Othmar Spann and the Sombart of Deutscher Sozialismus were almost unknown, and the most influential writers were probably François Perroux, who had taught at São Paulo, and Manoilescu.[97]

Manoilescu's attitudes may have been as influential as his social ideas, at least among the industrialists who first championed him. They welcomed his unabashed elitism, his support of industrialization, his emphasis on the role of the state in the economy, and his insistence on the close link between nationalism and industrial development. The ideologues of Vargas's authoritarian Estado Novo (1937–45)—Azevedo Amaral, Francisco Oliveira Vianna, and Francisco Campos—wanted a strong state, rationalization of the economy (chiefly cartelization), and economic planning.[98]

As in the case of his vogue as social sage, Manoilescu's economic theories as a scientific rationale for Brazilian industrialization did not survive the 1930s, chiefly because of the attacks by Jacob Viner and other neoclassical theorists on his work.[99] Manoilescu's ideas were slowly abandoned for more practical and circumstantial arguments. Simonsen, who had frequently cited Manoilescu in the early 1930s, had ceased referring to the master by the Second World War. In the debate between Simonsen and Eugênio Gudin on economic planning in 1945, it was Gudin, not Simonsen, who referred to Manoilescu, viewing him as a discredited charlatan.[100] Meanwhile, in 1944, Simonsen presided at an industrialists' congress that called for the harmonious development of agriculture and industry and championed government aid to agriculture.[101]

Despite the general absence of theoretical foundations for industrial development, for those Latin American countries that had made industrial advances in the 1920s increased self-sufficiency in the 1930s was a second-best option, in view of the sustained crisis in export markets.

Over the decade of the 1930s, industrial spokesmen grew bolder, except perhaps those Brazilians who had initially followed Manoilescu. Note, for example, the themes chosen by Luis Colombo, the president of the Unión Industrial Argentina: In 1931, he supports a moderate and rational protectionism and defends the manufacturers against the charge of promoting policies inimical to the interests of Argentine consumers; in 1933, he even-handedly justifies protection for both industry and agriculture; and by 1940 he attacks the industrial countries as having themselves violated the rules of the international division of labor by developing large agricultural establishments, only choosing to buy abroad when convenient.[102]

During the 1930s, industrialists pointed to the vulnerability of export economies, which they more frequently dubbed "colonial" in the process. Governments, however, moved hesitantly and inconsistently toward addressing the problems of industry. In 1933 the Argentine Minister of Agriculture, Luis Duhau, proclaimed the necessity of producing industrial goods that could no longer be imported (for lack of foreign exchange), and he pledged his government's support for the process. Yet in the same month the Argentine government supported the U.S. initiative for general tariff reductions at the Pan American Union Conference in Montevideo. Furthermore, as late as 1940, Finance Minister Pinedo's Plan for the economic development of Argentina still distinguished between natural and artificial industries, implying further that industrial development would occur in concert with the needs of the agricultural and pastoral sectors.[103]

In depression-era Brazil, dictator Getúlio Vargas was proindustry. Was he not the friend of all established economic interests? But he opposed artificial industries (manufacturing) in his presidential campaign in 1930, and government loans to artificial industries were still prohibited in 1937. Osvaldo Aranha, Vargas's Minister of Finance in 1933, even termed industries fictitious if they did not use at least 70 percent domestic raw materials.[104] The contrast of these official attitudes with those in Romania is striking, since Finance Minister Emil Costinescu defended industries with imported inputs as early as 1902.[105]

Vargas only became committed to rapid industrial expansion during his Estado Novo dictatorship (1937–45). Although he said he could not accept the idea of Brazil's remaining a "semicolonial" economy in 1939, as late as 1940, when the coffee market was still depressed after a decade of attempts to revive it, Vargas wanted to balance industrial and agricultural growth. Only in 1941 did a division for industrial development of the Bank of Brazil begin to make significant loans.

In Mexico, industrialization in the 1930s made modest advances while agrarian reform was at the top of the Cárdenas government's agenda; during the war the pace quickened. Nacional Financiera, a partly government-owned development bank, was established in 1934, but only became seriously committed to manufacturing after its reorganization at the end of 1940, when the new proindustry administration of Avila Camacho took office. Protectionism in Mexico, according to one authority, "begins in earnest with the Second World War."[106]

In Chile, the Popular Front government of Pedro Aguirre Cerda proclaimed the need for state-sponsored support for industry in 1939, and Aguirre established CORFO, the government development corporation. But relief and reconstruction following an earthquake that year was another reason for creating CORFO; in 1940 the sum budgeted for the development of manufacturing was less than each of those for agriculture, mining, energy, and public housing.[107]

In Argentina, Raúl Prebisch was one of the government planners of the 1930s who gradually convinced himself of the need to abandon export specialization as the primary engine of economic growth. As director of the Central Bank from its inception in 1935, Prebisch began to formulate his theories of unequal exchange between center and periphery. He assumed a greater rate of technological innovation in industrial countries and argued that there were different responses to recessions by primary exporters and those exporting manufactures, because of the power of organized labor to maintain high wages, and therefore high export prices, in the latter. These propositions were not fully worked out until the latter 1940s and were in part based on U.N. terms of trade data available only after the war. The question of how much Prebisch owed to Manoilescu was raised by Jacob Viner, the neoclassical trade theorist, a year after Prebisch's manifesto of 1949, *The Economic Development of Latin America and Its Principal Problems*. It seems probable, however, that Prebisch's ideas followed a different route to similar conclusions about the international trading system and the urgency of industrialization in underdeveloped countries.[108] Nonetheless,

Manoilescu's theses in the 1930s must have created a sympathetic audience for Prebisch's views in the postwar era, and one of Manoilescu's major essays was published in Chile as late as 1947; it appeared in *Economía*, a journal of the University of Chile later edited by Aníbal Pinto, one of ECLA's outstanding economists.[109]

At all events, the fact that Latin American policy makers clung to the ideology of free trade throughout the Great Depression seems to illustrate how slowly received ideas die. The international trading system was in crisis over the whole period 1930–45, but only at the end of the 1940s did ideological shifts flow from the observed fact that, in Argentina and Chile, industry's share of the national product was greater than agriculture's. Mexico and Brazil would soon follow.

Admittedly, Latin American nations seemed to have more to lose than did Eastern European countries before the Great Depression. Romania, for instance, reacting to the agricultural protectionism of Central and Western Europe, had begun efforts to industrialize as early as 1886. Almost simultaneously that country was threatened by more efficient grain producers "overseas," among which was Argentina, as the Romanian publicist Petru Aurelian noted in 1890.[110]

Another thing the Latin American proponents of industrialization lacked, at least compared with their Eastern European contemporaries between the world wars, was the strategic argument—of great import in Romania, for example, a country that had doubled its territory at the expense of its neighbors at the end of the First World War. In the Western Hemisphere a Pax Americana had succeeded a Pax Britannica during the 1890s; thus Chile, Argentina, and Brazil never became combatants against each other after the downfall of the Argentine dictator Juan Manuel de Rosas in 1852, when Brazilian troops fought on Argentine soil.

In Latin America, industrialization was fact before it was government policy, and policy before it was theory. Contrary to the views of Dobrogeanu-Gherea, who held that superstructural changes in "local" or peripheral societies precede changes in the material base, here is apparently a classical instance of a material transformation preceding the change in ideological superstructure—although it should be clear, from previous references to the importance of the absence or the phasing of some ideas and institutions on the development of others, that the argument is something other than economic reductionism. And it is true that no matter how committed Latin American governments might be to the international trading system, government policy was sometimes incoherent or accommodationist for established interests, including industrialists. Still, before the 1940s, industrialization had few intellectual champions, though some other aspects of liberal ideology had been challenged much earlier.

When a theoretical justification of industrialization appeared in 1949, the Argentine economy would scarcely have been recognizable to intellectuals of

Sarmiento's generation. They had advanced a liberal project, if not a bourgeois one. Prebisch and ECLA would reverse that emphasis, in effect inveighing against imperialism without abandoning capitalism.

NOTES

1. Hernández y Sánchez-Barba, "Ciclos Kondratieff," p. 225.

2. Halperín Donghi, "Economy and Society," p. 304 (on export stagnation).

3. Mörner, "Latin American 'Landlords,' " pp. 459–60.

4. Hernández y Sánchez-Barba, "Ciclos Kondratieff," pp. 230–31. Nonetheless, these estates were highly differentiated across the region as to the modernity of their technology, business practices, and labor relations.

5. Glade, "Latin America," pp. 10–11.

6. Díaz-Alejandro, *Essays*, p. 2.

7. Dean, "Brazilian Economy," p. 685.

8. E.g., see Leff, *Underdevelopment* 2: 43–51; and Jacobsen, "Cycles and Booms," pp. 488–89.

9. Bauer, "Rural Spanish America," p. 177.

10. Jacobsen, "Cycles and Booms" (referring to southern Peru), p. 489.

11. Inferred from Bauer and Johnson, "Land and Labour," pp. 88–89.

12. Dean, "Brazilian Economy," p. 702.

13. Bauer, "Rural Spanish America," p. 185.

14. Kay, *Sistema señorial*, p. 76. In neighboring Peru, as late as 1920, the government introduced corvée labor (*conscripción vial*) for the Indian population. Bauer, "Rural Spanish America," p. 177.

15. Katz, "Labor Conditions," pp. 1–47.

16. Slatta, *Gauchos*, pp. 106–125; and Glade, "Latin America," p. 37.

17. Ibid., p. 38.

18. Kay, *Sistema señorial*, pp. 20, 45–46; and Laclau, "Modos de producción," pp. 300–308.

19. Bloch, *Feudal Society* 1: 279 and 2: 442.

20. Pablo Macera, cited in Bartra, *Modos de producción*, p. 81. Few now accept the view associated with Sergio Bagú, Caio Prado, Jr., and Andre Gunder Frank that a sempiternal capitalism characterized Latin America from the conquest onward; one reason for rejecting this interpretation is that it does not allow for a *transition* to capitalism. See Duncan and Rutledge, *Land and Labour*, "Introduction," pp. 4–5.

21. For a summary of the debate on the Brazilian case, on which the literature is largest, see Love, *São Paulo*, pp. 53–61.

22. Palma, "Growth and Structure," pp. 102, 328, 345; and Dean, *Industrialization*, pp. 3–9.

23. Thorp, "Latin America," p. 66.

24. Ibid., p. 61.

25. In 1911 Brazil exported 38,500 tons of rubber; by 1930, it only exported 6,000 tons. Dean, "Brazilian Economy," p. 695. As Dean notes, it is remarkable that Brazil, a country of continental proportions, should become dependent on a single crop, coffee, for three-fourths its export earnings in the latter 1920s. Ibid., pp. 695–96.

26. Thorp, "Latin America," p. 62.

27. Dean, "Brazilian Economy," p. 721.

28. There was less import substitution industrialization in other parts of Latin America. See Díaz-Alejandro, "Stories of the 1930's," p. 12.

29. Phelps, "Industrial Expansion," p. 281.

30. In the postwar era, note, for example, the impact of the essays *The Economic Development of Latin America and its Principal Problems* by Raúl Prebisch (considered below) and *Dependency and Development in Latin America* by Fernando Henrique Cardoso and Enzo Faletto, the most widely cited and reprinted statement on dependency.

31. Gamio studied anthropology at Columbia University with Franz Boas; see Hale, "Political and Social Ideas," p. 434, n. 138. I do not wish to exaggerate the differences between Romania and Latin America in this regard: the two Romanians who receive the most attention below, Constantin Dobrogeanu-Gherea and Mihail Manoilescu, did not hold doctorates. But they debated men who did, which fact surely affected the level of discourse.

32. Safford, "Politics, Ideology and Society," p. 353–54.

33. Hale, "Political and Social Ideas," p. 369.

34. Sarmiento, *Facundo: Civilización y barbarie*.

35. Molina Enríquez was a reformer facing a revolutionary situation. Written in 1909, one year before the outbreak of the Mexican Revolution, his book was legalistic in approach, and his denunciations of the latifundia included the evils of absenteeism and low productivity decried by the eighteenth-century Spanish philosophe Gaspar Jovellanos, whom Molina cites. He displays an ambivalence toward foreign capital and sees it as less sinister than the creole faction (those descended from "pure" Spaniards). While urging land reform, Molina concurred with the *científicos* (establishment positivists) in defending the Díaz dictatorship. He did so because he believed the regime was appropriate for Mexico given its state of evolution at the time, despite the fact that much of the concentration of property had occurred through Díaz's efforts to alienate public lands and village commons. Molina Enríquez, *Grandes problemas nacionales*, pp. 90, 313, 346.

36. On the association of liberalism and xenophobia in Romania, see Chirot, *Social Change*, p. 108.

37. They continued still later in Colombia, where the final Liberal reaction came in the War of a Thousand Days, 1899–1902, in which 100,000 people may have died. For an analysis of the war, see Bergquist, *Coffee and Conflict*, part 2.

38. Hale, "Political and Social Ideas," pp. 377–78.

39. J. Romero, *Pensamiento político*, p. 28.

40. Zea, *Latin American Mind*, pp. 216–17, 227. On Spencer's influence in Brazil, see Graham, *Britain*, pp. 232–51. Spencer's long-term influence, however, given his strong emphasis on individualism and hostility to the state, was probably less important that that of Comte, whose values were more in tune with the Latin American ethos. Personal communication from Charles A. Hale.

41. Zea, *Latin American Mind*, pp. 287–88.

42. Hartz, "Theory," pp. 3–6.

43. For a summary, see Kitching, *Development*, ch. 2.

44. See Venturi, *Roots*, ch. 1 ("Herzen").

45. Gerschenkron, "Economic Development," p. 189; and Herzen, *My Past*, pp. 253–83.

46. Mouzelis, *Politics*, pp. 3–4, 72.

47. Demetrescu, "Liberalismul," pp. 270, 274.

48. Berend and Ranki, *European Periphery*, pp. 83, 115, 123, 156.

49. Chirot, *Social Change*, chs. 6–7; Eidelberg, *Great Rumanian Peasant Revolt*; and Dobrogeanu-Gherea, *Neoiobagia*.

50. Stere, "Socialdemocratism" 2: 320–21, 323.

51. Ibid., 2: 188–89, 330 and 3: 60–61, 68. In citing Kautsky, Stere did not mention that the former remained an orthodox Marxist and showed in *The Agrarian Question* how capitalism had revolutionized agriculture, albeit in more complex ways than industry. This fact owed, in part, to the phenomenon of (noncapitalist) ground rent and the peasant's willingness to engage in superexploitation of his own and his family's labor. Publishing in 1899, the same year Lenin's *The Development of Capitalism in Russia* appeared, Kautsky believed the vast majority of German peasants were already proletarians or semiproletarians selling labor power.

52. Lenin, *Development*, pp. 151, 172–74, 182, 250, 347, 555.

53. Dobrogeanu-Gherea, "Mic Răspuns," pp. 456, 458–60.

54. Dobrogeanu-Gherea, "Post-scriptum," pp. 478–82. The Junimea was a cultural and political grouping founded at Iasi (Jassy) in 1863 by Titu Maiorescu and others who had studied abroad, principally in Germany. (Maiorescu, who had been a student at Berlin, Paris, and Giessen, held a doctorate from the University of Vienna.) The Junimea argued that Romania had not attained a state of development corresponding to its adoption of Western institutions and that the (failed) revolution of 1848 against the Turkish Empire had not been the result of real aspirations of the country. Maiorescu was deeply influenced by Hegel on the evolution of culture and, like the German philosopher, believed that institutions, such as the state, could not change the organic "base," i.e., society; rather, change had to flow from the latter. See "Junimea," pp. 935–36; and Academia de Ştiinţe Sociale, *Istoria filozofiei romaneşti* 1: 353–96 ("Titu Maiorescu").

55. Dobrogeanu-Gherea, "Post-scriptum," pp. 498–99, 503.

56. Dobrogeanu-Gherea, *Socialismul*, pp. 8–9.

57. Ibid., p. 27. A similar idea was expressed by Marx regarding the Germany of the 1860s and was echoed by Lenin with respect to the Russia of the 1890s. Marx, *Capital* 1: 9; Lenin, *Development*, p. 659.

58. Dobrogeanu-Gherea, *Socialismul*, p. 34.

59. Kautsky in 1899 had implicitly touched on, but had not developed, the articulation of capitalist and precapitalist modes of production.

60. Dobrogeanu-Gherea, *Neoiobagia*, p. 64.

61. As Cristian Racovski noted in 1909, peasants had to sign formal contracts, a characteristic feature of capitalist labor relations, but such contracts included stipulations for the payment of feudal dues. Racovski, *Roumanie*, pp. 10–11.

62. Dobrogeanu-Gherea, *Neoiobagia*, p. 281.

63. Ibid., p. 34.

64. Ibid., p. 80. Cf. Racovski's similar analysis in "Chestia Agrară," pp. 40–41.

65. Dobrogeanu-Gherea, *Neoiobagia*, p. 82.

66. E.g., Zeletin, *Burghezia*, p. 18; Manoilescu, "Curs," p. 224; and Madgearu, *Imperialismul*, p. 5.

67. Sir Reginald Hoare to Foreign Office, 21 June 1940, FO 371.24992, Public Record Office, London.

68. Manoilescu, *Théorie du protectionnisme*, p. 177.

69. Ibid., p. 183.

70. Ibid., p. 161.

71. Manoilescu, "Teoria Schimburilor," p. 128.

72. Notably, Bertil Ohlin and Jacob Viner. Ohlin criticized Manoilescu's assumptions: Why should the average productivity of all national industries be considered representative of that of the export industries? What justified the assumption that the price level of factors is everywhere equal, when it was known that money wages in the United States were more than ten times higher than in Romania? Why did Manoilescu only consider labor productivity in his calculations and ignore capital and land? Ohlin's "fundamental criticism" was that, as Manoilescu assumed that factors of production can move from activities with low productivities to those with high productivities, he also assumed that protection causes the transfer. But why, Ohlin asked, did this transfer not occur *without* protection, since price signals should favor the industries with higher productivities? See Ohlin, "Protection," pp. 34–36. Viner made similar criticisms in his review of Manoilescu's book in the *Journal of Political Economy*, (1932), pp. 122, 125.

73. In philosophy, neoidealism found an effective proponent in the Argentinian Alejandro Korn.

74. E.g., the philosopher José Gaos, the sociologist José Medina Echavarría, and the economist José Urbano Guerrero, all resident in Mexico in the late 1930s and early 1940s. To be sure, Latin American readers of Ortega's *Revista de Occidente* were aware of German thought, and many Spanish intellectuals had visited Latin America before the Civil War. Ortega, a neo-Kantian, had lectured in Buenos Aires in 1916 and 1928. *Exilio*, pp. 814, 868, 975; Romero, *Desarrollo*, pp. 128, 134. In our own day some German language classics are available in Spanish, but not English; still others appeared in Spanish before their publication in English. Major studies by Werner Sombart, Henryk Grossman, Karl Kautsky, and Fritz Sternberg have been published in Spanish, but still await their English editions. Both Weber's *Economy and Society* and Hilferding's *Finance Capital* appeared in Spanish first.

75. Anderson, *Considerations*, pp. 25–37. Anderson notes a new generation of French intellectuals entering the Parti Communiste Français in 1928, but perceives no "generalization of Marxism as a theoretical currency in France" until the German occupation (p. 37).

76. As noted, the "peasantist" Madgearu and the corporatist Manoilescu also drew on Hilferding.

77. Aricó, *Marx*. On the points mentioned, see pp. 40, 107, 116–17.

78. On the relatively early appearance of Marxism in Argentina, see Ratzer, *Marxistas*.

79. Mariátegui, "Point de vue," p. 113; Paris, *Formación*, p. 145.

80. Internacional Comunista, *VI Congreso*, 2:180–81, 367.

81. Miroshevski, "Populismo," pp. 55–70, especially p. 68; and Paris, *Formación*, p. 183.

82. Walicki, *Controversy*, pp. 26, 132; Venturi, *Roots of Revolution*, pp. 365, 384, and passim. Gerschenkron argues that populism shaped Russian Marxism, the opposite of Walicki's thesis, but the two writers have different phases in mind for these long and intimately related movements. Gerschenkron, "Economic Development," p. 190.

83. Ionescu, "Eastern Europe," pp. 98–99.

84. Hennessy, "Latin America," p. 42. It seems more appropriate to use Ionescu's term "peasantism" than "populism" to describe peasant political mobilization, as Hennessy does (p. 40).

85. Outside the Communist parties of the region, other voices attacked British and

U.S. imperialism, notably Víctor Raúl Haya de la Torre in Peru and radicals of the Mexican Revolution, such as the anarchist Ricardo Flores Magón.

86. Díaz-Alejandro, *Essays*, pp. 55–56.

87. Justo was not even a Marxist. He considered Marx's theory of surplus value "an ingenious allegory." Justo, quoted in Ratzer, *Movimiento*, p. 34. As Nils Jacobsen notes in his essay, the German Social Democrats also opposed protectionism before World War I, but their position was obviously not based on accepting an "agricultural" role for Germany in international trade.

88. Brazil. Ministério da Fazenda, *Relatório . . . 1899*, p. xiii.

89. Paying their costs in local currency and receiving hard currencies for their exports, such groups profited by obtaining more local currency as its exchange value fell. An unintended byproduct of this exchange policy was a degree of protection for national manufactures, but this effect was partly offset by higher costs of capital imports.

90. Concha, "Balanza," pp. 327–28, and *Lucha*.

91. E.g., List was cited in the Argentine tariff debates of 1875–76, but the episode had no significant effect on Argentina's "open economy" orientation. See Chiaramonte, *Nacionalismo*, p. 136.

92. Sáenz Leme, *Ideologia*, p. 161. More aggressive arguments, e.g., challenging the artificiality of Brazilian manufacturing, had been advanced by the Centro Industrial do Brasil in 1904–5, but to little effect. See Carone, *Pensamento*, pp. 8–9.

93. See Bunge, *Economía*; Colombo, speeches in *Anales de la Unión Industrial Argentina*, año 44 (Dec. 1931), pp. 25, 27, and año 46 (July 1933), p. 37; *Argentina Fabril*, año 53 (Jan. 1940), p. 3; Simonsen, *Crises*, p. 6; Pupo Nogueira, *Em torno da tarifa*, pp. 91–112; and Siciliano, *Agricultura*, p. 18.

94. Estrada, *Ensayo*, p. 77. Paul W. Drake brought this work to my attention.

95. Siciliano, cited in Pupo Nogueira, *Em torno da tarifa*, p. 133; ibid. pp. 3, 131, (on Manoilescu); Siciliano, *Agricultura*, pp. 12, 62; and Simonsen, *Crises*, p. 58.

96. Simonsen, *Crises* p. 88; Pupo Nogueira, *Em torno da tarifa*, p. 136; and Siciliano, *Agricultura*, pp. 27–28.

97. In addition to Manoilescu and Perroux, Gaetan Pirou and Sergio Pannunzio also influenced Brazil's leading theorist of corporatism, Francisco Oliveira Vianna. Vieira, *Autoritarismo*, p. 31.

98. Ibid., pp. 27–70; and Diniz and Boschi, *Empresariado*, p. 59.

99. Additional possible causes of Manoilescu's unfashionability were his open adherence to fascism in the latter 1930s and his support for Germany in World War II.

100. Simonsen and Gudin, *Controvérsia*, pp. 108–9.

101. Congresso Brasileiro da Indústria, *Anais* 1:225–26.

102. See Colombo's speeches in *Anales de la Unión Industrial Argentina*, cited in note 93.

103. "Argentine Industrial Exhibition"; and Villanueva, "Economic Development," p. 78.

104. G. Vargas, *Nova Política* 1 (1938): 26–27; and *O Estado de São Paulo*, 8 March 1933. Interestingly, the artificiality charge came from the left as well. Caio Prado, Jr., Brazil's leading Communist intellectual of his generation, condemned the restrictive practices of Brazilian industrialists in 1935 as an indication of the artificiality of manufacturing, which lacked a mass market. It was necessary to create such a market through the redistribution of wealth before industry could thrive, he believed. Prado, "Programa," pp. 128, 133–35.

105. Thery, *Situation*, p. 67.

106. Villareal, *Desequilibrio*, pp. 43–45; Blair, "Nacional Financiera," pp. 210, 213; Izquierdo, "Protectionism," p. 243 (quotation); and Navarrete R., "Financing," p. 119.

107. Presidente, *Mensaje*, pp. 21–22, 95.

108. Viner, *International Trade*, pp. 61–64; and Love, "Raúl Prebisch" and "Manoilescu."

109. Manoilescu, "Productividad," pp. 50–77.

110. Aurelian, *Viitorul*, p. 21.

2

THE EMERGENCE OF ECONOMIC LIBERALISM IN COLOMBIA

Frank Safford

This chapter is a survey and analysis of salient economic opinion in New Granada (now Colombia) from approximately 1760 to 1880. It also seeks to give a sense of the texture of the economy and of economic thinking. It emphasizes two periods in which economic liberalism was *not* dominant: first, the late colonial era, when economic liberal ideas remained implicit or latent and were part of a variegated stew of economic perspectives, and then, more particularly, the economic crisis of the early 1830s. The study concludes with a summary discussion of the period when economic liberalism enjoyed virtual hegemony, from the end of the 1840s to 1880.

Joseph Love recently offered a definition of economic liberalism as "that corpus of ideology, theory, and policy prescription which sought to free economic activity from all constraints on the market, and promoted the international division of labor through the alleged complementarity of parts of the world economy (given their differing factor endowments)."[1] This brief definition usefully points to two aspects of economic liberalism: first, the general liberal stricture against governmental or institutional constraints upon the operation of market forces, and secondly, the international application of the open market precept. Although these two aspects are two faces of the same principle, it is useful to distinguish between them in our treatment of the incorporation of economic liberalism in Colombia, because they were not always conjoined in practice. At times there was a tendency for economic liberalism to be applied to foreign trade before it was given more general application in domestic policy.

Between 1760 and 1860, it is possible to identify several different phases in the incorporation of liberalism. In the Bourbon reform period (1760–1810), liberal, or protoliberal, notions began to be detectable in discussions of trade questions and, to a lesser degree, in aspects of domestic policy. Independence brought a more general commitment to economic liberalism in the 1820s by the Colombian government. It adopted free trade and attempted both to reform some taxes and to privatize Indian communal holdings in accord with liberal prescriptions. Economic crisis in the 1830s prompted an important policy debate among the elites; liberal dicta were questioned by some and partially abandoned both in foreign trade and in tax policy, though they continued to prevail in other areas, such as the division of Indian community lands. In the 1840s there occurred a renewal of liberal faith, first in tariff policy in 1847, then more broadly in measures affecting national institutions in the 1850s. Indeed, the seeming success of free trade in fostering exports after 1847 provided legitimation and reinforcement for the adoption of liberal doctrines more generally in domestic institutions in the 1850s. By the middle of the nineteenth century, important elements in Colombia's political and economic elites, both Liberal and Conservative, had committed themselves both to the general principle of economic liberalism and to its various applications in domestic economic and foreign trade policy. Particularly in the 1850s, the hegemony of economic liberalism was so complete among many elite sectors that it was virtually a dogma.

THE GEOGRAPHIC CONTEXT

Colombia's ultimate embrace of economic liberalism in the nineteenth century is in some ways surprising. Because of its geographic structure, the country would seem to have been ill suited for a commitment to economic liberalism. Liberal doctrines as elaborated by Adam Smith assumed the existence of effectively functioning markets; the larger the market, the greater the possibilities for increased productivity through the division of labor and economies of scale. Yet, Colombia, because of the combined effects of its mountainous topography and its tropical climate, was broken into many small local markets, while interregional trade was scant and confined to relatively few commodities.

This economic fragmentation partly reflected high freight costs. Because of the rough terrain of the Colombian interior and the difficulty of maintaining transportation routes in a region of seasonally heavy rainfall, pack mules carried almost all overland freight until nearly the end of the nineteenth century. The cost of such transportation was very high: from the 1820s to the 1860s, the rate was about 35 to 65 cents per ton-mile over mountain flanks in dry weather; in time of rain, the rate went up to 80 to 95 cents per ton-mile if mules could be obtained at all.[2] By contrast, in the United States, overland freight costs were dropping rapidly in these same years: from the 1820s onward, goods moved over wagon roads at 12 to 17 cents per ton-mile; by 1851 railroad rates averaged 4 cents per ton-mile, and a decade later they were only 2.2 cents, while canal rates after 1850 dropped below a penny per ton-mile.[3] Thus, while transportation improvements during the nineteenth century created an ever larger and more efficiently integrated national market in the United States, in Colombia such integration would by and large have to wait until the twentieth century.

While high freight costs were an important factor in the atomization of the Colombian economy, there were others too. The combination of mountainous topography and tropical climate created a considerable variation in temperature over relatively short distances, from the hot low country to the cold highlands. Along mountain flanks the differing thermal levels were closely bunched, making possible the cultivation of a considerable variety of crops within relatively restricted areas. Low country sugarcane, *yuca*, and cotton gave way, at successively higher elevations, to maize, other grains, green vegetables, potatoes, and sheep. The proximity of a great variety of crops made long-distance trade unnecessary except for a few commodities. This meant that the integration of a national market, and therefore transportation improvement, may have been less fundamentally important to Colombians than might have been true in the temperate zone. But it also meant that large markets, the division of labor, and economies of scale were slow in coming.

Colombia's geography also deterred its effective participation in the international division of labor. The bulk of its population and much of its best farming land were locked in the mountainous interior of the country, making it extremely difficult, especially with poor and costly transportation linkages, to compete effectively in world markets. Thus Colombia entered into international trade with serious disadvantages.

In contrast, some other areas in Latin America were relatively well endowed for effective competition in the export of primary products. Most notably, Buenos Aires, with its rich pampas hard by the sea, could easily be "born liberal" in foreign trade, as Tulio Halperín Donghi argues elsewhere in this volume. A similar case is Venezuela, with rich valleys near the coast, permitting effective export of cacao, indigo, coffee, and other tropical products. Brazil, with its long coastline of plantations, had played the role of tropical exporter from an earlier period and on a much larger scale. By comparison, Colombia, like Mexico, because of its topographical structure and the location of its population, was at a disadvantage in the export of agricultural products. Surprisingly, the country's elites nevertheless became committed to an essentially liberal trade policy early on in the republican era. Further, at midcentury, they went extremely far in giving expression to the tenets of free market liberalism in domestic institutional arrangements and policies, deliberately restricting the fiscal capacity and the policy purview of the national state. Indeed, between 1850 and 1880, Colombian elites probably were unequaled in the Western world in the extent to which they intentionally fragmented and minimized the power of the national state. If Colombia was not born liberal (economically) in the same manner as Buenos Aires, it was baptized liberal in the independence era and reaffirmed that commitment in still stronger terms at midcentury. The development of a pronounced economic liberalism in a country without an integrated national market and with great disadvantages as an exporter presents an interesting paradox.

ECONOMIC IDEAS IN THE BOURBON REFORM PERIOD OF THE COLONIAL ERA

Our principal sources on economic ideas in the Nuevo Reino de Granada (later Colombia) are the reports of Spanish viceroys and other officials and the writings of native sons, many of whom also were serving as colonial administrators or in semiofficial positions. There is not much evidence of consciously articulated economic concepts in their writings. The authors, after all, were government administrators, primarily concerned with practical economic and fiscal problems, and they were writing in the notably untheoretical, ad hoc tradition of the Spanish *arbitristas*. The economic concerns and the economic proposals expounded in their writings appear to have been shaped for the most part by policy signals emanating from Spain and by New Granada's geographic and economic realities. Shards of economic ideas may be found in these expositions, but inferences about commitments to particular economic theories must be drawn with caution.

Many of the problems that Spanish officials sought to address between 1760 and 1810 were those confronted by republican elites after independence. Not surprisingly, the collection of revenues was a constant preoccupation of administrators in both regimes. The problem of contraband bothered officials in both the colonial and republican eras, though it was more frequently harped on in the colonial era. Colonial administrators, like their republican successors, worried about the imbalance of New Granada's foreign trade. In the 1760s and 1770s, as in the 1820s and 1830s, New Granada exported little besides gold. Because of its lack of adequate exports, the country suffered a drain of specie in payment for imports. Thus, despite substantial exports of gold mined in its western provinces, New Granada remained poor and lacked the capital needed to undertake new economic initiatives.[4] Most viceroys after 1765 therefore sought to expand exports beyond gold. They also tried to keep North American wheat flour out of the markets on the Caribbean coast, so that wheat producers in the interior might supply them. Such a measure would help to stanch the outward flow of wealth from the realm, while providing income to the wheat-growing regions of the eastern highlands. Finally, the viceroys recognized that movement toward any of their economic objectives depended on improvements in overland and river transportation. Better overland trails were needed to supply the western goldmining regions, to promote other export commodities, and to make wheat flour from the eastern highlands competitive with that from North America on the Caribbean coast.[5]

The cast of mind of most of New Granada's eighteenth-century viceroys was a mix of traditional *arbitrismo*, focusing particularly on increasing revenues and preventing contraband, and of enlightened mercantilism. In general they assumed the state should play an active role in controlling, even in managing, commerce.

Frequently they advocated or established fiscal monopolies over the production of commodities.

One of New Granada's viceroys, Manuel de Guirior (1772–76), stands out as at least a selective exponent of a kind of protoliberalism. Guirior's report of 1776 took as its dominant theme the lack of commerce in New Granada and the need to stimulate it. Guirior was the first viceroy to focus much attention on the development of exports of tropical fruits to complement gold exports. He blamed existing taxes for the lack of agricultural exports. And he was unusual among New Granada's viceroys in tending to favor free enterprise, rather than state management, as the best way to encourage the development of new commercial activities or the resuscitation of ailing ones.[6]

Yet, even Guirior was not consistent in his protoliberal tendencies. Some two decades before Gaspar Melchor de Jovellanos's *Informe de ley agraria*, Guirior inveighed against latifundia that left land unused. His focus on the importance of land may reflect French physiocratic influences. Yet his remedy for the blight of latifundia was a rather unliberal, and unphysiocratic, one: the state should "oblige" *latifundistas* to alienate their land, so that others might use it. Similarly, seeking to develop wool manufacture in the interior, Guirior wanted to forbid the slaughter of sheep and require large landowners to raise sheep if they did not already do so. He advocated the rigorous enforcement of local price controls on basic foods, a long-standing feature of Spanish economic tradition. And his rhetoric now and again tended to have more the flavor of mercantilism than of protoliberalism: for example, he encouraged the sale of flour from the interior on the Caribbean coast, arguing that it would deny wealth to Spain's enemies, as well as enrich New Granadan producers.[7]

Guirior's protoliberal leanings did not mark the beginning of a consistent liberalizing trend among Spanish officials. On the contrary, subsequent viceroys of the 1780s, particularly the Archbishop-Viceroy Antonio Caballero y Góngora (1782–89), in accord with the general tendency of Spanish policy at the time, favored the use of state fiscal monopolies. Viceroys Francisco Gil y Lemos in the 1780s and José de Ezpeleta in the 1790s sought to choke off the export of some commodities from the coast on the ground that this trade provided an avenue for contraband. Still, Ezpeleta and his successor, Pedro de Mendinueta (1796–1803), were, like Guirior, strongly interested in developing exports of tropical products, and they generally opposed state monopolies or taxes on exportable commodities.[8]

It is hard to detect in any of these officials a clear and self-conscious adoption of liberal precepts. The most general hint of developing liberal tendencies is the increased orientation toward exporting and a corresponding opposition to taxes on exportable commodities. However, while both of these phenomena are consonant with liberal positions, they need not have been motivated by liberal convictions; they just as easily could have been a consequence of a practical assessment of the realities of the situation.

If the existence of liberal influences on Spanish administrators in New Granada remains unclear, liberal tendencies, and even direct influences, are more evident, albeit in an inchoate way, in some of the late colonial *criollo* economic writers. The most notable of these were Pedro Fermín de Vargas (b. 1762), author of several economic tracts around 1790, and José Ignacio de Pombo (b. 1761), whose known economic writings date from 1807–10. Both writers opposed government fiscal monopolies and supported more freedom of trade. Pombo, who had read Adam Smith by 1810, asserted the fundamental liberal tenet of the harmony of the economic interests of the individual and society.[9]

Vargas, who had served as a viceregal bureaucrat and then as a corregidor, borrowed eclectically. He quotes the physiocrat Mirabeau the Elder—but to an end that was not characteristically physiocratic—to justify the establishment of basic manufacturing industries in poor regions. Five years before Jovellanos's *Informe de ley agraria*, Vargas decried the predominance of large estates, which led to extreme inequality and hindered population growth and prosperity. His views on latifundia may not have been based on theory so much as upon historical experience and his own observation. He cites early Roman examples and the positive results of Henry VII's permitting the sale of feudal domains in England. He also points to the region of his birth (San Gil and Socorro) as demonstrating that small holdings were much more productive than latifundia.[10] Elsewhere, in an attack on government fiscal monopolies, Vargas makes use of a slogan usually identified with post-Smith political economy: "the government makes a bad businessman." Once again, however, the slogan is backed by reference to local experience—the poor results of government-run emerald and silver mines.[11]

In Pombo one finds a similar eclecticism. His *Informe* of 1807 is a consistent argument for the end of all taxes and monopolies on exportable agricultural products. Pombo's later *Informe* of 1810, however, combines elements of Bourbon reformist mercantilism and an enthusiasm for the principles of Adam Smith, whose *Wealth of Nations* had recently come into his hands. He cites Francisco Peñaranda and Bernardo Ward in support of government action to establish *hospicios* (poorhouses or workhouses). He quotes José del Campillo y Cossío on the barbarity of taxes on agriculture, on the physiocratic ground that "the products of the earth . . . constitute true wealth." He calls on his province of Cartagena to grow wheat in order to end its dependency on foreign flour (in the face of the absolute advantage of North American wheat). He also cites Adam Smith's labor theory of value, but does so in order to advocate protective duties for some types of manufacturing in New Granada.[12] Clearly we have here an undogmatic adherence to a variety of imported ideas, not necessarily mutually consistent.

THE STATE OF ECONOMIC KNOWLEDGE IN COLOMBIA, 1820–70

In 1810, at the dawn of the struggle for Colombian independence, José Ignacio de Pombo, clearly aware that the moment held great possibilities, recommended the establishment of a university chair in political economy.[13] A decade later, legislators in a newly independent Colombia included political economy in the standard curriculum for law students in universities and *colegios*, with Jean-Baptiste Say providing the prescribed text.[14] During the 1830s instruction in political economy was offered in universities and *colegios* in every section of the country.[15] It is not clear whether Say's text was read in all of these courses. Say was used by Ezequiel Rojas, one of the leading exponents of political economy at this time.[16]

Inventories of libraries of the period may suggest the diffusion of modern economic ideas. In libraries of four important figures in politics and/or education, dating from the years 1840 to 1852, Say appears in two. A third contained a book by the now obscure Charles Ganilh (1758–1836), a French apologist for protection. Three of the four had Jeremy Bentham's *Defense of Usury* as part of large collections of Bentham's works. Eighteenth-century Spanish writers were also represented: Francisco Cabarrús and Jovellanos (the *Informe de ley agraria*) appeared in one library, Pedro Campomanes and José Canga Argüelles's *Elementos de la ciencia de hacienda*, in another.[17] Of course, the fact that these volumes were in these libraries does not necessarily mean that they were read or their contents absorbed.

Recently Jesús Antonio Bejarano, a Colombian economic historian, has disparaged the extent and quality of Colombian economic knowledge for the whole of the nineteenth century. In that period, Bejarano says,

there continued a tradition situated half-way between that of physiocracy and mercantilism. . . . Santander liked to cite Necker and Colbert, and Murillo Toro as well as Salvador Camacho [mid-century Liberals] shamelessly invoked Quesnay a hundred years late to support an extravagant proposal for a single tax. The English classical liberalism of Smith and Ricardo was beyond the ken of the Frenchified modes of Colombian culture. . . . [Also] because of its abstract character [that culture] was less well adjusted to the political realism with which economic problems were dealt with than were the more pragmatic mercantilism, which, without achieving the status of theory, nevertheless provided practical and easily understood recommendations. Reading Jean-Baptiste Say's popular manual and Bentham was perhaps the only contact with classical economics; . . . even Florentino González, seemingly the only one who had seriously read Smith, ended up reducing him to the free trade message.[18]

There is some truth in Bejarano's acerbic commentary, as regards the extent of economic knowledge and the sophistication of economic discussion. It does appear that Say was the principal source of political economy for the Colombian elite (as he was also in the United States, for that matter). Few in the Colombian elite read Adam Smith; *The Wealth of Nations* is noticeably absent from the library inventories. And there is scant evidence of Ricardo's influence in nineteenth-century economic writers.

But the statement needs some refining, for the sake of both accuracy and fairness. First, it is not possible to make general statements for the whole of the nineteenth century. There were, in fact, distinct economic attitudes characterizing different periods. The ideas and policies of the period 1821–47 might be characterized as a pragmatic mix of economic liberalism and neo-mercantilism; as noted, liberalism was present particularly in the early fiscal reforms and legislative efforts to divide Indian community lands in the early 1820s, while protectionism became more evident as economic conditions worsened in the early 1830s. The years from the late 1840s through the early 1860s were marked by the hegemony of laissez-faire liberalism, often expressed in a rather dogmatic form. The period from roughly 1864 to 1880 continued the hegemony of economic liberalism, but now in a less absolute mode.

Secondly, Bejarano greatly exaggerates the extent of the ignorance of the Colombian elite about contemporary economic theory in Europe. Few may have read the latest economic treatises, but some at least knew who the leading theorists were. They kept up with the European press and would have gleaned from it whatever it might convey about current economic thinking. For example, Francisco de Paula Santander as a political leader made no claim to sophistication in economic science, yet Bejarano's suggestion that Santander took Jacques Necker and Jean Baptiste Colbert as models is a slander. The only reference to these mercantilists in Santander's collected papers in no way suggests a commitment to their ideas. In 1820 Santander, who was concerned about raising enough revenue to sustain the wars of independence, opposed on practical grounds Pedro Gual's effort to institute a sweeping liberal reform of the tax system in the province of Cartagena. Writing to Bolívar about his differences with Gual, Santander noted:

On this subject of political economy everyone thinks in his own manner. Necker differed from Colbert, and the economists of today will have different opinions than they [Necker and Colbert]. . . . I don't understand all this, nor do I have reason to understand it, but I understand fourteen months of experience of being in charge of providing pecuniary aid for whatever is needed. . . . Gual may have seen the United States, but I am carrying on the [fiscal] struggle in Cundinamarca.[19]

This quotation clearly does not support the notion that Santander was a mercantilist two centuries out of date. In fact, he knew not only of Smith and Say by 1826, but also had heard of Malthus and Ricardo, though one may doubt that he had actually read any of them except perhaps Say. Santander made use of the names of these political economists, in little fiscal jokes, essentially to transmit the same message—that, as the person in charge of the national executive, he had to be governed by practical necessities rather than by theories.[20]

Similarly, Bejarano defames Manuel Murillo Toro and Salvador Camacho Roldán with the suggestion that their economic knowledge in the early 1850s was limited to the eighteenth-century physiocrat François Quesnay. Murillo Toro, for example, in 1853 quoted, and was deeply influenced by, Simonde de Sismondi and Frédéric Bastiat; the latter's writings dated primarily from the late 1840s.[21]

THE ECONOMIC CRISIS AND THE POLICY DEBATE OF
THE EARLY 1830s

As already indicated, the early years of the independence era, from 1820 to 1845, were characterized by a relative lack of dogmatism in the making of economic policy, in contrast with the marked commitment to laissez-faire of 1849–63. Legislative debates and discussions within the Council of State make clear that there were marked differences of opinion over appropriate institutions and policies among liberals, pragmatic moderates, and traditionalists. Economic liberals in the 1820s tended to support a general reform of the fiscal system inherited from the Spanish, the lowering of import duties, and the elimination of export taxes. Pragmatic moderates, like Santander, tended to be cautious about changes in the tax system in fear of a drastic decline in revenues, while embracing other changes such as the abolition of slavery or the proposed division of Indian community lands into individual properties. Traditionalists tended to resist almost all alterations in the existing system, including the abolition of slavery. But though there are clearly observable differences of opinion, a generally practical spirit tended to prevail. In debates on economic or fiscal policy, it is noticeable that, while the views of some speakers clearly are informed by liberal theory, they tend not to appeal to the authority of liberal theorists. Nor do their opponents appeal to theoretical authority. Rather speakers tend to focus upon the practical consequences of policy.[22]

This undogmatic practicality, already evident in the 1820s, took on a more conservative cast during the difficult years between 1830 and 1845. This was a period marked by a tendency to preserve existing economic institutions and economic policies, in contrast with the tendency to optimistic liberal experiments that had been more characteristic of the early 1820s. Whereas the Congress of 1821 had sought to begin the end of slavery through a law of free birth, those who were politically dominant between 1830 and 1845 sought in various ways to evade or to delay the effect of the commitment of 1821. The legislators of 1821, guided by liberal economic ideology, had also sought to end the fiscal monopolies and the many vexatious and counterproductive taxes, such as the *alcabala*, an ancient Spanish sales tax, replacing them with a direct tax. Later in the 1820s, legislators, finding the direct tax virtually unenforceable, felt compelled by fiscal necessity to restore the *alcabala* and other taxes recognized as contrary to liberal theory, but which the harness of habit made it possible to enforce. Throughout the 1830–45 period the Colombian political elite retained such remains of the Spanish fiscal system as government monopolies over tobacco, salt, and *aguardiente*, because they feared the fiscal consequences of abandoning them. One innovation reflecting liberal economic thinking did occur, however: in 1835, on the initiative of the liberal Ezequiel Rojas and of Mariano Ospina Rodríguez (later leader of the Conservative party), the interest rate was freed.[23]

While the period from 1830 to 1845 was for the most part one of adherence to the status quo in terms of economic and fiscal institutions, the early 1830s (roughly 1831–34) were marked by a sharp debate about the general orientation of economic policy. This debate pitted economic liberals against protectionists. It was prompted by a severe economic crisis, which had multiple origins. First, recruitment during the independence wars had disrupted and reduced the labor force, both slave labor mining gold in western Colombia and free labor growing wheat, cotton, and tobacco in the eastern zone. As a consequence, in the independence period Colombia's production and export of gold declined, and its capacity to supply wheat flour to domestic markets virtually collapsed. In addition, when independence opened the possibility of free trade, imports of war materials, cloth, some foods, and consumer goods in general greatly increased. Thus, while Colombia's capacity to export, slight in any case, was disrupted by war, its import bill expanded. The adverse trade balance that developed, principally with Great Britain, for a time was financed in part by bond issues in London early in the 1820s. For a brief time around 1825 a fraction of the capital raised by the bond issue of 1824 actually reached Colombia (an estimated two million pesos) and provided a transient economic stimulus. According to contemporaries, this brief infusion of capacity to import further encouraged Colombian consumers to shift from coarse domestic cloths to finer imported ones.[24] But financial crisis in London and growing skepticism about Colombia's economic potential curtailed further flows of British capital. As foreign investment slowed to a halt, Colombians once again faced the consequences of the country's negative trade balance. By the end of the 1820s imported goods were being paid for by substantial remissions of specie, which, it was believed, exceeded New Granada's total gold production.[25]

The problems created by a chronic foreign trade imbalance were aggravated by the political crises that Colombia suffered from 1826 through 1831. The turmoil of these years was said by contemporaries to have discouraged enterprise. It probably also prompted the flight of Colombian capital as well as providing a further deterrent to European investments.

The combination of specie payments for imported goods and capital flight had drained the country of much of its circulating media. And as New Granada lacked banks or any other institutional devices for creating alternative means of exchange through credit, by 1830 the country was suffering a severe currency contraction, an equally severe depression of land and commodity prices, and extremely high interest rates (2 to 5 percent per month).[26] The price of one basic commodity, wheat, on the other hand, was unusually high, because for a decade wheat rust had ruined harvests, bringing substantial losses to growers.[27] Landowners in many parts of the country, unable to pay interest on their loans, were calling for the suspension of the *diezmo* (tithe) and even for the low 5 percent annual interest rate charged on loans from ecclesiastical sources to be scaled back to 3 percent.[28] Furthermore, rural weavers and urban artisans were suffering from the general fall of prices and the constriction of domestic demand, as well as from the competition of British and other foreign goods.

The crisis of the early 1830s prompted a surge of protectionism that was expressed in some manner in many parts of the country. There were two rather generalized explanations of the need for protection: First, protectionist measures were required to cut down on imports in order to reduce the outflow of specie, thereby keeping means of payment in circulation and preventing prices from falling further. Secondly, the competition of imported goods had reduced certain urban artisans, rural weavers, and some agricultural groups to misery.

Given the emphasis in protectionist writings on curtailing the outward drain of specie and the tendency to lament the fate of artisans, weavers, and farmers, it appears paradoxical that protection was first, and quite frequently, sought for Colombian import-export merchants. It is, of course, hardly surprising that pleas for protection of Colombian merchants from British competition were heard. After all, these merchants formed part of the urban elite and in not a few cases were politically prominent. What is surprising is that no one, not even liberal free traders, pointed out that protecting Colombian importers from the competition of British merchants would do little if anything to alleviate either the exchange problem or the misery of artisans, weavers, and farmers.

The felt need to protect merchants from foreign competitors dated from the early 1820s. To protect the position of national merchants, the Colombian government in 1822 had required foreign importers to consign their goods to Colombian merchants. This obligation, however, was removed by the 1825 treaty between Colombia and Great Britain, which granted the merchants of each country the right to trade on the same basis. By 1830, Colombian commercial interests were complaining that British merchants were "annihilating" local competition. The need to restrict the British merchants was, along with the need for political stability, the most commonly voiced aspiration made in reports from eight commericial cities in 1830–31.[29] The 1825 treaty, the defenders of New Granadan merchants asserted, was only formally equal and reciprocal, as the Granadans were unlikely to operate in England, while British merchants were taking over Colombia. New Granadan merchants, they argued, could not compete with British ones, since British traders, with superior credit, shipping, and manufacturing contacts in England, could bring their goods directly from Great Britain; thus they could easily undersell their Colombian counterparts, the most substantial of whom brought their goods from Jamaica. From 1830 through 1833, therefore, there were repeated calls for the revocation or revision of the 1825 treaty and a return to the requirement that foreign merchants consign their goods to local ones.[30]

Urban artisans in the early 1830s asked for two kinds of protection, the prohibition of imports of all manufactured goods and protection from the competition of immigrant artisans. Bogotá's artisans pointed out that their foreign competitors enjoyed privileges that the Granadan artificers lacked. To wit, foreigners were exempt from military service and from some kinds of taxes; further, as non-Catholics, they could work on religious festival days.[31] There was, however, little elite support for restricting the immigration of artisans; even protectionists among the governing class for the most part wanted to encourage the immigration of European capital and skilled labor. There was more sympathy for providing urban artisans with some protection from imported finished goods.

Many contemporary writings lamented the impoverishment of the rural weavers, but it is hard to tell how much real support there was for protecting their product. A number of articles called for prohibiting the importation of "manufactured goods," leaving unclear whether that term referred to cloth or finished goods, or both.

The protection of domestic agriculture from imports had advocates in at least certain parts of New Granada. The canton of Ocaña was particularly insistent on the protection of wheat flour, for which it wished to recapture markets on the Caribbean coast.

It was in the context of these specific concerns that a broader debate developed on the economic strategy that New Granada ought to pursue. An analysis of the crisis of the 1830s from a liberal perspective was most elaborately and persuasively stated by the British merchant William Wills. Wills emphasized political instability and the flight of capital as the root of the crisis, downplaying the role of imports. He further argued that New Granada, as a gold-producing country, ought to be exporting precious metals anyway, rather than hoarding them. The long-term solution to New Granada's problems, he suggested, lay in the development of agricultural exports. The protection of cottage weavers was a hopeless cause, as they could never compete with British machines. The only effect of such protection would be to burden consumers in order to favor a minority of producers. In sum, New Granada ought to play to its absolute advantage in tropical products; its future ought to lie in more international trade, not less.[32]

Despite the protectionist wave of the early 1830s, Wills's views were echoed by more than a few New Granadans. Some indeed were considerably more dogmatic than Wills in their adherence to economic liberalism. One anonymous writer placed his faith in the idea of a perfect market-adjusted monetary equilibrium. If New Granada was exporting gold and silver, it was clearly because the New Granadan market contained more than it could use; to try to retain it would only raise prices artificially. The free flow of currency would be "the true regulator of the amount of currency necessary for the movements of commerce"; it would "liberate us from the superabundance of unused precious metals"; and it would "constantly maintain the quantity at the required level of circulation."[33]

Perhaps few New Granadans were quite so sanguine about the perfections of the exchange market. There was a broad consensus among the elite, however, that the country had to stake its future on the export of tropical products, rather than autarchic development. Some who were most committed to the export model of development, like Wills, blamed New Granada's failures in this area on lack of enterprise.[34]

Toward the center of the liberal-to-protectionist spectrum were some leading public figures who intellectually accepted the doctrines of liberal political economy but who gave at least lukewarm support to some protection simply as a pragmatic response to crisis. Characteristic of these was Rufino Cuervo, the Governor of Bogotá province in 1831. Cuervo accepted the basic contention of liberal political economy that, because of its ample supply of fertile land and its scanty population, New Granada would have to give its preference to agriculture, with particular attention to exportable tropical crops. Cuervo believed, however, that the development of tropical exports could not come quickly enough to solve the immediate problems associated with the current trade imbalance. He therefore was willing to put aside the doctrines of political economy in response to the general pressure to restrict commerce.[35]

A little further toward the protectionist pole of the ideological spectrum were those whom the crisis drove to such desperation that they began explicitly to question the precepts of liberal political economy. In January, 1833, a junta of twenty-eight notable merchants and hacendados in Bogotá, contemplating the monetary scarcity, the drastic fall of prices, and the general bankruptcy of all economic sectors, announced that "most of the [economic principles] that European authors establish as encouraging economic activity of the Old World are not applicable in the New. . . . Experience . . . sadly has convinced us that the theories of the European economists have been the ruin of this country." The authors of the statement clearly were aware of some of the liberal principles that they were rejecting. For example, they agreed with liberal precepts in rejecting the mercantilist tendency to equate wealth with money. Yes, they understood, they said, that it was better to have fifty thousand pesos in productive capacity than in money. But this was only true, they pointed out, if there were enough currency in circulation to keep the economy moving. Because of the need to keep some means of payment in circulation and also to fight the social malaise brought on by unemployment, they supported restrictions on foreign merchants, high duties on imported luxuries, and prohibition of the importation of products already made in New Granada.

The junta also understood that, in theory, New Granada's imports of manufactures should stimulate agricultural exports. But that had not happened, because of lack of capital and the high cost of transportation over mule trails in the mountainous interior. They still held out hope of exporting tropical products from the lowlands. (In fact, they sought to encourage the establishment of large plantations for tropical crops by prohibiting the importation of such products.) But they wondered how the mass of population in the interior highlands would survive. Viewing the general depression affecting all sectors, they asked plaintively, "In what kind of work can Granadans employ themselves?"[36]

The junta's tone of perplexity reflected the fact that, while conditions seemed to put liberal economic theory in question, they did not have an integrated countertheory to replace that body of doctrines. A few in the political elite, however, soon began to develop structured arguments for protection as part of a strategy of economic autarchy. Salient figures in the creation of an alternative vision to liberal political economy were two residents of Bogotá, Dr. José Félix de Merizalde, a physician who was a frequent and vituperative participant in the polemics of the capital, and the more sedate Alejandro Osorio, who had held important positions in the government of Bolívar.

The importance of Merizalde's reasoning is somewhat obscured by his abusive tone and a certain lack of selectivity in his comments. He began his protectionist writings early in 1833 with a series of virulent attacks on foreigners, among other things celebrating as an act of divine providence the sinking of a steamboat loaded with a foreign merchant's imported goods. But mixed in with such sallies were some perspicacious observations: He noted the cleverness of the British in deliberately making low-quality cotton goods, which not only could undersell the local product, but would also wear out quickly, thus sustaining demand. He also alleged that the diabolic English were willing to sell their products at less than cost in order to ruin the manufacturing of other countries, after which they could charge monopoly prices.[37]

Whereas his bewildered contemporaries could bring themselves only to question the validity of liberal economic doctrines, Merizalde scornfully rejected these precepts. Jean-Baptiste Say, he claimed, was a "writer paid by England to bewitch" other nations. Merizalde said that Say had been combatted "victoriously" by Malthus, "in a work that the English have succeeded in preventing from being diffused, so that they could monopolize commerce." He also noted that the British themselves had not adhered to free trade precepts when they were founding their own industries.[38]

Among his many acrid observations, Merizalde also touched briefly on points that were fundamental to the construction of an alternative economic vision. He pointed out that the ruin of the weavers hurt agriculturalists too, as the farmers of the interior provinces produced goods, like wool and cotton, that could not be exported competitively and for which there would be no domestic market if the rural weavers disappeared. Like his contemporaries, he also noted the social costs of the decline of handweaving, which would increase idleness and undermine habits of industry in the weaving regions.[39]

Some of Merizalde's observations were restated, more soberly and dispassionately, by Alejandro Osorio in 1834, in a more coherent and systematic analysis, one with a surprisingly modern orientation toward employment as the key to prosperity. Osorio started his argument with a penetrating critique of free trade. Free trade, he admitted, offered the benefits of keeping prices low through competition. But the system could not work well for a country like New Granada, if the other nations with which it traded maintained, as Great Britain did, restrictions on the importation of goods New Granada might sell them. Indeed, he pointed out, all of the most powerful nations of the world, including Russia and the United States, maintained protectionist policies. It was foolhardy for a poor country like New Granada to adhere to free trade when the most advanced countries did not practice this preachment. In any event, free trade principles could not be applied to a country that lacked industry, shipping capacity, or commerce. "A country with neither agriculture nor industry, whose commerce of little consumption is in foreign hands is, as I see it, *a colony—simply a market for the foreigner.*" From the point of view of Great Britain, in fact, it was the best kind of colony, one that consumed British goods without involving any colonial administrative costs.

Free trade doctrine, Osorio pointed out, placed too much emphasis upon consumption, that is, upon the benefits of keeping prices low. Without anything to export, consumption meant simply handing over scarce means of exchange, depressing the economy. New Granadan free traders, he noted, had accused their countrymen of lack of enterprise, but enterprise could hardly be expected unless money were circulating and profits could be made.

In emphasizing consumption, Osorio thought, free traders were focusing upon the wrong thing. Instead of seeking low prices for consumer goods, they should be focusing upon creating employment so as to build internal demand. It would not do any good for prices to fall if laborers were unemployed or underemployed and could not afford goods at any cost. The government, he insisted, had to pursue a policy aimed at creating jobs. Manufacturing was an important means of creating jobs and building consumer power. Among its advantages in both respects was the fact that it offered year-round work and it employed women and children. It was important to develop agriculture, of course. But the contrasting cases of Poland and Russia on the one hand, and of England and the United States on the other, showed that a purely agricultural country would never become rich. Solely agricultural countries could not become wealthy, because they could not export all of their agricultural surplus. An industrial economy, with its demand for raw materials and with an urban workforce to feed, would provide a better internal market for agricultural surpluses. Osorio further emphasized the reciprocal relations of manufacturing and agriculture, each providing markets for the other. New Granada, he concluded, needed a general plan for coherent national economic development, emphasizing the creation of employment and the development of internal commerce.[40]

Osorio's sustained argument, too briefly summarized here, was an impressive intellectual achievement, both in its critique of the assumptions and real consequences of free trade and in his well-reasoned advocacy of a policy of balanced, autarchic growth. Reasoned argumentation, however, does not always carry the day. Osorio's argument, effectively presented though it was, never gained currency among the Colombian elite. One finds no subsequent repetition of it, or even of significant parts of it, in the New Granadan press. That his argument had so little resonance is testimony to the fact that, largely because of the weight of European authority, liberal political economy already had a substantial hold on Granadan elites. The crisis of the 1830s created widespread doubts about the faith but led only a few to abandon it.

For all of the rhetoric spilled upon the pages of newspapers and the reports of citizens' juntas, the protectionist wave of 1830–34 did not lead New Granada to the absolute import prohibitions asked by many protectionists. José Ignacio de Márquez, from Tunja, in the wool-growing and woolen-weaving region, supported protection as secretary of finance in 1831 and as acting chief executive in 1832. But beginning in 1833 those shaping economic policy in the executive branch, President Santander and especially his secretary of finance, Francisco Soto, were fundamentally liberal in economic as well as political principles. During the protectionist storm, however, they both trimmed toward protection. Soto opposed prohibiting any imports on the standard liberal ground that this would artificially raise prices to consumers. But, while maintaining that New Granada ought not to be involved in manufacturing given its agricultural resources, he granted that those provinces already engaged in weaving ought to have a right to a livelihood. He therefore proposed a balanced policy of moderately protective tariffs for weavers without excessively burdening the country's consumers.[41]

Santander, as already indicated, was not a dogmatist in economic matters and therefore probably did not find it difficult to support some kind of protection. But the moderation of his rhetoric is telling:

Popular opinion in New Granada demands this measure in favor of some agricultural products and nascent manufactures supplying consumers in the interior provinces. And the Executive believes that it should be adopted, if for no other reason than to enlighten ourselves through our own experience.[42]

Experience, he seemed to suggest, might teach New Granadans that tariff protection was inadvisable.

With considerable pressure for protection coming from the most important provinces, the Chamber of Deputies in 1833 prohibited a number of items by an overwhelming margin. The vote in the Chamber, however, represented the high water mark of protectionist influence in Congress. The bill was beaten down in the Senate, and the Chamber accepted the Senate's insistence on duties, without absolute prohibitions. Yet some of the duties were, in effect, prohibitive.[43] Flour, for example, would have to pay roughly 100 percent of its value. Duties on ready-made clothing, at 30 percent of value in 1831, and 35.5 percent in 1832, also went up to the neighborhood of 100 percent in 1833. Duties on common cloth, on the other hand, rose less sharply (by about 43 percent from 1831 to 1833) and appear to have been less prohibitive (25 percent of value).[44]

Thus the legislators favored the wheat growers of Ocaña and the urban artisans much more than they did the cottage weavers of Socorro and Boyacá. This difference in treatment may be explained in terms of political and economic leverage. Urban artisans were less poor, more frequently literate and politically active; moreover they were better located to put pressure on the political elites than the cottage weavers. Besides, the urban artisans typically were men, while the cottage weavers were women, whose work supplemented the incomes of male agriculturalists. Finally, the governing class probably still had some interest in the survival of local tailors and bootmakers, not yet having reached the epoch when the better-heeled had such frequent contacts with Europe as to order custom-made clothing in Paris.

The difference in treatment can also be explained, however, in terms of economic concepts current at the time. William Wills had argued in 1831 that it made more sense to protect urban artisans, whose production processes did not require much machinery, than to protect the cottage weavers, who could not possibly compete with highly mechanized British factories. Wills, taking a position that would become dogma among the Colombian governing class at mid-century, suggested that the rural weavers, rather than wasting their labors in a doomed attempt to compete with European factories, should abandon weaving for the production of tropical products, which he presumed would be more profitable to them.[45]

After 1833, the influence of protectionism gradually subsided. Already in 1834 the legislators halved the duty on foreign flour because the prohibitive duty of 1833 had left flour practically unavailable in the Caribbean coastal markets. The 1834 Congress also began to trim the duties on common cloth, and did so more significantly in the 1840s. Duties on some ready-made clothing, such as boots and capes, also declined during the 1830s. Duties on some other products of urban artisans, however, remained high until 1847.[46]

While urban artisans received considerable help, New Granadan merchants got little. President Santander reported in 1834 that the British were unwilling to modify the 1825 treaty that put British merchants on an equal footing with Granadan ones. Although a few newspaper articles subsequently called for restrictions on foreign merchants, the issue tended to fade away during the 1830s. It seems likely that the measure lost much of its constituency because New Granadan merchants were securing a large share of the import-export trade. Scattered data suggest that the merchants may have exaggerated the extent of the British merchant takeover even during the early 1830s.[47] In any event, it appears that by 1839–41 New Granadan merchants had developed their own commercial links to Europe and were bringing most of the merchandise shipments from European ports on their own account.[48]

It is not clear how much Colombian merchants were aided by the fact that goods brought on Colombian ships paid lower duties than those introduced from ships under other flags. Though this system varied in detail over time, it existed throughout the period from 1821 to 1847, and no major changes in the law occurred in the 1830s.[49] It is possible that in the late 1830s Colombian merchants were in a better position to take advantage of this preference than they had been in earlier periods.

The other notable protective device affecting elite enterprise throughout this period was the concession of limited monopoly privileges, in effect patents, for companies introducing technical innovations. This concession was used in the 1820s in an effort to put steamboats on the Magdalena River and to encourage an ironworks. In the 1830s the same privilege was granted to several small factories in Bogotá. It is important to emphasize, however, that these concessions were limited. They granted monopoly rights, for a specified area and time period, and only for the production of a good by modern techniques not previously used in Colombia. They did not prevent the continued manufacture of the same product by traditional methods. Nor did they in any way restrict the importation of the same product.[50] These concessions therefore protected not against foreign imports but against local competition. Interestingly, the factory entrepreneurs of the 1830s did not seek tariffs against foreign competition.

In part because the privileges or patents did protect against competition from other Colombian entrepreneurs, they began to fall out of favor during the 1830s. In the latter half of the decade it was increasingly argued that the privileges, rather than promoting the establishment of new industries, might be delaying their implantation by preventing competitors within the concession area from having a try. In 1835 and again in 1840 a group in Antioquia complained that the privilege enjoyed by an ironworks near Bogotá had prevented them from creating another in their province. On these grounds President José Ignacio Márquez, who throughout the 1830–45 period supported protection against imported goods, in 1840 opposed extension of the ironworks privilege. By 1840, exclusive privileges had fallen out of favor as instruments for promoting industrial development, though a privilege limited to Antioquia was extended to ironworks there as late as 1844. The increasing aversion to such privileges may be viewed as one indicator of an increasing commitment to the idea of unrestrained individual enterprise. It also reflects, of course, the fact that the protected industries either had failed or had been only modest successes.

Finally, in treating the protectionism of the 1830s, the relationship of economic issues to partisan alignments must be considered. The leadership of the Santanderista faction, from which the Liberal party ultimately emerged, was fundamentally committed to liberal principles, in economic as well as in other matters. However, as indicated, not only Santander but his followers as well were not so dogmatic about economic liberalism that they were not willing to make practical adjustments. Some of the men identified with the moderate faction that ultimately provided the core of the Conservative party were protectionists in the 1830s. José Ignacio de Márquez and Alejandro Osorio are salient examples. On the other hand, a number of men who were equally important in the conservative strand—such as José Manuel Restrepo and Lino de Pombo—remained ardent free traders even in the worst of the 1830s crisis. As strongly as the protection question engaged the concerns of the elite in the early 1830s, it appears not to have become a basis for partisan division.

Similarly, in regional terms, protectionism had its strongest and most persistent support in the eastern highland regions of Cundinamarca and Boyacá, where farmers, weavers, and artisans were all gravely affected by the crisis. Yet there were also many strong defenders of liberal economy hailing from both regions. And protectionist voices were heard on the Caribbean coast, in Antioquia, and the Cauca Valley, regions that were less adversely affected.

The crisis of the 1830s, and the whole of the 1820–45 period, in Colombia

demands some comparison with Peru in the same era, as treated by Paul Gootenberg in this volume. In both cases a protectionist coalition, including merchants, became politically important. However, the cases differ in important
ways: In Peru, according to Gootenberg, the protection question reflected opposing regional interests, became a political issue that defined partisan alignments, and was an important element in the political instability of the era. In
New Granada, by contrast, while the issue was important, particularly between
1831 and 1833, it did not lead to regional conflict, did not define party alignments,
and did not contribute to political instability in the 1830s and 1840s.

Why do the two cases differ so radically in their political significance? One
can point to various differences in the operative factors noted by Gootenberg.
For example, in Colombia the leading Bolivarian free traders were natives (e.g.,
José Manuel Restrepo, Lino de Pombo) rather than foreigners, as in Peru, so
that free-trade commitments may have had a stronger political base.

But these and other specific political features seem less important in explaining
the differences between the cases than the contrast between the structures of the
two economies. If Gootenberg finds a high degree of articulation of regional
economic interests and of expression of those interests in political action, this
probably is because geographic circumstances permitted or encouraged the development of such clearly delineated interests. The most clearly identifiable
players in Gootenberg's analysis were in important population centers on or near
the coast, both in Lima and the north coast on the protectionist side and in
Arequipa on the liberal side. Particularly in the case of the interests of the north
coast, relatively efficient maritime communication permitted the emergence of
strong and clearly identifiable economic interests.

In New Granada, by contrast, the development of strong, clearly identifiable,
and conflicting regional economic interests was inhibited by the fact that the
country was, in effect, economically invertebrate. As noted above, the mountains
of the interior and the tropical environment combined to fragment the most
populated part of the country into many small local or regional economic pockets.
These relatively self-sufficient markets in many places had scant connection to
foreign markets, and, though there was some interregional trade in textiles and
salt, there really was not a national market. Thus, in the mountainous interior,
where the great mass of the population lived and where the country had its center
of political gravity, there was little basis for the articulation of clearly identifiable,
conflicting regional economic interests, at least until about 1870. Before that
time it is possible to specify only a few cases of conflicting regional interests.
The most notable was the competition among Colombia's three principal Caribbean ports (Cartagena, Santa Marta, and Barranquilla), but this competition
occurred in a region that was lightly populated, not significant economically,
and less significant politically than the eastern cordillera or the Cauca Valley in
the interior. There also was regional competition among various mountain communities for government support in the development of mule trails to the Magdalena River. But intraregional rivalries over mule trail routes did not figure in

national politics before 1845, in part because New Granadan legislators, unable or unwilling to identify clear national priorities, or perhaps deliberately defusing the issue, doled out public works funds to the various provinces on a per capita basis. Conflicting regional economic interests became an important factor in Colombian politics only in the 1870s, when in sponsoring railway construction the national government began to make priority decisions favoring one region as against others.[51]

It may be also that Colombia's lack of economic integration and economic articulation provides part of an explanation for the tendency of its elites to accommodate themselves to liberal economic doctrines, even when these doctrines did not seem to serve the national interest very well. These doctrines had the authority of Great Britain, with its notable economic and political power, behind them. And, given the general lack of economic articulation, there were few strong and clear economic interests to defend.

THE UNCHALLENGED HEGEMONY OF ECONOMIC LIBERALISM, 1847–80

Economic ideas in Colombia after 1847 were distinguished from those of the 1830s in two ways. First, more economic writers and political actors became more dogmatic in their economic liberalism. And, secondly, there was a broad consensus among the elite, across both parties, in support of the tenets of economic liberalism.

Several elements entered into the decisive shift from pragmatic, moderate liberalism in the 1830s to the dominance of a more absolute variety in the 1850s. First, the small manufacturing establishments with modern equipment that were set up in and around Bogotá in the 1820s and 1830s had proven by 1840 either to be failures or at best survivors. The unimpressive performance of local manufacturing enterprise reinforced preexisting beliefs that Colombia's future had to lie primarily in the export of tropical products. That same lack of success had soured many in the elite, whether politically liberal or conservative, on the idea of using monopoly privileges as an instrument to encourage new enterprises.

A second important factor in the transition to more liberal policies was the ascent to the presidency in 1845 of General Tomás Cipriano de Mosquera, who set in motion a broad program of modernizing reform. In 1846 the Mosquera administration permitted the free export of gold dust, and his finance minister, Lino de Pombo, a political conservative but a free trader, began to press for lower tariffs. When fiscal conservatives and protectionists in his cabinet opposed these measures, Mosquera accepted their resignations and pressed on with his liberalizing program.[52]

The shift toward more liberal policies that had begun in 1845 was reinforced by an important external event, the repeal of the Corn Laws in 1846. The new British free trade policy had an impact on Colombia in two ways: First, ideologically, it seemed to be a signal that Great Britain was really committing itself to the economic liberalism that English economic theorists for a long time had been advocating. Secondly, in Colombia, the repeal of the Corn Laws was perceived as opening up a new opportunity for the export of agricultural commodities to England, as producers of sugar and other tropical products in the British Caribbean no longer would be favored in the British market. In response to the repeal of the Corn Laws, Colombians now experienced a renewed belief both in the country's destined role as an exporter of tropical products in the international division of labor and in free trade policies as the best road to that destiny.

The preeminent spokesman for the new, more fervent liberalism was Florentino González, who in 1846 had recently returned from England, where free trade opinion was becoming ascendant. In newspaper articles in 1846, and then as Mosquera's finance minister in 1847, González clearly articulated an integrated argument for free trade. There was nothing particularly new in what González said. Most of the elements had been expressed by Wills and other economic liberals in the 1830s. For one thing, because of its geographical situation and factor endowments, New Granada's future lay in the export of tropical products. It made no sense economically to protect artisans and weavers, whose labors would be more productively applied to tropical agriculture. High tariffs offered a special privilege to a minority that simply raised the costs of European consumer goods for the mass of the population. For another thing, if New Granada lowered its import duties, more imported goods would come from Europe, and revenue collections on imports would increase. Finally, if New Granada imported more, it also could export more and more effectively, as more ships would be coming to Colombian ports.[53]

González's particular contribution was in expressing these ideas in a clearly integrated and forceful manner. The principal difference between González's formulations and those of Wills in 1831 lay in their boldness. Whereas Wills, as a foreigner writing amid a protectionist reaction, had simply suggested that weavers might be better employed in tropical agriculture, González in effect called for government policy, through the lowering of the tariff, to force them to do what would be best for them and for society as a whole. In accord with González's argument, the Colombian Congress in 1847 substantially lowered import duties.

Another element in the conjuncture of the late 1840s was the emergence of Colombia as a producer of tobacco and, less important, cinchona bark. Beginning in the early 1830s William Wills, in his role as merchant, had carried out experimental tests in European markets of the tobacco of Ambalema, in the upper Magdalena Valley. Experiments in the 1830s did not yield encouraging results. But by the early 1840s Colombian leaders were persuaded, in part by an offer of British investment, that there might be a good market for Colombian tobacco if the country could produce enough. One of the central concerns of the governments of the 1840s was to expand tobacco production under the government monopoly by bringing private capital into the industry. The Mosquera government did this by giving companies of private capitalists exclusive rights to operate in already existing or newly established production areas. Under this system of local monopolies, tobacco production expanded considerably and effective exporting to England began.[54]

The success of the tobacco industry, and subsequent spurts of cinchona exports, served to legitimize the whole of liberal economic ideology. The fact that lower import duties and expanded exports had coincided, as Florentino González had predicted, reinforced beliefs in other aspects of liberal political economy, particularly the idea that the government did not make a good businessman and could best serve the economy by staying out of the way of private entrepreneurs. One of the first expressions of this new commitment to economic liberalism in domestic policy was the decision in 1848 to abolish government controls over tobacco production and open it completely to free enterprise in 1850.

The movement toward a more unqualified liberalism had the strong support of a new generation of university students and professionals, most of whom had been taught political economy according to Say. Politically the new generation was reacting to the rigidly conservative university regime, and the generally conservative politics, of the Herrán administration (1841–45). Its political enthusiasm was stimulated by the European revolutions of 1848. But the atmosphere of optimism induced by growing tobacco exports and the economic movement they created also encouraged a tendency to ideological and institutional experimentation and boldness. Under such stimuli, the new generation sought to carry forward the liberal revolution, which, they thought, had been begun but then aborted in the Independence era.

As Gerardo Molina has pointed out, there were two strains among the Liberal elite of the 1850s. The dominant one, which he calls the liberal strain, was firmly, indeed dogmatically, committed to economic laissez-faire. Leading spokesmen of this school were Florentino González, Miguel Samper, and Aníbal Galindo. Allied with them politically, but differing with them in their economic vision, was what Molina calls the democratic strain, which Molina identifies with Manuel Murillo Toro. Actually, there were several democratic strains. Murillo Toro in the 1850s accepted the doctrine of laissez-faire, in the sense of favoring a weak state and economic competition, but, an egalitarian, he also believed that the monopolization of land by a small elite made true competition, and democratic government, impossible. Murillo therefore favored state action to prevent the monopolization of land in order to level the playing field somewhat. In 1853 he also called for government control of interest rates to protect the little man. These and other heterodox views provoked strong criticisms from the dominant element that was committed to conventional laissez-faire views.[55] The other democratic strain was that of the artisans of Bogotá and their political allies among an earlier generation of Liberals, whose attention was focused primarily upon the issue of tariff protection for the artisans.

The new generation of Liberals, both the "liberals" and the "democrats," came to power with the Liberal administration of General José Hilario López

(1849–53). The general thrust of the new Liberal administration was to promote individual liberties (economic as well as political) by reducing the power of the central government. The López administration handed many sources of revenue over to provincial governments (with the hope that the provinces would abolish some of them). It also abolished the tobacco monopoly, leaving that industry to free competition. The Liberals' commitment to laissez-faire was also manifest in an 1850 law permitting Indians to sell the individual plots carved from community lands. It also can be discerned, along with evident moral concern, in the contemporaneous abolition of slavery.

The López administration's continuance of the low-tariff policy initiated by Florentino González in 1847 soon ruptured the Liberal coalition. López had come to power with the critical assistance of the artisans of Bogotá, who had mobilized politically in reaction to González's lowering of the tariff. To obtain artisan support, the Liberals had promised the artisans a return to tariff protection. Once in power, the Liberals broke this promise and continued to follow the low-tariff policy. With a remarkable dominant-class insouciance, the new generation of young Liberals even went so far as to give lectures on liberal political economy to the Society of Artisans in an attempt to instruct them on their true interests. By 1853 conflict over the protection issue had created a deep gulf between the young Liberals of the political class and the disgruntled artisans, a gulf which was expressed in open class warfare. The artisans found allies in the professional military, who resented the young Liberals' insistence on cutting back the standing army and their antimilitary attitudes, and some Liberals of an older generation, who felt that the policy of weakening the central government had gone too far. In 1854 the military-artisan coalition staged a coup, which took on aspects of a social revolution. Ultimately the military-artisan coalition was put down by the allied forces of dominant-class Liberals and Conservatives. With the defeat of the artisans, the dissident professional military, and the old-style, moderate Liberals, the exponents of free trade stood virtually unchallenged.

The relative success of the export economy in the 1850s (in relation to its near nonexistence in the 1830s and early 1840s) and the confirmation and reinforcement it gave to liberal economic ideas had important social and political effects. Both the growth of the export economy and the liberal notion of the international division of labor that it confirmed had the effect of legitimizing activities associated with the export economy, and delegitimizing activities not associated with it. Young men from the dominant class ventured down to the Magdalena Valley to establish tobacco plantations and later tried indigo and cotton. The apparent success of tropical exports made that seem a good idea. Also, the economic ideas that were confirmed by the success in exporting tended to imbue such tropical enterprise with an aura of heroism. These young men thought that they were fulfilling the liberal prescription of aiding society as a whole through individual enterprise.[56] By the same token, the growth of the export economy and the dominance of the liberal economic ideas that that growth reinforced tended to delegitimize the artisans, who were viewed by elements of the elite as outmoded and counterproductive relics in a more efficiently specialized export economy. That delegitimization underlay the attempt of the dominant class to annihilate the artisans politically in the 1850s. Government officeholders were supposed to be similarly delegitimized, since they simultaneously symbolized lack of enterprise and government, which hindered individual initiatives.

After the defeat of the artisans in 1854, differences of elite opinion over economic theory resurfaced, essentially over the degree of their commitment to laissez-faire. Such differences were evident, for example, in debates in the newly created federal State of Santander in 1857–58. Murillo Toro, clearly influenced by Bastiat, sometimes went so far as to argue that the state should not even take responsibility for building roads. Others, while favoring a limited state, did see primary education and road building as state functions. The tendency to strong laissez-faire commitments continued in the 1863 Constitutional Convention at Rionegro, which wrote into law, among other things, absolute freedom of commerce in arms.

The tendency to laissez-faire in government policy began to be moderated from the mid–1860s onward, primarily because it became evident that a more active government would be needed to carry forward the development of overland transportation. By 1864 Murillo Toro, now president of the country, was supporting a modest governmental role in public works; and in 1872, after having traveled in Europe and the United States, he was championing government development of transportation even more strongly.[57] The transition is also clearly illustrated in the writings of Salvador Camacho Roldán. In 1858 Camacho Roldán relied entirely upon heroic individual enterprise to get a major road built; by 1871–72, with doubts and quavers, he concluded that an active role of the national government was unavoidable.[58]

But while practical concessions were made in actual government policy, many of the Liberals who became politically active in the 1840s and the 1850s remained wedded to the principles of liberal economy for the rest of their lives. Most particularly, they retained an unwavering faith not only in the virtues of unfettered individual enterprise, but also in the notion that there is a fundamental harmony of interests between the individual and society as a whole.[59]

Conservative political leaders, for the most part, were also economic liberals from the late 1840s through the 1870s. Conservative governments attempted to divide Indian communal lands in the 1840s. Conservatives supported low tariffs from the late 1840s onward, though a few individuals occasionally called for a protectionist policy. The Conservative party programs, as late as 1878 and 1879, while calling for political centralization, continued to subscribe to liberal political economy.[60]

The first significant challenge to the hegemony of economic liberalism occurred in the 1880s, when Rafael Núñez—with a vision of a stronger, more active national government, derived in part from experience as a consul in Imperial Germany—defied the conventional wisdom. Núñez first moved to establish protective tariffs and then brought the national government into banking and note issue, theretofore a strictly private activity. His banking and monetary policies—including first the requirement that government banknotes be accepted as legal tender, then the prohibition of privately issued banknotes, and finally substantial government issues of paper money, of obligatory acceptance as payment—provoked a flurry of writings defending liberal economic orthodoxy. Núñez's liberal opponents were not able to defeat him politically, in the sense of removing him from power. But in a sense the economic liberals emerged victorious, in that, through their many attacks on Núñez's heterodoxy, they were able to stigmatize his policies. Until the 1940s there was a pronounced tendency in Colombian economic and historical writing to view Núñez's economic policies as a kind of crazed aberration. With the development of interest in a more state-directed economy in the 1940s and afterward, Núñez's economic policies for the first time began to be looked to as a model.[61] This tendency to take Núñez seriously as a forerunner of modern economic and monetary policy continues among recent generations of Colombian economists.[62]

In sum, economic liberalism was an important force in Colombia from 1820 until well into the twentieth century. During the 1820s and 1830s a significant element in the political elite at least had a knowledge of the basic principles of liberal political economy. Many in the 1820s and 1830s accepted it as established doctrine sanctioned by British and French authority, even though in a practical spirit they did not always adhere strictly to that doctrine. Precisely because of their awareness of the doctrine of liberal economy, many were disconcerted when it did not seem to work well for Colombia in the 1830s. Only a few were able to develop a coherent alternative vision. When the export economy began to grow in the middle of the nineteenth century, the whole of liberal political economy was legitimized, to the extent that the political elite, Conservative as well as Liberal, tended to adhere to liberal orthodoxy. Having been won over to economic liberalism by the perceived success in export growth, most held firmly to that orthodoxy through one economic crisis after another.

NOTES

1. Personal communication from Joseph Love, January 1987.
2. Safford, "Commerce and Enterprise," Table 1, pp. 460–64. Rates quoted in Colombian pesos, which for most of the period were close to the U.S. dollar in value.
3. Taylor, *Transportation Revolution*, pp. 133–37.
4. *Relaciones de mando*, pp. 64–65, 73, 88.
5. *Ibid.*, pp. 48–50, 60–62, 126–29, 178–80, 219.
6. *Ibid.*, pp. 64–65, 68–72, 87–88.
7. *Ibid.*, pp. 71–72, 74, 82.
8. *Ibid.*, pp. 141–42, 144–45, 162, 174–77, 215–16, 219.
9. Vargas, *Pensamientos políticos*, pp. 28–32, 43n; *Escritos de dos economistas coloniales*, pp. 123–34, 152.

10. Vargas, "Memoria sobre la población," in Vargas, *Pensamientos políticos*, pp. 77–78, 81, 83–84.

11. Vargas, *Pensamientos políticos*, p. 43n.

12. *Escritos de dos economistas coloniales*, pp. 142–44, 150–52, 171, 173–77, 179, 182–87, 193, 198, 219–20.

13. *Ibid.*, p. 179.

14. Decree of 20 October 1828, *Codificación nacional* 3: 438. See also Decree of 26 October 1830, regarding Say.

15. Archivo Nacional de Colombia - República (ANCR), Instrucción Pública, tomo 112, fols. 578–86; tomo 113, fols. 529–57, 726–54; tomo 115, fols. 115–18, 421–31, 467–73; tomo 125, fols. 515–30; and tomo 126, fols. 672–82, 745–856.

16. Molina, *Ideas liberales*, p. 79; and Rodríguez, *Ezequiel Rojas*, pp. 128–29.

17. The libraries were those of José Duque Gómez, a jurist and university professor; José Vicente Martínez and Juan Clímaco Ordóñez, merchants and moderate Conservative politicians with ministerial experience; and Domingo Ciprián Cuenca, a lawyer and Liberal politician. (ANCR, Notaría 2a, 1840, tomo 43, fols. 57r–58r; Notaría 3a, 1848, tomo 435, fols. 534v–36r; Notaría 2a, 1851, tomo 264, fols. 759r–63v; Notaría 2a, tomo 269, fols. 26r–29v).

18. Bejarano, "Aníbal Galindo—Economista," pp. x–xi.

19. *Cartas y Mensajes de Santander*, ed. Cortázar 2: 400–01.

20. "The honorable chamber will be frightened on hearing the name of head tax in the century in which political economy has discovered the irregularity and inequality of this tax; but he who is about to shipwreck does not take care to prepare a board that is strong and well worked, but rather seizes the first that he encounters . . . If we lose ourselves to financial discredit, what good will it do us to have the consolation of having respected the doctrines of Smith, Say, and Malthus?" (Message to Chamber of Representatives, 24 Apr. 1826). Writing to Bolívar in the same year, Santander noted that the Council of Government had decided to reestablish such Spanish colonial revenue devices as the *alcabala* and government control of *aguardientes* (cane liquors). "If these reforms produce money for the administration of the republic and for repairing our national credit, while arousing the least discontent of the people, we ought to throw Say, Malthus, Ricardo, etc. into a bonfire." (Santander to Bolívar, 9 Dec. 1826). Both in *Cartas y Mensajes de Santander* 6: 290 and 485.

21. Molina, *Ideas liberales*, pp. 325, 330.

22. Cf. discussions in Congreso de Cúcuta, *Libro de Actas*, and ANCR, "Libro de rejistros de los acuerdos del Consejo de Estado," meeting of 19 Feb. 1829, fols. 158v–60v. For a comprehensive discussion of the issues in play in the 1820s, see Bushnell, *Santander Regime*.

23. Rodríguez, *Ezequiel Rojas*, p. 175.

24. "Numerario," *Constitucional de Cundinamarca*, 16 Dec. 1832; "Pobreza," *Constitucional de Antioquia*, 10 Feb. 1833.

25. Report of junta of notables to Governor of Bogotá, 19 Jan. 1833, ANCR, Miscelánea general, tomo 134, fols. 683–88.

26. Safford, "Commerce and Enterprise," table 3, p. 470.

27. "Enfermedades que padece el trigo," *Constitucional de Cundinamarca*, 15 Jan. 1832.

28. Plea from Villa del Rosario (Cúcuta, 1831) in ANCR, Miscelánea general, tomo 161, fols. 283–85; "Censos," *Constitucional de Cundinamarca*, 12 Feb. 1832; "Abusos

ruinos a la agricultura," *Constitucional de Boyacá*, 6 Jan. 1833; "Interés legal de los censos," *Constitucional del Cauca*, 20 July 1833; and "Reducción de censos," *Constitucional de Cundinamarca*, 16 Feb. and 16 Apr. 1834.

29. Pleas to restrict the British merchants came from Medellín and Rionegro in Antioquia, the Canton of Atrato in the Chocó, the Magdalena River ports of Honda and Mompos, and Bogotá. (ANCR, Miscelánea general, tomo 161, fols. 75–85, 116–17, 172, 180, 185v, 200, 204–5.)

30. *Constitucional de Cundinamarca*, December 18, 1831; November 25, 1832; May 5, 1833; "Tratados con Inglaterra," *El Pensador Granadino*, 5 Mar. 1833; and *El Neo-Granadino*, 15 and 29 Dec. 1833.

31. Petitions of Bogotá and Cartagena artisans, 1831–32, ANCR, Miscelánea general, tomo 161, fols. 112–15, 120–25.

32. Wills, *Observaciones*. Wills restated some of his arguments in *Constitucional de Cundinamarca*, 8 Jan. 1832.

33. "La estracción del dinero aumenta nuestra ruina?" *Constitucional del Cauca*, 16 Mar. 1833.

34. "Comercio," *Constitucional de Cundinamarca*, 15 Jan. 1832; "Prohibiciones comerciales," ibid., 28 Apr. 1833.

35. Cuervo to Minister of Interior, 15 December 1831, ANCR, Miscelánea general, tomo 161, fols. 75–78.

36. ANCR, Miscelánea general, tomo 134, fols. 683–88.

37. *El Pensador Granadino*, 27 Jan. and 17 Mar. 1833.

38. Ibid., 17 Mar. 1833.

39. Ibid. Interestingly, the same point about the connection between agriculture and manufacturing (in the case of wool and weaving) was made on the same date by an anonymous writer in Boyacá. ("Tunja 17 de marzo," *Constitucional de Boyacá*, 17 Mar. 1833.)

40. *El Proletario*, no. 1 [undated, probably the end of March 1834] through no. 9, 29 May 1834.

41. Nueva Granada, Ministerio de Hacienda, *Informe 1833*, pp. 8–9.

42. "Mensaje del Presidente del Estado de la Nueva Granada al Congreso en la sesión de 1833" (1 Mar. 1833), in *Constitucional del Cauca*, 6 July 1833, suplemento al número 34.

43. Archivo del Congreso, Cámara, Actas, 1833, no. 5, morning sessions of 23 Apr. and 30 May 1833, fols. 161–62v, and unnumbered folio; Restrepo, *Diario político y militar*, 2: 285.

44. Ospina Vásquez, *Industria y protección*, p. 170. The duties cited are for goods brought in foreign-owned ships. Duties were slightly lower for imports brought on New Granadan ships. But as the New Granadan merchant marine was insignificant, presumably most goods came on foreign ships.

45. Wills, *Observaciones*, pp. 50–51.

46. In some cases the duties on artisans' finished goods were even higher in 1844 than they had been in the 1830s. See Ospina Vásquez, *Industria y protección*, p. 170.

47. In 1832–33 less than 13 percent by value of the imported goods brought to Cali were introduced by merchants with non-Spanish names. And the biggest shipments belonged to New Granadans. ("Alcabala de Cali," *Constitucional del Cauca*, 16 Nov. 1833.)

48. Cf. "Relación de las cantidades que adeudan a esta aduana varios individuos de

la provincia de Bogotá por derechos de plazos cumplidos," Aduana de Santa Marta, 9, Mar. 1842, *Constitucional de Cundinamarca*, 8 May 1842.

49. See Ospina Vásquez, *Industria y protección*, pp. 97, 106, 110, 141, 147, 160, 167, 210.

50. Ibid., pp. 124, 160–64.

51. The role of the Northern Railway project in provoking regional jealousies, political realignment, and the emergence of the Núñez regime is well told in Delpar, *Red against Blue*, pp. 112–14, 121–22, 190; and Park, *Rafael Núñez*, pp. 68, 92–97, 156–58.

52. Helguera, "The First Mosquera Administration," pp. 312–25; and Ospina Vásquez, *Industria y protección*, p. 206, n. 28.

53. "Hágamos algo de provecho," *El Día*, August 23, 1846; and "Vamos adelante," *El Día*, 30 Aug. 1846.

54. Safford, "Commerce and Enterprise," pp. 188–218.

55. Molina, *Ideas liberales*, pp. 53–91, 319–33; and Johnson, "Social and Economic Change," 29–31.

56. Rivas, *Los trabajadores*, celebrates this notion.

57. Molina, *Ideas liberales*, p. 79.

58. Camacho Roldán, *Escritos varios*, segunda serie, pp. 183–85, 298–301, 329–32 and tercera serie, pp. 195, 225–29.

59. See Samper, *Escritos politico-económicos*; and Galindo, *Estudios económicos y fiscales*.

60. Ospina Vásquez, *Industria y protección*, pp. 206–10, 246–55; and *Programas del conservatismo*, pp. 97–114. Bergquist, in *Coffee and Conflict*, contends that a commitment to economic liberalism in the nineteenth century was peculiar to political Liberals, and Conservatives in Antioquia, holding that it was incompatible with the world view of Conservatives of Bogotá. Bergquist errs here in imagining that all Bogotá Conservatives shared the experiences and world view of Miguel Antonio Caro. In fact, many nineteenth-century Conservatives in Bogotá and environs were economic liberals (e.g., Leopoldo Borda, Pastor Ospina, José María Samper), and there were many more in Santander, the Caribbean coast, and other areas outside of Antioquia.

61. Liévano Aguirre, *Rafael Núñez*.

62. E.g., Urrutia, "El sector externo"; Bustamante Roldán, "Efectos económicos," 559–660.

3

BELEAGUERED LIBERALS: THE FAILED FIRST GENERATION OF FREE TRADERS IN PERU

Paul Gootenberg

One of the most widely accepted myths about Latin America is that our backwardness results from the principle of economic laissez-faire adopted in almost all our constitutions when we achieved independence from Spain and Portugal early in the last century. According to this myth, the opening of our economies to market forces made us easy prey to imperialists, whose voracious business practices brought about the inequities between rich and poor. . . . Peru [Latin America; the majority of third-world nations] never had a market economy. The economic freedom guaranteed by our constitution is as much a fiction as political freedom.

Mario Vargas Llosa,
New York Times Magazine,
February 22, 1987

THE LIBERALISM OF FREE TRADE

For two decades now, Latin Americanists have pointed to the triumph of economic liberalism in the external sector—free trade—as the formative economic policy shift of the nineteenth century. The adoption of free trade by the nascent republics both exemplified and, some insist, caused the region's mounting secular dependence on the world economy. In 1760, exotic notions of free trade remained practically unheard of in Ibero-America. By 1860, the free flow of international factors, low tariffs, and export/import promotion were the region's reigning

economic orthodoxy, if not universal practice: this reign would irrevocably structure Latin American society for over the next half century. Yet despite this
theorized centrality of free trade, next to nothing is known about the inner
workings of the sea change.[1] How did liberal doctrines enter and win over the
region, what political transformations accompanied their rise, and what social,
regional, and political realignments buttressed the new liberal regimes? In short,
nineteenth-century trade policy has not yet earned the attention lavished by
historians on other issues of liberal-conservative strife.

The conventional view—from our suggestive corpus of *dependentista* speculation—holds that free trade, while the crucible of conflict for modern political
economy, had a much easier task rooting itself in Latin America than did related
branches of economic liberalism. Free trade evoked little of the overt political
struggle waged, for example, around the secularization of church functions or
the privatization of property rights in land.[2] Indeed, in this arena, Latin America
must have pioneered the new global praxis of commercial liberalism. For even
before the new trade theories of Adam Smith, David Ricardo, and Jean-Baptiste
Say had congealed—much less gained official sanction in Britain and France—
their implications had been fought out on the battlefields of Latin American
independence. Eighteenth-century Bourbon reformers first planted the seeds of
these ideas into the Americas, which turned roundly subversive by 1810. Free
trade, we are told, then incubated American ideas of separation from restrictive
Spain, along with the wider prospects of liberal trade integration with Britain,
propagated by far-sighted diplomats like George Canning. Anxious to reap the
rewards of unfettered commerce, the elites of the new Latin American states
had little use for countervailing economic nationalist plans and interests. Not
only had foreign proselytizing elevated free trade into uncontestable scientific
truth, but—should reason falter—British diplomats, traders, and gunboats stood
ready to batter down the redoubts of tottering mercantilism and the early sporadic
regional experiments in economic nationalism. In fact, little imperialism of free
trade was required. For Latin America's incipient colonial exporters—miners,
merchants, and landed elites—were willful collaborators with the internationalist
agents and doctrines of free trade. As the three legs of a wobbly social table,
these groups dominated the bankrupt, torn states of the region, states supremely
ill equipped in any case for resisting the overwhelming pressures and lures (fiscal
or otherwise) for full integration with the world economy.[3] By the 1840s (when
codified nationalist alternatives like Friedrich List's first appeared in Europe),
Latin America was so committed to export development, that these policies and
the comparative disadvantages they inscribed endured without question well into
the following century, until at least the 1929 crash. In part a question of timing,
in part of necessity, Latin America emerged as the purest and most tenacious
pole of liberal orthodoxy of the modern world economy.

This portrait of the reception, adoption, and implementation of free trade in
Latin America—a billiard ball theory, from center to periphery—can no longer
be sustained. Recent research suggests that nineteenth-century liberalism was

instead poorly received, ill adaptive, and half-heartedly implemented. Emerging critiques, while too broad for discussion here, stress three points of revision. First, the brisk initial imports of "political economy" hardly achieved instant intellectual prestige: throughout much of the region, rudimentary nationalist regimes (saner kin of José Gaspar Francia) blocked any easy transmission of liberalism, leaving foreigners far from free to trade. Second, the reputed hegemony of liberal exporters seems, at best, a projection back in time of the social alliances of the high age of export liberalism after 1860.[4] It begs the pivotal question of where liberal interests came from and how they achieved their sway. The postindependence depression represents a long wait between colonialism and neocolonialism, in which caudillismo, and a resurgence of colonial norms and interests, inundated the initiative of protoexporters. Trade policy ferment was one basic theme in the sharpening subterranean struggles here between Bourbon and more ancient visions for neohispanic societies. Finally, neither was the apogee of free trade an unmitigated triumph: few liberal states abdicated all interventionism, and this creeping neomercantilism now seems precursor of the nationalist policies embraced wholesale after 1930.[5] In sum, the new views question our notions of discrete liberal phases, alliances, blocs, and states in the region and make analysis of their original transplant and bloom even more compelling.

Peru offers an instructive case study for this dual process of resistance and accommodation to free trade in postindependence Latin America. In 1800, the Viceroyalty of Peru was the diversified center of a preliberal Spanish bullion empire; and during independence, Lima, its capital, became the vortex of South American reaction against imperial free trade. Yet by 1860, Peru had become the liberal Peru of the Age of Guano—the legendary monoexporter of bird droppings to Europe. The radical free trade of the guano age, besides being the textbook case for export riches gone awry, was part of a century-long autocratic domination of liberal elites, which left Peru especially marked by the kinds of structural disparities commonly ascribed to liberal misdevelopment.[6] The shifts in Peru could not be clearer. Moreover, in Peru, free trade stands out as the singular issue of early economic liberalism, for Peru's exceptionally complacent elites barely clashed over the complex of property, religious, and political reforms that characterized liberalism elsewhere. Whatever the causes (and some seem unique), European economic and political individualism made little lasting headway in the Andes, while North Atlantic free trade certainly did.

The historiography of Peruvian liberalism is also striking, for it starkly affirms propositions found for all of Latin America. Peru, it is said, was hobbled by a particularly precocious and ingrained liberal elite dominance. Independence from Spain signified little more than the swift transfer of mercantilist masters for the neocolonial subjection of free trade. British interests held such sway during this transition—"control" is the favored term—that alternative policies never stood a chance. In 1821, Peruvian elites, lacking any credible nationalist project, much less a viable state, surrendered the country to the foreign trade juggernaut, in marked contrast to their stubborn resistance to other imperatives of nineteenth-century liberalism. The resulting social hybrid of the guano age—extreme external dependence wedded to an atavistic domestic social order—led Peru down a grotesque path of underdevelopment, nay, even to absolute national catastrophe by the War of the Pacific.[7] All these disasters, historians maintain, stemmed from the incorrigible, misguided, and warped liberal consciousness of Peru's founding elites.

This essay takes a harder look at the genuine transmission agents of free trade to postindependence Peru, for a new version of the story just told. Peru's first generation of free traders—overseas liberal powers and traders, Bolivarians (and their intellectual and military progeny), and southern economic elites—all proved congenital failures. They could not complete their mission of transplanting free trade ideas onto thin Andean soil. Besides weakness in numbers—these groups were not Peru's dominant class—special features of their social, geographic, and political makeup bred contradictions and splintering that paralyzed their efforts to mount a viable free trade movement between 1820 and 1845. Instead, independence begot a protracted and radical phase of Peruvian protectionism, more in line with the obscured nationalist proclivities of Peru's truly dominant elites. Only in the late 1840s, with the dissolving of this nationalist movement, could a second generation of Andean free traders step forth: new liberals, unrelated to their foreign, Bolivarian, and southern forefathers, advocating new varieties of free trade and responding to greatly altered political and social contexts. These men, not the failed first generation, finally achieved a coherent free trade crusade and built Peru's enduring liberal state after 1852. This Peruvian liberalism remained truncated, to be sure; nevertheless, structural, not ideological or personal deficiency, best accounts for the problematic legacy of free trade.

Two caveats may help the reader of this brutally synthetic essay. First, individual liberals here are considered mainly as "free traders" and ought not to be taken literally for all the country's liberal politicians. This reductionism is warranted by the facts, for the role of trade policy actually helps explain why other liberal-conservative strife remained so muted in Peru. Second, for want of space, the other half of this story, the rise and fall of Peru's vibrant early protectionist movements, is kept offstage. In fact, the economic nationalism of postindependence elites—native merchants, shopkeepers, planters, millers, northern and sierran oligarchs, master artisans, textile magnates, miners, treasury officials, and caudillos—was born of the shocks of independent Peru's first frontal encounter with the world economy in the 1820s, though some might trace conception to the penumbra of colonialism.[8] This amalgam of national interests spawned ideologies and practices directly at odds with the rising doctrine of free trade, and their unique strategic, regional, and political attributes allowed them, and not only elites, to forge a compelling protectionist alliance. While not terribly successful as economic policy, this nationalism (surely a controversial term) did prove essential to the definition of Peruvian statehood itself. In the early 1840s, however, novel pressures broke up the old protectionist bloc; by 1850, diehard nationalists became the beleaguered ones, and the new free traders could triumph with their guano-age Leviathan. It had been, nevertheless, a long and rocky road from silver to guano.

FAILED FREE TRADE IMPERIALISTS

The initial foreign consuls, chargés, and ministers to Peru—U.S., French, and, above all, British—are frequently charged (on the basis of scant direct evidence) with free trade imperialism. It is alleged that foreign officials coerced, cajoled, or successfully persuaded Peruvian elites to adopt liberal trade policies against their own national interest. (Alternatively, foreign historians have used consular reports to completely exonerate their nationals from the charge of meddling in the name of free trade.) Peru's leading trade partners, the story goes, met particularly easy success here because of the marked weakness of their prey: the chronically unstable and bankrupt Peruvian state.[9] The nonstop interference of consuls in local politics and their proximity to and intense social relationships with Peruvian elites made them, in effect, members of the political elite, though with clear foreign allegiances.

Under close scrutiny, the evidence overwhelmingly supports half the imperialism argument: overseas political interests did indeed massively intervene in Peruvian affairs in a push for free trade, far more, in fact, than historians even imagined. However, the second half of the imperialism equation—that they succeeded—is wrong. Over time, the isolation and setbacks of ever active foreign liberals only intensified.

All three sets of diplomats harbored similar objectives in Peru: to expand their commerce with Peru through low uniform import tariffs, guarantees of access and safety for their traders, and commercial treaties designed to seal a liberal system upon an erratic Peruvian state. Partly zealous missionaries of the new universalist doctrines of free trade, and partly cynical defenders of their countries' narrow economic interests, the consuls as a group shared one broad vision. Their ultimate aim, quipped one famed British envoy, was to make Peru's relation to their countries "one of miner to manufacturer."[10]

Only their specific liberal interests and strategies diverged in this difficult mission. The British worked mainly to promote the consignment trade of their large import houses in Lima and their ancillary export activities in the south. British interventions in trade politics appear sporadic, yet most approximated a genuine imperial strategy. Informed by a "realist" assessment of the antiforeign proclivities of the Peruvian elite (and of the instability endemic to Peruvian politics), the British chose to throw political support to extraregional military forces. These liberal surrogates, like the Bolivian Andrés Santa Cruz, could forcibly impose the full edifice of a free trade regime upon Peru's notoriously recalcitrant elites.[11] Once established, these regimes were to provide a stable institutional framework for British investments in exports and state finance, thus transforming Peru into an integral outpost of the expanding British world economy. British efforts peaked in the mid–1820s (with Consul Ricketts's intimate ties with Bolivarians) and the mid–1830s (with B. H. Wilson's active sponsorship of the Peru-Bolivia Confederation of Andrés Santa Cruz). Yet when the British saw their great liberal hopes falter—as happened in both the late 1820s and late 1830s—they rapidly withdrew from Peruvian politics or adopted purely defensive postures against the ensuing nationalist reprisals. For the British, it was all or nothing, a sensible attitude indeed, since their overall stake in Peru counted for little in global terms.[12] In any case, British goods and traders were not really the main target of Peruvian protectionists.

The fact is that the scale and persistence of British free trade campaigns actually pale next to those of their closest rivals: the impetuous North Americans. Contrary to prevailing historiography, the United States was Peru's most strategic trade partner in the aftermath of independence, and consequently had the most aggressive agents in Peruvian trade politics.[13] Yankee shippers dominated the critical flour and coarse textile trades to the north-central coast (which deflected commerce from the region's coveted Chilean connection), were most conspicuous in coastwise shipping, and included in their sphere the key urban market area of Lima. Unlike the initially upscale British trade, these staples of U.S. merchants posed an immediate challenge to the most organized and commercialized sectors of the Peruvian economy, and not surprisingly, for the two economies shared related market structures and factor endowments. In contrast to European goods, the U.S. exports of 1820 were directly competitive, not complementary, to Peru. As a result, the influential Lima elite protectionists, merchants and planters, immediately targeted U.S. trade. They aimed to eliminate the North American presence altogether, through complete import prohibitions or their galvanizing alternative of a closed market system with Chile.[14]

The United States fought back tooth and nail, in a series of political interventions to save this critical commercial foothold in the Pacific basin. North American efforts culminated in a decade-long free trade drive from 1827 to 1837, orchestrated by their energetic, ubiquitous, and imaginative chargé d'affaires, Samuel Larned. The tactics of the U.S. contrasted sharply with British liberal strategy: rather than remain aloof from Peruvian politics (which the United States could ill afford to do), consuls enthusiastically jumped into the messy ring of local political struggles. They hoped to win over, piecemeal, decisive allies among members of the Peruvian political elite. With each new tariff controversy, the United States launched new missionary efforts in an endless quest to sway Peruvian "Publick Opinion," to cultivate high-ranking allies, or to strong-arm congressional voters. Their hearts-and-minds approach is exemplified by the fact that North American consuls actually produced, clandestinely, much of the liberal propaganda of the era, in effect defining the terms of early debates. The covert press suggests again the frailty of Peru's home-grown liberalism. Washington ordered the special Larned mission to revoke Peru's unfriendly trade policies (and made no fuss over extra printing bills).[15] Despite these daily and multifarious interventionist activities, however, few Peruvians flocked to the U.S. cause, and the campaign dragged on fruitlessly over the decade.

French diplomats, on the other hand, were at once the least important and most hostile participants in Peruvian trade politics. Obsessed with safeguarding the luxury trades of the numerous French retailers based in Lima, French officials adopted a third strategy: instead of concerted efforts to win allies, the French relied on intermittent displays of military might aimed at inculcating Peruvian officials with a healthy respect for the property rights of French nationals. The "moral effects" of French gunboats, however, were short-lived, requiring on-going applications, since each round of coercion itself renewed anti-French sentiment, particularly among excitable Lima shopkeepers.[16] The French also conducted a relatively diplomatic campaign to lower the extraordinarily high imposts on French wines, brandies, and crafts—protests diplomatically ignored by Peruvian officials over three decades.

If the campaigns by foreign officialdom fared poorly, overseas private interests (in some ways more closely enmeshed with Peruvian elites) made even less headway against hostile trade policies and practices. Associated with the top twenty import firms that replaced the peninsular import elite after 1821, the four hundred or so resident foreigners in Lima were by instinct and profession fervent liberals. Three avenues lay open for foreign merchants to spread their free trade gospel. While often cited as the major ways a free trade imperialism on private account operated in Peru, in fact each method was blocked to foreign merchants until the mid–1840s.

First, free trade could filter into the Peruvian body politic via their immediate business clients and contacts: the scores of leading national merchants dependent on foreign houses for overseas goods, credit, and graces. Nevertheless, the embryonic national commercial elite (which, penurious yet concentrated, was the closest thing Peru had to a dominant class) staunchly resisted any political blending with their overseas suppliers. Instead, from the earliest days of independence, reliance on foreigners actually had an opposite and paradoxical effect—mounting merchant antipathy to North Atlantic interests, so much so that the Peruvian merchant class came to form the bedrock of persisting nationalism among the Lima elite.[17]

A second possibility was direct foreign merchant immersion in liberal trade politics. Given their unusually exposed position in Peru's volatile political scene, no major merchant dared follow this path. The risks far outweighed any possible gains; business survival itself depended entirely on cordial and "neutral" relationships with changing Peruvian authorities. Otherwise, foreign merchants could easily become the favored targets of nationalist politicians and, on occasion, even mobs, with disastrous results. Only those with nothing to lose—small or itinerant foreign traders—ever gambled in Peruvian politics (and usually lost), and these were the men least able to change or interested in changing trade policy.[18] Similar constraints precluded indirect strategies to undermine high tariffs, such as the often-claimed use of contraband. The clear risks of smuggling were an effective deterrent, at least in Lima, where policy took shape.[19]

The last option for the capital-rich foreign houses lay in their capacity for financial inducement, legal or otherwise. Here too the foreign liberals proved intelligent risk-averters. Lending to the bankrupt Peruvian state or bribing officials and caudillos for specific trade concessions was economically and politically unprofitable, but above all, fraught with danger.[20] Bitter experience with loans in the 1820s taught foreigners several lessons: loans were rarely repaid; they rarely produced reliable tariff reductions (or even better treatment); and they invariably exposed merchants to arbitrary (if retaliatory) perils of escalating exactions and forced loans. These risks loomed even larger outside Lima and the major ports. The foreign merchants quickly realized that financial entanglements of any kind were the chief threat to profitability and survival in Peru, far overshadowing the discriminatory trade policies themselves. Their economic resources did not translate into power against predatory caudillos; they made them sitting ducks.

With the concerted help of the consuls—the only realm where coercion really worked—the major foreign merchants made clear their principled refusal to fund caudillo regimes and conflicts, no matter what their ideological complexion or promises on trade policy. This enforceable tax exemption amounted to a kind of de facto extraterritoriality in Peru's convulsive environment and helped foreigners consolidate their economic position.[21] Yet, it simultaneously cost foreigners their most promising tool for molding commercial policy. In the financial sphere (which by Peruvian norms defined one's basic juridical and political relationship to the local polity), the liberal foreign elite proved unwilling to fully integrate with Peruvian society. Most caudillo-forced finance then fell to Peru's nationalist *consulado* (merchant guild), which came to mold the essentials of policy. Despite the obvious (and growing) economic and social standing of foreign businessmen, they remained outsiders, whose liberal beliefs counted for little in trade politics.[22] When Peruvian politics and finance finally settled down in the 1850s, this context for foreign influence dramatically changed.

Merchants aside, all three sets of foreign diplomats, whatever their tactics, ultimately failed in their liberalization crusades. Condensing a good deal of intriguing political history, the essential fact is that the transition to free trade in Peru during the 1840s, when the elites and state first reconsidered their protectionist orthodoxy, occurred in a veritable xenophobic context, when foreign political influence had actually reached its lowest ebb. The British might temporarily press for, and shore up, their surrogate liberal empires, but—bereft of any local social base—these quickly collapsed, bringing on anti-British reprisals in their wake. Twice Britain withdrew its diplomats, in 1828–33 and 1839–45, or was forced to defend its merchants from the discrimination, depredations, and outright attacks—attempts on consuls' lives included—that British intervention itself provoked.[23] Nationalist backlash more than rolled back any British gains in policy.

The United States suffered a more drawn out and lasting defeat. None of its local political allies, so assiduously cultivated, proved capable or even willing to overcome the forces of Lima protectionism, targeted so clearly against U.S. interests. North American propaganda failed to enlighten South American opinion. The bald U.S. intervention in Peruvian politics only worked to further taint free trade as a hopelessly foreign cause. By the late 1830s, despite some fleeting successes, North American commercial and political stock had plummeted in Peru. Officials in the United States abandoned all pretense of changing Peruvian commercial policies, devoting their sapped energies to the retrospective task of collecting old damage claims for their merchants.[24] Ironically, in several ways, this U.S. defeat determined the subsequent age of British predominance in Peru once the liberal order of the guano age took shape. British economic interests had expanded while U.S. trade suffered. The French, with their sporadic violence and threats, became progressively less safe and popular in Peru, if not a symbolic affront to Peruvian sovereignty and nationalism.[25]

Among a host of specific political circumstances that explain the failures of foreign liberals, two general factors stand out. First, the very "weakness" of the Peruvian state, which at first glance seems to make a victory by powerful foreigners inevitable, was actually the greatest obstacle to foreign interests. The chronic instability of caudillo-style Peruvian governments, politics, and finance paradoxically protected national economic sovereignty in a larger sense. Each time consuls managed to score a liberal gain, their favored regime or allies quickly fell from office. No lasting liberalization was possible through the pressures of free trade imperialism alone, for no foreign power could ever hope to stabilize, much less capture, Peruvian political institutions.[26] (Nor did Peru exhibit a statelessness of the sort that later drew Europeans into direct rule elsewhere in the nineteenth century; it possessed a recognizable core of westernized functionaries willing to deal with foreign powers, if on their own terms.) In many ways the foreign interventions exacerbated the original dilemma by stimulating continuous nationalist backlash that readily translated into trade policy. Antiforeign tirades became the standard war cry of disaffected caudillos, perhaps the easiest way to discredit specific officials and mobilize for new revolts.[27] Interventions only weakened the positions of liberals in the elites, led to further instability and polarization, and ultimately (during the early 1840s) to total state disintegration. And if intrusions by foreign states proved risky and counterproductive in this climate, their wary merchants stayed completely out of the fray. In short, Peru's main asset against foreign domination was her sheer unpredictability.

Second, as a general proposition, the precondition for success of nineteenth-century free trade imperialism was the existence and cooperation of a strong local collaborating elite that, for its own profit, would mediate, construct, and enforce the wishes of North Atlantic traders and nations. Once established, the empire of free trade was conceived as a relatively costless and self-regulating hegemony of the metropolis, diametrically opposed to the inefficient precapitalist

Spanish colonialism it replaced.[28] In Peru, however, this critical element was wholly missing: British, U.S., and French free traders, as shown, found no such willing and dependable collaborators; quite the opposite. Even efforts to nurture collaborators, such as the secret North American press, had no perceptible impact.[29] In the long run, the compradors would emerge, but primarily from Peruvian processes of change.

How does the Peruvian evidence on foreign elites relate to the general debate on nineteenth-century free trade imperialism? It affirms and denies aspects of both schools and shows a more interactive process between external and internal actors. Foreign powers were anything but the withdrawn innocents abroad portrayed in most European historiography. The British, French, and U.S. imperialists tried their best to mold Peruvian trade policy. But neither were they omnipotent, able to translate their economic prowess into control, as many Latin Americanists suppose. Strong states could not automatically subdue weak states. The missing variable in both interpretations was the structure of political and economic risk, if not the entire sphere of politics itself.[30] The "excessive" weakness of the early state, and this instability combined with its "excessive" bankruptcy, made Peru impenetrable to direct external political control or to financial integration into a liberal world economy. This, however, leaves the discussion at the level of direct pressures; indirectly, the external actors still wielded enormous influence by defining the broadest options available for both national elites and their state.

WOULD-BE LIBERALS: BOLIVARIANS AND INTERNATIONALISTS

The dearth of sturdy collaborators for overseas liberal interests did not mean a total absence of liberal groups in the region. Three identifiable sets of liberal elites operated in postindependence Peru: Bolivarians, the ideological internationalist pressure group of high civil functionaries, and a diffuse regionalist movement led by southern economic elites. Besides weakness in numbers, however, this first generation of Andean free traders remained isolated from each other and politically incapable of expanding into a type of national liberal alliance that could conquer the Lima-based state. Only the southern liberals would survive to affect Peru's actual transition to free trade in the late 1840s, that is, when such an alliance finally became feasible. Like the foreigners without collaborators, Peru's first liberal elites lacked a meaningful social base.

Strictly speaking, Bolivarians were foreigners, too, and foreign invaders at that. Yet, before their liberalism helped trigger Peruvian nationalism itself, the prelude to Peru's actual definition as a separate polity, the Bolivarians remained regional forces. (Even after, Peruvian nationalists continued to distinguish their South American brethren from the North Atlantic aliens.) The Bolivarians also bequeathed a few liberal orphans to Peruvian soil: a weak wing of military chiefs, functionaries, and *políticos* loyal to Bolívar's vision long after the Liberator's forced exit in 1827.

Both liberators of Peru, José de San Martín and Simón Bolívar, were free traders by conviction, not for political expediency alone, which perhaps explains why they played trade politics so poorly in Peru. Their personal visions for independent South America had coalesced in the two most dynamic commercial territories of Bourbon liberalism, La Plata and Caracas—areas that saw Anglo-Saxon merchants as allies more than rivals. In those territories, their free trade proclamations, and those for de facto liberal alliances with North Atlantic capitalism, helped rally elite support against restrictive Spanish colonialism.[31] In Peru it did not. Both San Martín and Bolívar arrived in Lima ready to transplant free trade by fiat, in 1821 and 1824, in the naive hope that free trade ideas could survive transplant and wean Lima elites from their protracted royalist sympathies. In the case of San Martín, historians clearly recognize how free trade backfired, mobilizing Limeño elites against independence—a key factor in San Martín's Peruvian fiasco.[32] For Bolívar too, the negative consequences were at least as severe.

Opposition to Bolívar's planned trade policies played a critical role in inciting (or inventing) the Peruvian nationalism that ousted the Colombian occupiers from 1826–27. Palpable grievances against the new freedoms and lower tariffs Bolívar promised to foreign traders in 1826, and well-publicized plans to make Peru into a liberal British protectorate, aroused as much opposition as his flamboyant authoritarian political designs. (In Bolívar's case, liberalism and authoritarianism probably went together). Elite Lima merchants organized this resistance, launching broad appeals to "popular" artisans, miners, and shopkeepers, already agitated by the initial effects of foreign competition. Lima shopkeepers proved most effective as shock troops against Colombian forces during the mob and political confrontations of 1826–27; in fact, the opening of free trade in the 1820s had most directly hurt the native retailing classes.[33]

Apart from the gathering storm of anti–free trade interests—who deftly combined anti-Colombian invective with economic nationalist demands—liberals faced internal obstacles to success. The only national stronghold potentially poised to support free trade in the 1820s, the Arequipeño aristocracy, was far from Lima, both geographically and socially. Moreover, disillusioned with Bolívar's centralist political scheme, southern leaders like Luna Pizarro actually spearheaded the political challenge to Bolivarians in Congress. Separated by geography and radically different conceptions of the state, early free trade elites could not act as a unified bloc. Instead, influential southern liberals helped to throw Bolivarian troops and collaborators out of Lima and to consolidate national institutions—and then watched helplessly as the economic definition of the new Peruvian nationalism became clear. This movement climaxed with the prohibitions policy of 1828, the fruit of Peru's first genuinely national (and bitterly anti-Bolivarian) Congress.[34] Anti-Colombian camouflage continued to fuel economic nationalists into the 1830s.

Three political legacies stemmed from these mid-1820s anti-Bolivarian struggles, which were to hamper free trade over the next generation. First, free trade became tainted as an irredeemable "foreign" cause, the antithesis of Peruvian nationalism. Its connection to North Atlantic interests was only part of the problem. Second, free trade also acquired its antipopular cast. Liberals showed nowhere near the capacity or inclination to cater to restless popular groups (such as shopkeepers and artisans) as protectionists could and did. Both nationalism and republicanism became, in a sense, protectionist properties, increasing its mobilization range.[35] The failure of liberalism was, in part, just as some suggest, a failure of social reactionaries unwilling even to consider the plight of Peru's popular classes. Third, free trade was firmly associated with authoritarian centralism, blunting its appeal to its sole natural constituency, Peru's federalist liberals of the south. (The Yankee republicans, too, soon abandoned Bolívar with similar dismay.) This political legacy endured until the mid–1840s, when a new brand of decentralist liberal surfaced in Peru, independently, unrelated to Bolivarian free trade. To some degree, these political handicaps represented the genuine distribution of losses and gains from freer trade. Together they doomed any national liberal alliance.

A more notorious Bolivarian legacy was *caudillismo*. The Liberator's Andean lieutenants rapidly divided into the rival military cliques that would fight over Peru for two decades after 1825. A few caudillos remained loyal to the Bolivarian ideal of turning greater Peru into an "emporium of free trade," which was itself an extension of Bourbon policies. The majority read political signs correctly and defected to the protectionist camp. Andean caudillos, generally viewed in personalistic terms alone, actually espoused well-defined trade policies; despite fluctuations tuned to the changing fiscal and political climate, their programs also appealed to recognizable regional or social blocs. Generals Domingo Nieto, Luis José de Orbegoso, Manuel Ignacio Vivanco, Juan Francisco Vidal, and Andrés de Santa Cruz emerged as liberal caudillos, mainly intertwined with the free trade aspirations of southern regionalism. However, until the 1840s such caudillos (along with civil functionaries brought up in the Bolivarian milieu) were hopelessly outclassed, particularly in the strategic north and interior, by self-proclaimed nationalist warriors—Gen. Agustín Gamarra and his followers, the *gamarristas* Antonio de La Fuente, Juan Bautista Eléspuru, Felipe Santiago Salaverry, Juan Crisóstomo Torrico, José Félix Iguaín, Miguel de San Román, and Ramón Castilla. For their part, the free trader Bolivarian caudillos, like Bolívar himself, lacked a secure and broad social base in Peruvian territory.[36] Thus, for example, Santa Cruz's proto-Bolivarian Peru-Bolivia Confederation (1836–38) remained utterly dependent on outside forces, which sealed its destruction by the nationalist caudillo "party," itself helped by Chile. More could be said about the nationalist and liberal chiefs and their effects on the shifting ship of state, but—however messy the alignments—sectionalism, Bolivarianism, and their trade policies became recurrent themes in caudillo struggles.

The second group of would-be national liberals were ideologues and state functionaries best deemed internationalists: distinguished members of the political class like Manuel de Vidaurre, José María Pando, Juan García del Río, and Manuel del Río. Stepsons of the Bolivarian occupation, these men never tired of expounding their liberal plans, frequently from high posts in the finance and foreign ministries, and seemed (at least at first) particularly cozy with North American interests. In their origins, these men reflected what one recent historian aptly calls the Atlantic "network of trade and revolution," even in distant Peru. García del Río had served Bolívar on finance missions to London; Vidaurre (a key convert to free trade) wrote from Boston; and Pando enjoyed extensive European and Bolivarian contacts.[37] (The foreign liberals were deeply enmeshed too. The aggressive British consul, B. H. Wilson, had been Bolívar's trusted aide-de-camp in the 1820s; Larned had trained against Chilean protectionists before moving on to tougher foe in Peru.)

Yet they were internationalist in the deeper sense of what they advocated: an economic transformation far more sweeping than merely lowering the tariff barriers that mushroomed in the wake of Bolivarian defeat. The internationalists envisioned the development of a full international export economy directly integrated with North Atlantic commerce, a far cry from Peru's time-worn provincial patterns of Pacific commerce and comparative advantage. Apart from lower tariffs, they advocated lifting all restrictions on bullion production and trade and, as centerpiece, the creation of a free port in Callao. The latter had considerable significance, as a virtual commercial revolution. A free port, with incentives like unlimited storage and transshipment rights, would turn Peru into the leading entrepôt for European imports in the eastern Pacific. (Ironically, Chile itself was rapidly implementing this strategy, yet remained the hope of the Peruvian nationalists seeking a commercial union of Pacific states.) Moderate taxation of direct overseas commerce, which had shunned risky Peru for Valparaíso since independence, would provide revenues and stimulate a new style of liberal development enhanced by nontraditional exports.[38] In this internationalist ideal, Chile became Peru's natural competitor, if not archenemy.

Off and on during the 1830s, the internationalists were catapulted into power by friendly or desperate caudillos, entranced by lavish promises of instant revenues. Yet all their frenetic activity, decrees, and political economy sermons, as in 1831–33, came to naught. Their liberalization schemes were blocked by Congress and other disaffected groups. It was they who first spoke of Smith and Say, whose theories were invariably lambasted by their foes as "slavish," "inappropriate," and "ruinous" for Peru. ("Hypocrisy," however, was the standard charge: if novices in economic theory, Peruvians scored high in economic history and practice and constantly reminded internationalists and foreigners alike of the critical role of protectionism in the North Atlantic's own worldly ascent.) And Pando, usually baptized as the father of Peruvian free trade, was, if anything, an impotent one.[39] The reason is simple: The internationalists remained mere ideologues with no elite support. All their anticipated allies, those central to the plan, opposed it.

First and foremost, Peruvian merchants would have to comply with the liberal transformation of Callao import structures, when in fact the Lima Consulado viewed internationalist trade strategy as anathema. Merchants, for a range of motives, yearned to revive once lucrative local patterns of trade, especially with Chile, the sheltered market route unifying Peru's northern elites. Here merchants might recover from the vicissitudes of direct foreign commerce, which had taken such a toll in the 1820s. Second, mining interests of the central sierra, the sole functional export sector in the aftermath of independence, would have to rally as well. Instead, silver miners expressed no particular leaning toward free trade. But miners did vehemently fight Bolivarian attempts to open the sector to international speculators in the 1820s, accepted much neomercantilist regulation of bullion, and, above all, remained highly dependent on the anti-internationalist Lima merchant guild. Other potential exporters, like the powerful coastal sugar planters, were even less enthusiastic in their crusade to recover their former Chilean markets.[40] Internationalists' third possible base were the southern liberals. But the south wanted its own free ports, not dependence on a grand Lima entrepôt. Finally, the genuine financial elites of *caudillismo*—the Lima cliques who took on the fiscal role foreigners had refused—were heady partisans of nationalist trade and fiscal policies, which went hand in hand.[41] Thus, the internationalist vision never advanced beyond blueprints until the late 1840s, long after its theorists had vanished from a transformed political scene.

THE LIBERAL WAR OF SOUTHERN SECESSION

Native liberalism found one other fount besides this scattered assortment of post-Bolivarian caudillos and ideologues: southern agriculturalists, exporters, and merchants. From Moquegua to Ica, with Arequipa as its core, lay fertile social ground for Peruvian free traders. Arequipeño liberalism grew from four basic roots: a general market orientation to the south, distance from the colonial institutional matrix of Lima, "oppression" by monopolistic Limeño commercial policies, and incentives of new British-financed regional exports like nitrates, quinine, and wool. The promise of true liberal elites, however, exceeded the reality. The movement was torn by contradictions and ultimately proved incapable of merging with other liberals until the 1840s. Instead, the south opted to secede, failed, and rose again.

While northern and Limeño economic elites collectively gravitated toward Chilean markets and protectionism, southern agriculturalists saw Bolivia as the Mecca. Upper Peru and the southern sierra had been thriving markets for late-colonial coastal wine and brandy producers; as well as the lifeline for the thousands of southerners in related transport and commercial services, from lowly alfalfa farmers to international trade firms. For a complex web of economic and political complications (typical of Latin America's early nineteenth-century balkanization[42]), Bolivia and Chile made wholly incompatible commercial allies for independent Peru. The country thus emerged effectively divided into two broad zones of commercial interests, north and south.

The larger commercial dynamics at work started with the creation of Bolivia and the opening of her own import route through a desert outpost, Cobija, in the mid–1820s. With the help of discriminatory duties, this port diverted traffic from Bolivia's more natural Peruvian link to the outside, the port of Arica. Chilean interests also favored this new arrangement—transshipments for Cobija traveled through Valparaíso—which meant, in turn, endorsement by Peru's northern elites, ever anxious as they were to retain their Chilean markets and political friends. Naturally, southern Peruvians, who suffered the brunt of intermittent trade wars with Bolivia across all sectors of the regional economy, were incensed. They needed open frontiers with Bolivia, wanted direct imports through Arica, and opposed all Chilean pretensions. This meant a southern liberal alliance with Bolivia—or at least with those segments of that also divided country seeking free trade.[43] Besides sparking a bewildering array of international alliances, tensions, wars, and policies between 1825–45, internally, in ever clearer fashion, this commercial axis pitted the Peruvian south against its north.

Most concretely, southern and northern elites came to loggerheads over a series of critical trade issues. For example, southern grape distillers felt ruined by the postindependence conversion of northern sugarcane into the cheap cane alcohol that flooded sierran markets; the fertile Arequipa granary appeared mortally threatened by the Chilean wheat imports encouraged by northern pressure groups; the lingering southern wool *obrajes* (manufactories of colonial origin) wanted restored access to Bolivian markets and seemed to blame the free trade in textiles on Lima; and southern desert enclaves (such as Iquique) needed the duty-free food supplies blocked by Lima.[44] Second, Arequipeño merchants, while dependent upon Lima, desperately hoped to break the closed-port system upheld by the Lima Consulado, which increased costs through transshipment and legal surcharges as it thwarted all local commercial autonomy. Third, the relatively rapid initiation of new regional exports—wool, nitrates, and bark—in the 1830s, helped along by British investment and organization, gave southerners, unlike the remainder of Peruvian elites, some hope that a profitable future might lie in changing comparative advantages and free trade. (This contrasts sharply with the north, where many regional economies were in perpetual decay from the early eighteenth century.) And British imports were gradually extending Arequipa's commercial sphere toward Cuzco itself, opening new possibilities for those southern elites pushed out of competing activities.[45] Finally, institutional and social—even mental—frameworks in the south differed radically from those of the north. As one example, slavery, still a major institution in northern agriculture, was by 1820 practically extinct south of Cañete. Even this was reflected in trade disputes.

Despite the incentives in play, the southern liberal impulse remained, at least until the 1840s, too feeble and isolated to serve as the social pillar of a national free trade movement. Regional hacendados were still not consistent liberals; for example, they fought to ban all foreign wine imports (like the French imports savored by Lima aristocrats) and grains (favored by Lima plebeians). Initially, the new British merchant presence found little welcome in Arequipeño commercial circles, who felt just as beleaguered as other Peruvian merchants by foreign inroads into local trade, more so because British development was so visible in Arequipa. In fact, the south produced the sharpest nationalist outbursts (repeated calls to expel foreign merchants, periodic attacks on consuls), which punctutated its painful transition into the British orbit. The benefits of British expansion of Arequipa's market area could not be fully appreciated until the 1840s. The old protectionist strongholds in Cuzco were only gradually giving way to the south, while the austral nitrate regions were but slowly entering Arequipa's liberal realm.[46] And although there remained, at best, this imperfect alignment with Britain, North American trade was barely perceptible in the south, ensuring that alliance with Peru's most articulate and active liberals could never develop.

Perhaps most important, in political terms, Arequipa seemed destined to remain a regional liberal movement. The south leaned toward liberal secessionism, not hegemony. Its spokesmen, despite other similarities, would have little truck with the centralized liberal state proposed by Bolívar and the internationalists. Federalism, decentralized liberalism, was essential to their cause, as much as reintegration with Bolivia. Geographic reality meant in fact that the south could exert little ongoing pull over the "national" state in Lima (where trade policies were resolved); the effective influence of such a state, even if it were well disposed toward southern demands, rarely extended beyond the central coast. The north, at least, with its willing protectionist planters, merchants, and Limeños, fell within the military orbit of Lima, and Lima-centric caudillos found at least a semblance of a permanent army and administration at their disposal. The south, in short, was not integrated into the initial Peruvian state, nor strong enough to conquer it and create it anew.[47]

This left rebellion under regionalist caudillos like Vivanco and Santa Cruz as the sole means of altering commercial policies. Arequipa became the legendary pueblo caudillo of Peru, and political unification with Bolivia became their utopian aim. The south's particular commercial demands always played a critical role in the smoldering regional revolts of the 1830s and 1840s, revolts whose impact became ever more serious with the international complications of shifting Bolivian and Chilean allies.[48] Liberal caudillismo had a separatist flavor, since a lasting conquest of the protectionist north proved impossible within Peru's prevailing national military and political balance. The main legacy of southern liberal separatism was the chronic instability—political stalemate—of the post-independence era, not free trade.

Paradoxically, southern liberalism established its foothold in Lima in the mid-1840s, following the region's effective pacification and subsequent forced integration by the expanding Lima-based state. It was not just the more consistent liberal impulse from provincial economic elites. By then, northern protectionism itself was in disarray, and Castilla's emerging state proved amenable to the free traders streaming in from the south.[49] By 1850, free trade had finally become an integrative, not divisive, ingredient in the formation of an elite national state.

Free trade elites were few, foreign, feeble and fractionalized in postindependence Peru. The liberal proclivities of later elites were as yet unknown. The stellar liberals were actually foreign consuls, mainly those of the United States. Yet their multifarious pressures could not succeed in the absence of a stable collaborating elite and state. Foreign merchants shied from involvement, knowing all too well the risks. Would-be liberal allies, the Bolivarians and their internationalist orphans, were easily outgunned by nationalist elites, for they lacked a credible economic constituency. The only palpable indigenous liberal movement arose in the south, yet it was truncated by the very regionalism of its liberal aspirations. In any case, the odds were set against liberals from the start, for Peru was dominated by its powerful protectionist elites.

BELEAGUERED NATIONALISTS: THE NEW LIBERALS' REVOLUTION, 1840–52

A whole generation passed before liberal dreams could gain credibility in Peru and translate into a consistent and winning drive for free trade. Underlying the ultimate victory of the second wave of Andean liberals in 1852 was the complex field of Peru's sweeping sociological and political transformations of the 1840s. These changes (more critical than even new creeds and practices in liberal politics) shattered the once formidable protectionist bloc, as they renewed opportunity for the new-style free traders. This time liberals stopped being beleaguered and multiplied.

Peru's dominant nationalist alliance did not break down until the early 1840s, when each of the issues and coalitions that had made protectionism tick ran into crisis or sheer obsolescence. First came widespread disenchantment with the protected Chilean market strategy, Peru's oldest roadblock to direct incorporation with North Atlantic capitalism. By 1840, northern planters, their miller and urban allies, merchants, and shippers discovered in dismay that new patterns of Chilean trade (chiefly the substitution of flours for wheat) had antiquated their hoped-for regional market integration. In its place, they began pondering new overseas markets (such as sugars for Europe) and contemplating a more receptive general outlook on direct ties with the world economy. The old internationalist critics of provincial trade formulas seemed vindicated.[50] In the south, too, enthusiasm for interregional trade networks flagged, blocked by the rise of new nationalists in the Bolivia of the 1840s; southerners now had to look to the north of Peru and accommodate their vision. The main effect, since new markets emerged slowly, was to quickly diminish the north-south regional conflicts that had so stymied trade policy (and the state's viability itself) for two decades. Political emotions defused, for the state stopped being the battleground of every commercial dispute.

A parallel development occurred within provincial commercial oligarchies, as their traditional antiforeign postures yielded to decentralized export promotion. Here, a fall in risks and shipping costs and the final death throes of colonial *obrajes* and backwoods artisanates paved the way, so that by 1845 most regional elites were seeking faster communications and direct linkups to world markets via freer coastwise trade. Sometimes good prospects for new exports, such as wools and nitrates in the south, precipitated these liberal conversions. But for many provincials, regionalist free trade represented simply their last-ditch effort to save depressed hinterlands pushed out of competing lines.[51] Most important for politics, the nationalists of Lima, upholding archaic port restrictions, now looked like the oppressive centralist party, which indeed they were. More nationalists defected on these issues. For Peru's state, soundly triumphant in arms over the south by 1845, these regional pressures could go either way. Tutored by the new liberals, who for once took regional grievances seriously, Lima officials began to regard free trade favorably, as now a possible integrative (if not blatantly co-optive) route to a more national state.[52] In short, by 1845 roles had reversed: protectionists now opposed the regions, while liberals offered them freedom and material hope.

Indeed, developments within the state best explain the other ways nationalist unity and resolve dissolved during the 1840s. For twenty years, Peru's endemically unstable caudillo-dominated state had, in complex fashion, fed into and supported protectionism on many fronts. A pivotal symbiosis between caudillos and Limeño merchants (who looked to the state for protection against risks as well as foreign traders), reinforced by their underlying financial nexus, had kept the Gamarrista generals afloat and kept them staunchly nationalist. However, excessive instability could ruin the protectionist cause too, as it did with the unprecedented round of national bloodletting and disintegration following Gamarra's own death in 1841. In four years of nonstop war, leading national merchants failed by the score, and their most cherished nationalist projects and symbols, such as the statist Asian Trade Company, drowned in the havoc as well.[53] In effect, desperate Consulado merchants and their allies reached the dead end of their statist protectionism; there was neither a state to serve, nor could it protect.

With startling speed, starting with their crisis of 1841, Lima merchants underwent a deep ideological crisis as well, which ended only with social peace in 1845 and a radical rethinking of their then peaking nationalism. All prior nationalist strategies had been premised on unswerving support from a strong state—for example, to enforce commercial monopolies and high tariffs. Clearly, this strong state had failed to emerge in Peru, and with the risks and outright predation Peru's real state engendered, the wisest path now appeared to be to lessen a destructive dependence. The liberal concept of a minimalist state, not to mention more utopian notions linking free trade to political stability, was their best (and final) option.

This move to a "private" sector was actually quite focused: it meant un-

precedented business partnerships and political alliances with their old antago-
nists. Liberal foreign houses (Peru's paragon of private enterprise) not only
offered profitable contacts, they were also shielded from attack by the local state.
The liberal turn of Limeño elites, though sparked by survival instincts, at the
same time neatly embraced four principles of liberalism: a reduced state role in
the economy, the supremacy of a stabilizing civil society over arbitrary despot-
ism, the supposedly civilizing tonicity of commerce, and regulation by and from
the external sector. Ideological embellishments came later, but, if unwittingly,
Peruvians were telescoping several centuries of liberal capitalist thought into
these few short years, 1841–45.[54]

This process also meant that national merchants, who once had orchestrated
the protectionist bloc, progressively distanced themselves from lesser allies such
as shopkeepers and artisans, Peru's expendable *menu peuple* still unenamored
of foreigners and free trade. Thus, the embrace of liberalism was, in part, a
move to a narrower and consciously elitist politics. That feature of Peruvian
liberalism would not change but only deepen over the years. Finally, after three
decades of uneasy coexistence, native elites could act as the natural conduits of
free trade policies from their liberal North Atlantic suppliers, creditors, and now
mentors. This political matrimony of commercial elites was sanctified in 1848,
when for the first time, foreigners were allowed to join the Consulado, that
hallowed ground of Peruvian nationalism.[55] This had more than symbolic import,
for the guild remained the state's critical institution for commercial policy. By
the mid–1850s overseas traders would actually dominate the Consulado.

The heightened caudillo fiscal crisis of the early 1840s also hastened the retreat
of protectionist fervor. True, the Peruvian state had suffered from militarist
deficits ever since 1821. But for a complex of reasons, most important of which
were the risks spawned by instability, the pressures of bankruptcy had not led
to a typical regimen of low tariffs, nor obsequiousness to free trading foreign
creditors, but to their opposite—elevated tariffs and symbiosis with the local
and nationalist merchant-finance cliques. In short, the usual liberal state-building
solutions were unavailable to this erratic regime. During the orgy of destruction
of the early 1840s, however, caudillos finally bankrupted their cherished native
fiscal intermediaries, or at least made their further lending improbable. The state
forced the improverished surviving *prestamistas* (money lenders) down the liberal
road, and they conveniently had forgotten to pack their checkbooks. Thus, by
1842, treasury officials and caudillos themselves began a hunt for new agents,
sources, and strategies of stopgap finance.[56] They did not have to look long or
far, for guano was just emerging as the miraculous fiscal panacea of the century.

By the mid–1840s, it looked as if liberal revenue tariffs might just become
workable for once (with Peru's new guano-induced imports and stability). Yet
these fiscal tariffs never really became the hallmark of liberal agitation; rather,
the whole issue was eclipsed by the state's direct access to huge guano export
fees. But guano, even if exploited under a nationalist export policy (the monopoly
system expertly modeled after traditional Peruvian protectionism), still required

accommodating postures toward the foreign houses and financiers now essential for managing the trade and, more important, for handling the new guano *adelantos* (advances on the receipts from future sales) to the treasury. After 1846, with mounting exports of bird dung, the novel free trade pressures mostly focused on this liberal realpolitik of guano. They were compounded, on the local side, by the irresistible distributive demands of national elites eager to divert guano funds for amortizing decades of defaulted debts from caudillo misrule. To Lima elites, liberalized tariffs, accelerated guano shipments, and institutionalized foreign credit seemed the most efficacious means for settling private debts, and such a policy was thriving by 1850, thanks to Peru's infamous $23 million "consolidation" of her formerly worthless internal debt bonds. Though nothing in liberal theory actually prescribed such a course (except for the midcentury Latin American variant that states should give to the rich), Peru's large public bondholders, the *consolidados*, became steadfast allies of foreign interests and the most strategic prop to the liberal cause.[57] Given the sheer weight of Peru's public bounty, the initial merchant postures for a private sector soon wore thin. It was the beneficiaries of the consolidation scheme, these nouveaux riches with ancient roots, who pressed on for foreign debt settlements and trade treaties and who bought wholesale the novel liberal notion that the true measure of liberty and civilization was one's ability, capacity, and propensity to import.

The relative political calm between 1844 and 1854, product of the pacification of the south (and the new monopoly of violence afforded by Lima's new monopoly over excrement), also made nationalism passé. These sorts of indirect influences, mediated by the evolving state structure, worked the critical transformations of guano wealth on elite consciousness, those which made free trade both thinkable and believable. Liberalism was not simply the handmaiden of opportunity cost or greed. A new breed of centralizing caudillos—Ramón Castilla and his ilk—were naturally sensitive to maintaining the fragile new hegemony of Lima, and export liberalism proved useful even if they and their Lima constituents still clung to much nationalist nostalgia. Increased guano revenues (for greater military and bureaucratic spending), restored overseas credit and diplomatic support, co-optive measures for the south (such as transforming Arica into a full entrepôt), and the lull in destabilizing pyrotechnics around deficits all made free trade a utilitarian imperative. Hard as it may seem to interpret these steps to a stronger state as a sign of *doux commerce*, most of the veteran caudillos tamed themselves, and the intransigent nationalists (provincials like Iguaín) would be liquidated for Peru's own good.[58] For civil elites, stability so reduced the risks and uncertainties of enterprise that, at last, export prospects could be estimated rationally under long-term vistas and acted upon. For foreign potentates, still reeling from the spree of reprisals unleashed in 1838, the new stability meant that Peru lost some of her unpredictability. The result was hardly Peruvian acquiescence, but ongoing foreign pressures, lures, and relations could at least now become normalized. Foreign prodding was not excessive, nor did it lead smoothly or swiftly to liberalization in the late 1840s (for external coercion became superfluous as soon as it was possible), yet foreign pressure did speed settlement of external debts and negotiations for trade treaties.[59] In short, this time foreigners met willing and able collaborators in the state. History, however, still left its imprint, both in Peru's ability to pursue its nationalist guano monopoly and in its choice of metropolis. The United States could not recover from its early Peruvian fiasco until late in the century, which helps explain British commercial and political ascendancy in the Age of Guano.

Stability led to other novel and far-reaching political consequences that directly undercut protectionist causes and, to no small degree, defined the coming liberal era. Peru's vintage nationalist warlords found themselves isolated or banished by the more versatile Castilla group, ever more attuned to liberal civilian advisers like Manuel de Mendiburu, Domingo Elías, Pedro Gálvez and Santiago Tavara. These men, a true liberal cabal, prescribed free trade as the cure-all for fiscal straits, national integration, and a lasting pacification. Since Castilla and his cohorts were the closest Peru had to typical caudillos of "Order and Progress," Peruvian liberals certainly partook then of the "contradictory, bastardized and denatured" liberalism that swept most of Latin America at midcentury. This type of regional adaptation (some say mutation) of liberalism was typically traceable to such liberal social alliances with centralizing states. Early rhetoric and hopes aside, by 1850 Peruvian free trade was not especially antimilitarist (linked to the Praetorian modernizers), nor exactly federalist (married to their centralizing project), nor minimalist (tied up with grounding a stronger and denser state). Nor did the liberal elites long hold to notions of creating an autonomous private sector, as partnership with the stabilizing state loomed far too lucrative. That much of the constituency for free trade emerged from conversions within the statist-protectionist camp also blunted its ideological purity and implications. The new and revived top-down forms of statism would persist into the liberal era, embodied in the guano monopoly, policy by fiat, and the persistent elite penchant for perquisites and privilege.

These outcomes were logical, for almost everywhere in Latin America midcentury liberalism closely reflected that generation that had come of age through the horrors and penury of the caudillo era. Liberalism adapted itself, in Peru as elsewhere, as a semiauthoritarian recipe for overcoming the pandemic instability that invited political decay and social chaos and that had thwarted economic growth since independence. Rather than showing deficient ideology or will, these circumstances help explain liberalism without much liberty and help explain why naive characterizations of discrete liberal phases, ideologies, and states prove wrong for much of the region.[60] Furthermore, as a deep-seated reaction to decades of nationalist instability (and no doubt failures), this type of liberalism would accrue its fantastic staying power not only in Peru, but in most of postcaudillo Latin America, for which Peru was but a hyperbolic case. The alternative to liberalism would remain clear—back to anarchy—a specter that later liberals lustily recounted, embellished, and distorted. It makes sense, then, to take early nationalist-caudillo episodes like Peru's quite seriously, as the truly formative experience of the new republics.

A new exclusionism of free trade, which erupted dramatically during the climactic tariff debates of 1849–52, was only new in the sense that by then an elite foundation had formed for successful exclusionary politics. The Bolivarian free traders were elitist too, but this trait had made a distinct handicap in the postindependence era. Then chaos and depression shrank social distances and lent initial republican politics its open and fluid air. Then, too, protectionist artisans, shopkeepers, and rustic patriarchs could not be shut out, nor did Peru's dominant elites want them out. But after 1845, propelled by the guano boom, foreign partnerships, and the Consolidation, a republican plutocracy was rapidly settling into place, along with its formal political institutions. Thus, while perhaps more national in a geographic sense, the new trade emerged as class based as, or more so than, its predecessor.

Indeed, the sharp tariff debates of 1850 show that the triumph of free trade (and a class struggle that helped bequeath it) were true benchmarks in the formation of an oligarchic consciousness in Peru. Until 1849, most Lima elites, while of a different mind about the issue, remained largely agnostic about trade policies, eager to concentrate on the business, not the politics, of exports. Their apathy vanished in late 1849, when assorted underclasses, abandoned by their old allies and shaken by the first dislocations of the guano trade, launched their aggressive, formidable, and largely autonomous campaign for a return to prohibitive tariffs. Led by avowed Jacobin artisans, this was Peru's own little 1848. The reaction of Lima elites proved decisive and swift. They were not to be cajoled by a protectionist rabble. Politicians quickly closed their ears to the artisans' pleas, and elites rapidly embraced an extreme, even reactionary, brand of free trade.[61] Liberal publicists goaded them on, with broadsides heralding the consumers' right to luxury over artisan claims of employment and sustenance and with free trade visions of an imported sybarite lifestyle suitable for Peru's reemergent aristocrats. These were entirely new arguments in Peru, and the victory of free trade in 1852 must be seen as part of a general drive to legitimate the unfolding elite privilege against possible threat from below.

This conflict in midcentury Peruvian political culture is striking, since other arenas of overt class strife were remarkably quiet. Peru had no rebelling peasantries, recalcitrant nobles, or striking workers to speak of. What differentiated Peru's 1848 from that of the continent (besides the one-year lag) was precisely the role of free trade. In Europe, nineteenth-century free trade was less critical (freedom of industry more so), but the issue still acquired distinctly popular overtones, opposed in the main against the "feudal" privileges of landed gentry, who starved urban groups (middle classes, laborers, the bourgeoisie) with their exorbitant corn. And when some artisans (like those in Paris and German towns) added protectionism to their revolutionary lists, liberals, libertarians, and socialists alike joined in strenuous efforts to purge these popular errors. In Peru—

or most of Latin America for that matter—there were few attempts to demo-
cratically persuade artisans, who by 1850 were the last major protectionist lobby.
In Santiago, Bogotá, and La Paz, more political energies went to exclude them,
and free trade, rather than aimed at rural oligarchs, seemed by now a major
issue conjoining urban and rural interests. National social structures were that
different from Europe and even small differences could affect emerging political
structures.[62] In Latin America, by 1850, the expendable groups were mainly
popular and (besides the peasant masses who were excludable for other reasons)
few in numbers. At one pole of the world economy, then, trade policy contributed
to democratization; at the other pole, in a situation like Peru's, it helped to detract
from democratization.

Against all these backdrops, a new liberalism surfaced by 1850 that could
deftly manage the changing social and political currents. It became, in short, a
broad-based elite social movement, an efficient carrier for free trade ideas from
abroad. Carryover from the defeated generation, however, was slight. Pando
and his entourage had long fled Peru, though Castilla rehabilitated some aging
internationalists (Manuel del Río among them) to implement the needed reforms.
By 1850, however, the novelty had worn off internationalist ideas, an indistin-
guishable common currency as viable protectionist alternatives faded. The constituency of free trade came mainly from the converted (and convertible) elites:
national merchants, *prestamistas*-turned-bondholders, regional oligarchs, tamed
caudillos, the anxious and responsible functionaries. They were joined by youthful ideologues, fledgling exporters, newly welcomed southerners, and foreign
houses (ensconced in the Consulado itself). Free trade gained ground swiftly,
for each new convert directly diminished protectionist ranks. Goaded from below,
most Peruvian elites, not tied to specific industries, could make the switch then
to liberalism with both profit and ease.

The ideologies in motion were indeed the latest European imports, but as a
port and a capital, Lima had always been a cosmopolitan's delight. More important for politics than theories was the example set by foreigners, who only
by the late 1840s shed their hypocrisy about free trade. Peruvians, even the
keenest free traders, had always been aware of, as well as irked and undermined
by, the fact that Britain and the United States preached free trade to them while
drawing on a long history of protectionism for themselves. Even the internationalists were nationalists enough to reject a one-sided deal. Now, William
Huskinsson, Richard Cobden, and Robert Peel became instant heroes in Peru,
outdoing any political economist, for the repeal of the Navigation Acts and Corn
Laws in 1846 proclaimed for all to see that free trade was good enough for
internal consumption as well as export.[63] In fact, British parliamentary debates
impinged directly on Peru, as Peruvian deputies and senators (and diplomats at
the treaty table) were able to quote their foreign peers verbatim, with the usual
year or so lag. More libertarian strains of free trade also filtered into Peru via
France and the refugees of 1848, yet these were luxuries readily discarded under
local artisan pressures. Along with other types of fallout from neighboring An-

dean countries, Francisco Bilbao and other Chilean leftists tried linking free trade to political concerns, but their followers remained a pitiful minority in Peru. Diffusion was thus a multilayered, multidetermined, and disjointed process. In Peru, only the concept of low tariffs would become more radical, perhaps as the typical reflex of repentant radicals, Peru's nationalist converts.[64] For example, the peripatetic French economist, Jean Gustave Courcelle-Seneuil (a notable influence in Chile, the region's first foreign economic adviser), proffered several stark recipes to the Peruvian government as well: among these, formal abolition of all tariff barriers!

By the late 1840s, the local propagation mechanisms were also far more convincing than the cranky press releases of a beleaguered U.S. consul. Free trade became a respectable, even universal, intellectual creed, removing, at last, the mercantilist remnants that had showed such staying power in Peru. (Perhaps, for a currency producer, bullionism had made some sense.) Liberal intellectual barnstorming was important and necessary insofar as new types of nationalist doctrines, like Norbeta Casanova's novel "infant industry" arguments (to legitimate new elite interests in Lima factory experiments), could still muster support after 1845, especially in official circles. The explicit idea of these new nationalists was to divert guano income into state-sponsored diversification. Yet the new liberals had still greater resources: *El Comercio*, the merchant paper par excellence, by 1845 had become a free trade mouthpiece that dashed off liberal editorials at all critical junctures in the tariff debates. So was *El Progreso*, the new house organ of Peru's "progressive" Civilian Club, led by Domingo Elías, with their direct line to Presidents Castilla and Echenique (the latter, southern reared, threw critical support to the victory of free trade).[65] The nascent political clubs, while talking vaguely of "promotion of industry" to artisan groups, espoused free trade in their programs. A new breed of professional free traders surfaced to replace the vanishing internationalist species. Dubbing themselves *los cursantes de economía política*, they publicly beleaguered protectionists and offered all kinds of economic (and of course political) advice to official bodies like the Consejo de Estado, the Ministry of Finance, and congressional tariff commissions, easing all of their transitions to free trade.[66] In fact, Peru had established its first official chair of political economy in 1847 (Eugenio Carrillo Sosa filled the post), and four young *cursantes* were its first, and immensely influential, graduating class. By 1850, the discipline had become compulsory in Lima's three elite *colegios*.

Intellectual imports bolstered free trade arguments, because this time liberals had acquired the political skills needed to seize the initiative in a shifting national balance of elites. Though often spiced with abstruse digressions on the political economists, the recipes of free traders were concocted with national, even nationalist, conditions in mind. Leaders like Elías and Távara were in fact Peru's first wide-ranging nationally based entrepreneurs; they could speak with greater compass than the Arequipeños of the 1820s. They capitalized on the deep-felt disillusion with protectionist promises and seemed to consciously distance themselves from foreign power. Indeed, compared with the 1820s, when consuls led self-defeating liberal efforts, this was a national movement, not a war of proxies. For example, liberals roundly condemned the ancient protectionist standard of alliance with Chile as the most "antinational" and dependent policy imaginable, and so it was by 1850. Free trade was also eminently national for its receptiveness to southern and interior developmental aspirations, which finally found their voice in the capital. Lima privileges, such as high duties on transport equipment or foodstuffs needed in export regions, were now denounced as fetters on national development.[67] In contrast to the 1820s, a new kind of Peruvian nationalism was possible, in which a politician's nativistic railings against foreigners no longer automatically earned him political credentials. This was a new sort of internationalism to help the nation as a whole to develop faster and to bolster the national state. Finally, though serious disjunctions and omissions remained, this wave of free trade seemed to ride the crest of other liberal issues, such as they were in Peru: for example, the abolition of slavery (only nationalists had supported the sordid "free trade" in human chattel), the spread of free labor (free trade would obliterate the last *obrajes* and guilds, emancipating their ensnared workers in the process), or the reform of precapitalist commercial and civil codes (legal modernization would spread the new economic boom).

In fact, the final push for free trade in 1852 had a great deal to do with the wider dictates of economic and political individualism, which also helped define both its radicalism and indigenous roots. The stunningly effective liberal arguments during the 1850–52 congressional debates—those that swayed skeptics— offered low uniform tariffs as the perfect antidote to privileged, personalistic, and politicized economic policy. For liberals like the *cursantes*, a single free trade standard was a kind of leveling device, to do away with irrational influence peddling. Protectionism had always favored privileged groups at the center, or, more dramatically, it had created a kind of combined pork-barrel demonstration effect (especially in Congress) whereby each group in Peruvian society escalated its particular protectionist demands, favors that politicians, naturally, found hard to resist. This was Peru's special plague, since the country harbored so many aggressive and competing protectionist interests and such hallowed traditions of patrimonial politics. This specter remained fresh in the minds of deputies and other policymakers after the latest barrage of artisan demands in 1849, which had galvanized a host of other protectionists. With their uniform and impersonal free trade standard (to be cast into statute to preclude all political tampering), liberals this time made beleaguered protectionists look like a contradictory, squabbling, and divided flock. Indeed they were, as factory owners publicly blasted artisans over duties and both lambasted agrarian nationalists. Elite liberals promoted a scorched earth free trade—for example, by sacrificing their own promising factory experiments in order to stem the populist contagion of protectionism. (The soon-emptied workshops became new mausoleums of nationalist failure.) All groups would henceforth receive the same Manchesterian favoritism—low input and subsistence costs—and no more.[68] In a remarkable turnabout, the 1852 Congress embraced the strict egalitarian premises of Manchesterian tariffs—one reason why Peru's free trade of the guano age turned out to be such an extreme and rigid policy.

Of course, the impersonal dictates of the world market were not really democratic, particularly in a country whose internal markets (much less the market for influence) could never be depersonalized. Most everyone concerned in 1852 could see that free trade, and the exclusionism sanctified in this form of tariff, privileged some sectors (connected foreigners, well-heeled city consumers, would-be exporters) over others, chiefly skilled workers and the rest of Peru without the resources or pull to take an easy path to an open economy. Artisans bewailed. And in a climax of inverted irony, one leading senator proclaimed the new tariff "In Protection of Commerce."[69] Freedom to trade was, like all liberal freedoms, a freedom for whom.

LIBERAL LEGACIES?

In the long run, free trade in Peru did not create an individualistic market society out of the market economy reinforced in the external sector, just as many historians suggest. There was no sweeping social transformation, as some early free trade proponents spoke of, though in a multiplicity of ways, trade policy struggles had always been about wider concerns of Peruvian nation and state building. We saw that in one sense free trade emerged long after independence and as a narrow elite response to the nightmare of social and economic retrogression in the caudillo era. But the chief reasons for liberalism's limited social impact and range came still later and seem more structural still. These were not ingrained ideological and personal defects (the "distorted" liberal consciousness) usually singled out by the historiography of Peru.[70]

In large part, the social failure of liberalism occurred because of the extraordinary *success* of the guano-age state: the rapid burgeoning of exports, imports, and foreign credit of the 1850s and the budgetary affluence this sudden prosperity allowed. On a world scale, few nineteenth-century states approached Peru in terms of the portion of national product captured and consumed by the state (around 25 percent). Because of Peru's unencumbered sovereignty over guano, bird dung, by the 1860s, came to supply some three-quarters of state income.[71] Few states anywhere, anytime, have enjoyed such a remarkable fiscal autonomy. Such freedom could also bring some paradoxical social consequences.

A handful of concomitant liberal reforms came from above, mainly from the largess of an enriched and enlarged state: the abolition of Indian tribute and black slavery in 1855, rationalized and secularized legal structures, or what amounted to a huge public buyout of church properties and entailed estates. However, most of the consequences of free trade remained within the confines of the state sector or the immediate environs of Lima. The core Peruvian entrepreneurs quickly seized investment in the state itself (guano contracts, state banking, public works and services) as the dynamic growth pole, a profit pattern enhanced by free trade, politics, and the peculiar fact that the Peruvian state actually owned and operated most of the export sector.[72] Thus, there was little private incentive felt, and there were few initiatives taken, to press for wider liberal-capitalist reforms that might have loosened the colonial (or even precolonial) social and economic constraints that prevailed nearly everywhere outside Lima and its state. Even Peru's most intrepid capitalist spirits soon became sycophantic creatures of this reconstituted colonial-style Leviathan. The extraordinary social autonomy of the guano economy stalled movement for change, whether by capitalists, by lords, or by peasants, groups mainly left alone and to their own devices in the nineteenth century.

From the public sphere, the feeble pressures for further liberal reforms also slackened. Peru's state enjoyed such a radical fiscal autonomy—it bowed to no one for its income—that few incentives came into play to develop the kind of ties to civil society that (in the classic guise of institutional change for fiscal and political support) accelerated capitalist development elsewhere in the modern world.[73] Tied to the state, Peru's free trade regime after 1852 remained an anomalous hybrid that left most of Peru's economy and society operating on blatantly precapitalist principles—anything but a paragon of nineteenth-century liberalism. In a schizophrenic neocolonial society, individualism came out as dualism instead, widening, not narrowing, the gaps between a reduced but hypermodernized external sector and the vast majority of Peruvians left behind, or pushed behind, in motley versions of the colonial past. In short, Peru acquired its syndrome of social dualism, which still plagues the Andes today.

NOTES

I thank the School of Social Science of the Institute for Advanced Study, Princeton, for their generous support for this research, as well as the Social Science Research Council. Most of the data and interpretations in this essay I have developed in "Merchants, Foreigners and the State: The Origins of Trade Policies in Post-Independence Peru" (Ph.D. diss., University of Chicago, 1985) and *Between Silver and Guano: Protectionist Elites to a Liberal State in Peru, 1820–1850* (Princeton University Press, forthcoming).

1. See, for example, introduction (p. 12) and various country surveys in Cortés Conde and Stein, *Guide to Economic History*, esp. Hunt and Macera, "Peru: Interpretive Essay," pp. 546–71. All recent textbooks on the region treat this shift as the fundamental policy change of the nineteenth century: Skidmore and Smith, *Modern Latin America*, pp. 39–45; Keen and Wasserman, *Short History*, pt. 2; and Burns, *Poverty of Progress*, chs. 2, 7.

2. Safford, "Politics, Ideology and Society," esp. pp. 384–86; and Arnaud, *Estado y capitalismo*.

3. Stein and Stein, *Colonial Heritage of Latin America*, ch. 5; Frank, *Lumpenbourgeoisie and Lumpendevelopment*, ch. 4; Cardoso and Faletto, *Dependency and Development*, ch. 3; Halperín, *Historia contemporánea*, chs. 3–4; and Véliz, *Centralist Tradition*, ch. 6. A typical country view from this vast literature is McGreevy, *Economic History of Colombia*, chs. 5–7.

4. White, *Paraguay's Autonomous Revolution*; Palma, "Growth of Chilean Manufacturing Industry," ch. 2; Rector, "Merchants and Commercial Policy in Chile"; Abel and Lewis, *Latin America*, esp. pp. 95–100 and chapters by Thompson (Mexico), MacFarlane (Colombia), Ortega (Chile), and, with a grain of salt, Platt; Gootenberg, "Merchants, Foreigners and the State," ch. 1; Gootenberg, "Social Origins of Protectionism"; Halperín, *Historia contemporánea*, ch. 3; and Coatsworth, "Obstacles to Growth."

5. The revisionist literature here is now too large to adequately survey: see, for example, Cortés Conde and Hunt, *Latin American Economies*, introduction and chapters on Brazil, Chile, Peru, and Argentina; Weaver, *Class, State and Industrial Structure*; Brown, *Socio-Economic History of Argentina*; Topik, "State Intervention in a Liberal Regime"; and Thorp, *Latin America in the 1930's*.

6. Thorp and Bertram, *Peru, 1890–1977*; Anna, *Fall of Royal Government*; Hunt, "Growth and Guano"; and Levin, *Export Economies*, ch. 2. The best study of postindependence politics is still Basadre, *Multitud, ciudad y campo*.

7. Bonilla, *Guano y burguesía*; Bonilla, *Siglo a la deriva*; Bonilla, "Perú entre independencia y guerra"; Bonilla and Spalding, "Independencia en el Perú"; Yépes, *Desarrollo capitalista*; Cotler, *Clases, estado y nación*; Flores Galindo, "Militarismo y dominación británica"; Piel, "Place of the Peasantry"; Tantaleán, *Política económico*; and Macera, "Algodón y comercio exterior." An opposing, antidependency view (with many of the same overtones) is Bollinger, "Bourgeois Revolution in Peru."

8. The argument is developed formally in Gootenberg, "Merchants, Foreigners and the State," chs. 2–3.

9. Bonilla, *Gran Bretaña y Perú*, 5, 76–77, and "Perú entre independencia y guerra," pp. 418–22; Bonilla et al., "Comercio libre y crisis andina," pp. 10–11; Flores Galindo, "Militarismo y dominación británica"; Macera, "Algodón y comercio exterior," pp. 287–88; Yepes, *Desarrollo capitalista*, pp. 43–44. The obverse view is Mathew, "Imperialism of Free Trade"; Platt, "Imperialism with Reservations"; or more generally, Platt, *Latin America and British Trade*, pt. 1.

10. Great Britain, Foreign Office, Series 61, 1821–60, "Correspondence between British Diplomatic and Consular Agents in Peru and the Foreign Office" (henceforth, FO61:vol. no. and date); and FO61:8, Ricketts to Canning, "Report on the Commerce of Peru," 17 Dec. 1826. British "Reports on Trade"—each running into hundreds of pages of commercial documents—and analysis exist for 1824, 1827, 1834, 1838, 1839, 1840, and 1841 (henceforth, BRT and year). Printed versions of some are Bonilla, *Gran Bretaña y el Perú*, vols. 1–4; and Humphreys, *British Consular Reports on Latin America*, pp. 107–207.

11. FO61:1–187, 1823–60. See esp. BRT 1827, FO61:11, Ricketts to Canning, all 1827, and FO61:37–53, Wilson to Palmerston, 1836–38 for the major interventionist campaigns. FO61:53, 29 Sept. 1838 (BRT 1837), FO61:82, Wilson to Palmerston, 15 Apr. 1841 (BRT 1840).

12. FO61:11, Ricketts to Canning, 11 May 1827, "A Few Remarks Connected with the Commerce of Peru," FO61:12, Ricketts to Canning, 20 Dec. 1827; FO61:13–21 (various), 1827–32; FO61:62, Wilson to Palmerston, 4 Sept. 1839, "Report upon the Trade of Peru for 1838" (BRT 1838); and BRT 1840. Defensive posture after 1839 documented in FO61:58–100 (various), 1839–43.

13. Based on U.S. National Archives Record Group 59, General Records of the Department of State, M154 (microfilm copies), "Dispatches from U.S. Consuls in Lima,"

vols. 1–6, 1823–1854 (henceforth, M154: vol. numbers, date), and T52, U.S. Ministers (vols. 1–16, 1826–61).

14. See esp. T52:1–3, Larned to Van Buren and Forsyth, 1829–35; BRT 1827; or XYZ, *Reflexiones sobre la ley de prohibiciones reimpresas y aumentadas con notas* (Lima, 1831). This early U.S. role is ignored in standard works on U.S. interests in Peru; for example, Bonilla, "Emergencia del control norteamericano." Exceptions are Bollinger, "Evolution of Dependence," or Clayton, "Origins of U.S.-Peruvian Relations."

15. For interests and strategy, see esp. T52:1, Larned to Van Buren, 5, 8 March 1830; "Conference on the Subject of Prohibitory Duties," 20 Apr. 1830; M154:1, Tudor to Pando, 2 Nov. 1826; Tudor to Clay, 15 Jan. 1827; Archivo del Ministerio de Relaciones Exteriores del Perú (henceforth, ARE), 1830, "Servicio Diplomático Extranjero 6–3, Legación de los Estados Unidos," 13 Oct. 1830; Anon., *Observaciones sobre el proyecto de Reglamento de Comercio presentado al Congreso por la Comisión de Hacienda* (Lima, 1828), 6–18; and [Santiago Tavara], *Análisis y amplificación del manifiesto presentado al Congreso del Perú por el honorable Señor Ministro Don José María Pando* (Lima, 1831) 1:42–53. For overall campaigns, see T52:1–4, Larned to Van Buren, Livingston, Lane, and Forsyth, all 1829–36; and T52:1, 5 Mar. 1830 (instructions). For secret propaganda efforts, M154:2, Tudor to Clay, 1 Mar. 1828; Prevost to Clay, 26 Apr., 17 May, 6 June 1828 (with large set of sample products); and T52:1, Larned to Van Buren, 25 Oct. 1830, 4 July, 1 Aug., 5 Sept. 1831.

16. Based on Archives du Ministère des Affaires Etrangères (Paris), Correspondance Consulaire et Commerciales, Lima, vols. 1–12, 1821–62 (henceforth, CCC:volume no., date); and Correspondance Politique (Pérou), vols. 1–16, 1798–1847. See esp. CCC:1, Chaumette, 8 June 1827; Barrére, 14 Oct. 1829, 29 July 1830, 26 Aug. 1831; CCC:2, Barrére, 17 Dec. 1832, 3 Jan. 1833; CCC:3, 18 July 1833; ARE, 6–14, Legación de Francia, 1829–44. For typical anti-French reactions, F061:33, Wilson to Palmerston, 7 Aug. 1835, and BRT 1837.

17. See, for example, British awareness of the merchant role in FO61:8, FO61:11, Ricketts to Canning, 15 Sept. 1826 and 11 May 1827; FO61:53, "Report on the Trade of Peru in 1837," Wilson to Palmerston, 29 Sept. 1838 (BRT 1837); and CCC:2, Barrére, "Tableau general du commerce," 6 June 1833. The merchant paradox is analyzed in Gootenberg, "Merchants, Foreigners and the State," chs. 2–3.

18. For examples, T52:5, Pickett to Forsyth, 4 Dec. 1840; T52:6, 31 May 1842; and FO61:26, Wilson to Palmerston, 5 Feb., 27 Apr., 5 May 1834. For this reason, consuls insisted throughout the period that merchants maintain strict neutrality; see "Notice: Legation of the U.S. in Lima," *El Comercio* (Lima), 16 Apr. 1842; and *El Peruano* (Lima), 25 Oct., 29 Oct., 6 Dec. 1845.

19. Bonilla, "Perú entre independencia y guerra," p. 418; on contraband, T52:3, Larned to Forsyth, 12 Jan. 1835; M154:5, Bartlett to Forsyth, 11 Jan. 1839; FO61:13, Ricketts to Canning, 9 Aug. 1827; CCC:1, Barrére, 14 Oct. 1829; Santiago Távara, *Informe sobre contrabando* (Lima, 1832); and "Medidas para ebitar el contrabando," *Comercio*, 7 July 1845.

20. Bonilla et al., "Comercio libre y crisis andina," pp. 9–11; or Tantaleán, *Política económico*, pp. 61, 223–24, for opposite views. See Gootenberg, "Merchants, Foreigners and the State," pp. 289–308, for full documentation of loan dangers and strategies. For hundreds of illustrations, see FO61:35, Humphreys to Palmerston, 16 Apr. 1835; FO61:47, H. Wilson to Palmerston, 17 July 1857; CCC:3, Barrére, 10 Apr. 1835; and

"Respuesta del Cuerpo Diplomático relativo a la lei sobre empréstitos extranjeros," *Peruano*, 6 Dec. 1845.

21. FO61:1, Rowcroft to Canning, 9 Aug. 1823, and "Memorial from British Merchants in Lima," 17 Mar. 1823; Archivo General de la Nación (AGN), Section H–1, Archivo Histórico de Hacienda, Cartas/Oficios 185:1207, Prefecturas, Dec. 1828–Jan. 1829 (henceforth, AGN H–1 OL); AGN H–1 OL 241:622–40, Tribunal del Consulado, Apr. 1835; speech of Deputy Alegre, *Comercio,* 8 Aug. 1845; and "El Artículo 61 del Reglamento de Comercio," *Comercio,* 26 Apr. 1842.

22. "Informe del Consulado," *Comercio*, 10–30 Jan. 1840; and "Los zeladores del Congreso," *El Telegrafo de Lima*, 21 Mar. 1828. This is best seen in Peru's futile forced naturalization campaigns: *Peruano*, Aug., Sept. 1840; FO61:70, Wilson to Palmerston, 27 Sept, 4 Oct. 1840; CCC:5, Le Moyne, Apr.-July 1842; and Gootenberg, *Between Silver and Guano*, ch. 5.

23. FO61:8, Ricketts to Canning, 15 Sept. 1826; FO61:11, Ricketts to Canning, "Secret," 6 Feb. 1827, 11 May 1827; FO61:17, Willimott to Palmerston, June-July 1830; FO61:51–60, Wilson to Palmerston, all 1838–40; and BRT 1839, 1840, 1841.

24. See statistics in Nolan, "Diplomatic and Commercial Relations with Peru," pp. 103–5; Bollinger, "Evolution of Dependence," pp. 1–22; T52:4, Larned to Forsyth, 1836–37; and FO61:33, Wilson to Palmerston, 7 Aug. 1835.

25. For France, CCC:4, Barrére, Aug. 1835; CCC:5, Saillard, 16 July 1839; CCC:7, Le Moyne, 15 May 1843; CCC:8, "Rapport sur l'état y la condition des étrangers au Pérou," 1 Nov. 1846; BRT 1837; FO61:88, Sealy to Canning, 26 Mar. 1842; and *Comercio*, 13 May 1842.

26. For this "weak state" argument, see Bonilla, "Perú entre independencia y guerra," pp. 418–22; and Flores Galindo, "Militarismo y dominación británica," pp. 119–20; Tantaleán, *Política económico*, pp. 223–24. For recognition as the obstacle, FO61:12, Ricketts to Canning, 20 Dec. 1827; FO61:45, "Petition of British Merchants in Lima," 28 June 1837; FO61:108, Adams to Palmerston, 8 Feb. 1845; CCC:3, Barrére, 21 May 1834; and T52:1, Larned to Van Buren, 1 Aug. 1831.

27. Examples are endless: T52:1, Larned to Van Buren, 8 March 1830, 4 July 1831; BRT 1837; FO61:58, Wilson to Palmerston, 27 Mar. 2 Apr. 1839; *El Rebeñique* (Lima), Sept. 1841; and *El Tribunal del Pueblo* (Lima), Sept.-Dec. 1839.

28. Robinson, "Non-European Foundations of Imperialism"; applied to Peru in Bonilla, *Guano y burguesía*, pp. 44–45, 63–64.

29. They discovered instead that their natural allies in the elite—practically the entire spectrum of agrarian, commerical, and financial interests—were vehemently antiforeign and averse to the very notion of free trade. As examples, the repeated "betrayal" of British and U.S. aims by their collaborators Pando, Benavides, and Santa Cruz: FO61:11, Ricketts to Canning, 11 May 1827; T52:1, Larned to Van Buren, 12, 16 Apr. 1830, 10 Sept. 1832; M154:1, Tudor to Clay, 2 Nov., 24 Dec. 1826; 6 Jan., 3 Feb., 23 Mar. 1827; and M154:2, Tudor, Prevost, and Radcliff to Clay, 7 Nov. 1827, 6 Feb., 17 May, 30 Aug. 1828.

30. Louis, *Robinson and Gallagher Controversy*. This new view is more compatible with the complex interpretations of intrastate relations in Doyle, *Empires*, pt. 2, esp. pp. 222–26.

31. Graham, *Independence in Latin America*, chs. 2–3; Jaramillo, *Bolívar y Canning*, pp. 228–35; and Temperley, *Foreign Policy of Canning*, app. 4, pp. 555–61.

32. Anna, *Fall of Royal Government*, chs. 6–8; and esp. Melzer, "Kingdom to Republic in Peru," chs. 5–8.

33. FO61:8, Ricketts to Canning, 15 Sept. 1826; FO61:11, "Secret," Ricketts to Canning, 6 Feb. 1827; also 3 Mar., 11 May, 16 May 1827; *Clamores del Perú* (Lima), March 1827, pp. 5–12; *Manifesto que se presenta a la Nación sobre reformar la aduana y comercio por el ciudadano F.L.* (Lima, 1827); AGN, Section H–4, Libros manuscritos de la sección Hacienda, no. 1584, Tribunal del Consulado, "Copias de oficios y informes," 18 Mar., Nov. 1825, June-July 1826 (henceforth, Actas); and AGN, Section H–8, Tribunal del Consulado republicano, Legado 1 (henceforth, AGN H–8, vol. no.), 30 Mar., 1 Sept. 1825.

34. Debates in *Mercurio Peruano* (Lima), Aug. 1827, 5–25 June 1828; "Comercio," "Nuestra Patria y el Bien de nuestra Patria," *Telegrafo*, Feb.-March, June 1828; "Comercio y fábricas," *Telegrafo*, May 1828; *Observaciones sobre el proyecto de Reglamento de Comercio de 1828*; [Tavara], *Análisis y amplificación*; and XYZ, *Reflexiones sobre la ley de prohibiciones*.

35. Popular memory lasted long, too; "Reglamento de Comercio: los artesanos," *Comercio*, 1 Aug. 1850. FO61:11, Ricketts to Canning, 11 May 1827, well expressed British revulsion at the marriage of "mob" republicanism and protectionism.

36. For liberal (and nationalist) caudillos, see Gootenberg, *Between Silver and Guano*, ch. 4, sec. a, or Vivanco decrees in *Peruano*, 6 Feb., 24 Mar., 5 May 1841, 10 May, 22 Apr., 3 July 1843. Tristán, *Peregrinaciones de una paria*, pp. 350–51, for a "fictionalized" account of protectionist "party of Gamarra" caudillos. Foreign observations are ubiquitous: e.g., T51:1, Larned to Van Buren, 8 Mar. 1830; and FO61/24, Wilson to Palmerston, 18 Dec. 1833.

37. Liss, *Atlantic Empires*; Baltes, "Pando: Colaborador de Gamarra"; Palacios, *Deuda anglo-peruana*, ch. 1; Pike, *Modern History*, p. 42; FO61:91, Foreign and Domestic, Palmerston, 17 June 1842; and CCC:4, Barrére, 1 June 1836.

38. "Exposición del proyecto de Reglamento de Comercio," *El Conciliador* (Lima), Nov.-Dec. 1832; "Economía política," May-Oct. 1831; Manuel Vidaurre, *Discurso sobre la acta de navegación pronunciada por el Diputado Manuel Vidaurre* (Boston, 1828), reprint, *Conciliador*, 18 Feb. 1832; José María Pando, *Memoria sobre el estado de la Hacienda de la República Peruana al fin de 1830 presentado al Congreso por José María Pando* (Lima, 1831); and [Tavara], *Análisis y amplificación; Apuntes relativos a la operación práctica del Tratado de Comercio llamado de Salaverry concluido entre las Repúblicas de Chile y del Perú* (Guayaquil, 1836).

39. Romero, *Historia económica*, pp. 268–71; Bonilla et al., "Comercio libre y crisis andina," p. 12; and Tantaleán, *Política económico*, p. 51. Their efforts and defeat are graphically illustrated in FO61:21–23, Wilson to Palmerston, 1832–33; T52:2, Larned to Livingston, 1832–34; CCC:2, Barrére, 4 Feb., 1 July, 26 Aug., 10 Oct. 1831; and *Telegrafo*, Jan.-Aug. 1833.

40. "Tratado de Comercio entre Chile y el Perú," *El Redactor Peruana* (Lima), 25 May 1836; AGN H–1 OL 248:485–93, Tribunal, May-June 1836; "Análisis de las proposiciones del Sr. Vidaurre," *Eco de la Opinión del Perú* (Lima), Aug.-Sept. 1827; Pedro de Rojas y Briones, *Proyectos de economía política en favor de la República Peruana* (Lima, 1828), pp. 6–8, 25–28; and *Clamores*, 13 Mar. 1827 (miners).

41. Gootenberg, *Between Silver and Guano*, ch. 5, explores this fiscal group.

42. *Balkanization* properly should be termed *Latin Americanization*, for the process unfolded here before the fragmentation of Balkan states.

43. CCC:8, Lima, Lemoyne, "Rapport sur le commerce d'Arica et Tacna (Pérou) 1845," 16 Mar. 1845; CCC:1 (Arequipa/Arica), Villamues, Apr. 1846; CCC:2 (Lima), Barrére, "Histoire de la contestation existante entre le Pérou et le Chile," 12 Oct. 1832 (and 24 July 1830); FO 61:71, "Mr. Belford Wilson's Report on the Trade of Peru during the year ending the 31st of December 1839," Wilson to Palmerston, 30 Apr. 1840 (BRT 1839); and "Breves reflexiones sobre el tratado de comercio concluido en Arequipa en 8 de Nov. de 1831 entre Bolivia y el Perú," *Conciliador*, 9–20 June 1832.

44. Dávila, *Medios para salvar Moquegua*, pp. 1–85; Rivero, *Memoria sobre la industria agrícola*, pp. 7–38; *Conciliador*, 25 Aug. 1830; *Comercio*, 9 Jan.–15 Aug. 1841, 10 June 1841; *Peruano*, 30 January 1841; 10, 20 May 1843; and *La Bolsa* (Lima), 9 Sept. 1841.

45. Flores Galindo, *Arequipa y el sur andino*, pp. 45–93; Ponce, "Social Structure of Arequipa," ch. 3; and Jacobsen, "Landtenure and Society in Azángaro," ch. 2; See esp. "Memorias del General Manuel Mendiburu" (MS., Biblioteca Denegri Luna, Lima, 1829–54), 1:115–18, 131–46; and "Representación del comercio de Arequipa al gobierno," *Comercio*, 14–15 Aug. 1850.

46. For one of many examples, Pedro José Gamio, *Representación que el comercio del Arequipa ha dirigido al Supremo Gobierno* (Arequipa, 1832); See also Mariano M. De Loayza, *Refutación a las observaciones de S.M.B. D. B. H. Wilson en el Correo n. 47* (Lima, 1840); CCC:2, Barrére, 14 Feb.–1 Mar. 1833; FO61:58–90, all 1839–45.

47. A compelling analysis along these lines is Wibel, "Evolution of a Regional Community: Arequipa," esp. chs. 9–12; earlier chapters are also informative on the region's trade orientation and policies.

48. Carpio, "Rebeliones arequipeñas del siglo XIX"; Herrera Alarcón, *Rebeliones*. For trade issues in southern revolts, *El Regenerador* (Arequipa), 12 Jan. 1841; *Peruano*, 12 Jan., 24 Mar. 1841, 2, 22 Apr., 10, 20 May 1843; FO61:64, H. Wilson to Palmerston, 3 Oct. 1839; BRT 1839; FO61:83, H. Wilson, 16 Jan., 3 Feb., 20 Apr., 15 May 1841; and FO61:100, Wilson to Earl of Aberdeen, 8 Apr. 1843. See Gootenberg, *Between Silver and Guano*, ch. 4.

49. Mendiburu, "Memorias," (1842–52) 1136–46, 3527–28; "Representación del Consejo de Estado sobre el proyecto presentado por el Ministerio de Hacienda," *Comercio*, 14 July 1850; "Comercio de Arica," *Comercio*, 7 Aug. 1851; and "Política económica," *El Progreso* (Lima), 10 Aug. 1850. Regional integration processes are examined in Gootenberg, *Between Silver and Guano*, ch. 4.

50. Santiago Tavara, "Paralelo entre el tratado denominado Salaverry y los de Santa Cruz," *Comercio*, all Nov. 1846; "Proyecto," *Comercio*, 13 Jan. 1843; Ledos, *Consideraciones sobre agricultura*, pp. 167–70; *Comercio*, 1, 13 Oct. 1845, 8–11 May, 15 June 1846; and "Política económica," 27 July 1849, *Progreso*. For the state's changing attitude to southern grievances, Mendiburu, "Memorias," (1842–43) 1:115–46.

51. See esp. regional tariff debates of 1845 Congress in *Comercio*, all July-Sept. 1845; *Los Intereses del País* (Cuzco), 13 Sept. 1849; Dávila, *Medios para salvar Moquegua*; and "Representación del Comercio de Arequipa al Gobierno," *Comercio*, 15 Aug. 1850. The best and only description of a regional transition is Jacobsen, "Landtenure and Society in Azángaro," chs. 2–4.

52. Mendiburu, "Memorias," (1842–52) 1:115–46, 3:517–36; "Política económica," *Progreso*, 10 Aug. 1850; "Representación del Consejo de Estado sobre el proyecto presentado por el Ministerio de Hacienda," *Comercio*, 12 July 1851; "Reglamento de

Comercio," *Comercio*, 4 Mar. 1852; and Dancuart, *Anales*, "Memoria de Hacienda de 1851," 5100–5104.

53. Gootenberg, "Merchants, Foreigners and the State," pp. 357–83, for detailed analysis of these developments; "Monopolio de Ana," *Comercio*, 22 June 1842; "Compañia de Asia," 20 June 1842; "Patentes: unos comerciantes," *Comercio*, 16, 21 Aug. 1845; and AGN H–4 1838, Tribunal del Consulado, Actas, 24 Dec. 1845.

54. Hirschman, *Passions and the Interests*, pt. 2. For two brilliant expressions of this sea change, see "El artículo 61 del Reglamento de Comercio," *Comercio*, 26 Apr. 1842, and "Rápida ojeada sobre las causas jenerales que han determinado la suerte del Perú, o sea ensayo político y económico," *Progreso*, Apr.-May 1850; "Política económica," *Progreso*, 3 Aug. 1850; and CCC:8, Le Moyne, "Rapport sur l'état y la condition des étrangers au Pérou," 1 Nov. 1846.

55. "Tribunal del Consulado," *Progreso*, 29 Dec. 1849; *Rejistro Oficial* (Lima), 25 Oct. 1851; and AGN H–8, 3, Tribunal del Consulado, Elecciones, 1843–61. For small business reaction, see, for example, *Comercio*, 8 July 1845, 7 Sept. 1846, and "Reglamento de Comercio," 4 Feb. 1853; José María García, "Representación que han elebado los gremios ante las Cámaras," *Comercio*, 17 Oct. 1849.

56. Gootenberg, "Merchants, Foreigners and the State," ch. 5, details these fiscal dynamics. See "Empréstito," *Peruano*, 10 May 1843, for new official attitude, or "Crédito Público," *Peruano*, 22 Apr., 20 May, 3 July, 25 Oct. 1843; and "Huano: Dictamen de la Comisión de Hacienda del Senado," *Comercio*, 26 Sept. 1851 (or "Empréstito y cuestión fiscal," 26–29 Sept. 1849).

57. Quiroz, "La consolidació de la deuda interna," a superb work; Gootenberg, "Merchants, Foreigners and the State," pp. 383–92; *Comercio*, Congress debates, 10 Oct. 1845; and Manuel del Río, *Memoria que presenta el Ministro de hacienda del Perú al Congreso de 1847* (Lima, 1847), pp. 18–24.

58. Mendiburu, "Memorias," vols. 1–3, (1842–54), is outstanding for all these processes. On Iguain group, see *Comercio*, all Aug.-Sept. 1845; FO61:104, Adams to Palmerston, Sept. 1844; FO61:108, 14 June 1845; and FO61:109, Paz Soldán to Adams, 3 Sept. 1845.

59. Mathew, "First Anglo-Peruvian Debt"; T52:7, Jewett to Buchanan, 25 Oct., 27 Nov. 1845, 28 Feb. 1847; T52:8, Clay to Webster, 11 Aug. 1848, 12 Jan. 1849, 12 Feb., 20 Oct. 1850; FO61:121, Adams to Palmerston, 29 Mar. 1849; FO61:130, 8 Nov., 8 Dec. 1851; CCC:9, Le Moyne, 26 Apr., 24 Aug. 1848, 29 Sept. 1849; and CCC:10, 23 Dec. 1849, 6 Feb. 1850.

60. Albert Hirschman pointed out the significance of these issues to me. "Rápida ojeada sobre las causas generales que han determinado la suerte del Perú," *Progreso*, Apr.-May 1850; "Necesidad de un tercer candidato dedicada al estado de la Hacienda Pública," *Progreso*, 10 Aug. 1850; Mendiburu, "Memorias," (1845) 1: 266–76. See Friedman, *State and Underdevelopment*, chs. 5–6, and Véliz, *Centralist Tradition*, chs. 6–7, for similar views on reactive liberalism; and Sinkin, *Mexican Reform, 1855–1876*, for a closer study of authoritarian liberalism.

61. Gootenberg, "Social Origins of Protectionism," pp. 329–58, amply documents this episode; see esp. *Comercio*, 17 Oct., 14 Nov., 12, 14, 27 Dec. 1849; "Reglamento de Comercio," 23 July, 5 Aug. 1850; and *Progreso*, "Política económica," 6 July 1850.

62. See, for example, Leguía, "Las ideas de 1848 en el Perú"; and "Estado de los artesanos de Lima," *El Correo de Lima*, 16 Oct. 1851. For Chile, see the excellent study

by Luis Alberto Romero, *Sociedad de la Igualdad*; for European parallels consult Semmel, *Rise of Free Trade Imperialism*, esp. ch. 7; and Kindleberger, "Free Trade in Europe."

63. See esp. Congress and Senate debates, *Comercio*, 19–23 Aug. 1851; "El Reglamento de Comercio en el Senado," 5 Aug. 1851; *Comercio*, "Reglamento de Comercio," 23 July, 14 Aug. 1850, and "Memoria del Ministro de Relaciones Exteriores," 23 Aug. 1851. (Compare all to attitudes to foreign free trade in even the 1845 Congress debates: *Comercio*, July-Sept. 1845.) "Política económica: leyes restrictivas," *Progreso*, 22 Dec. 1849; "De los peligros del réjimen prohibitivo y de las necesidad de remediarlos," 5 Jan. 1850; *Peruano*, 6, 10, 17 July 1850; and FO61:121, Adams to Pardo, 16–26 Mar. 1849.

64. Francisco Bilbao, *El Gobierno de la Libertad* (Lima, 1855), pp. 32–34; "De los peligros del réjimen prohibitivo (Blanqui)," *Progreso*, 5 Jan. 1850; "De las objecciones hechas ultimamente contra el réjimen de la concurrencia," March 1850; and "Sociedad de Economía Política," *Comercio*, 16 May 1856. See later influences in Felipe Masías, *Curso elemental de economía política por Felipe Masías* (Lima, 1860); and Manuel A. Fuentes, *Catecismo de economía política* (Lima, 1877).

65. Casanova, *Ensayo económico-político sobre la industria algodonera; Peruano*, 22 July, 13 Sept., 21 Oct., 25 Oct., 8 Nov. 1848; *Comercio*, 1849–52, esp. see editorial, 4 July 1851, and "El Reglamento de Comercio en el Senado," 5 Aug. 1851; *Progreso*, all 1849–51; and [Juan Casimiro Ulloa], *El Perú en 1853: un año de su historia contemporánea* (Paris, 1854), pp. 16–17.

66. "Los cursantes de economía política," *Comercio*, 23, 29–30 July, 5, 17–20 Aug. 1850; and *Peruano*, "Economía política," 17 Aug. 1850, 1 Apr. 1848. For one of their most enthusiastic students, see José Silva Santisteban, *Breves reflexiones sobre los sucesos ocurridos en Lima y el Callao con motivo de la importación de artefactos* (Lima, 1859), esp. his dedication.

67. "Política económica," *Progreso*, 27 July, 10 Aug. 1850; "Proyecto de reforma del Reglamento de Comercio y varios otros documentos para el excelentísimo Consejo de Estado," *Rejistro Oficial*, 12 Aug. 1850; "Reglamento de Comercio," *Comercio*, 23 July 1850; "Representación del comercio de Arequipa al gobierno," *Comercio*, 14–15 Aug. 1850; "Igualdad de derechos en los puertos," *Comercio*, 11 July 1851; José Simeón Tejeda, *La emancipación de la industria* (Arequipa, 1852); Santiago Tavara, *La abolición de la esclavitud en el Perú* (Lima, 1855); and "Legislación mercantil," *Progreso*, 28 July–25 Aug. 1849.

68. Gootenberg, "Social Origins of Protectionism," pp. 351–56; see esp. *El Amigo del Pueblo* (Lima), 14 May 1840; *Comercio*, 27 Dec. 1849, 5 Jan. 1850, 16 Aug. 1851; "El Reglamento de Comercio en el Senado," *Comercio*, 5 Aug. 1851, and esp. speech of Senator Seoane, 19 Aug. 1851; "Política económica," *Progreso*, 6 July 1850; Silva Santisteban, *Breves reflexiones*, pp. 32–34, 41–43; "Fábrica de papel," *Comercio*, 5 Oct. 1851; and "Reglamento de Comercio: informe al Consejo de Estado," *Comercio*, 4 Mar. 1852.

69. "Discurso del Sr. Seoane sobre que se moderen algunos procedentes de aduana en favor de comerciantes," *Comercio*, 23 Aug. 1851, and his "Reglamento de Comercio," 27 Sept. 1851; for artisan reactions, see *Comercio*, 25 July 1850, "Unos artesanos," 29 Nov. 1851, and "Día de Felicidad o de Luto," 20 Dec. 1850; *Correo*, 16 Oct. 1851; or later still, *La Zamacueca Política* (Lima), Jan. 1859.

70. Polanyi, *Great Transformation*, esp. chs. 7–8, a book that deserves more study by Latin Americanists; for orthodox views of liberal failure, see Yepes, *Desarrollo*

capitalista, chs. 2–3; Bonilla, *Guano y burguesía*; Bonilla, "Perú entre independencia y guerra," pp. 428–30, 463–71; and Cotler, *Clases, estado y nación*, chs. 2–3.

71. Hunt, "Growth and Guano," pp. 69–85. Berg and Weaver, in "Reinterpretation of Political Change in Peru," also stress a version of guano state autonomy. Hirschman, "Rival Views of Market Society," may help elucidate the paradoxes of my position here.

72. Quiroz, "La consolidación de la deuda interna," chs. 4–5; Camprubi Alcázar, *Historia de los bancos*. For an extended discussion of these issues, see Gootenberg, *Between Silver and Guano*, ch. 5, sec. e, or in another vein, Gootenberg, "The Patterns of Economic Institutional Change."

73. North and Thomas, *Rise of the Western World*; Hicks, *Theory of Economic History*; and Coatsworth, "Obstacles to Growth." Cortés Conde and Hunt, *Latin American Economies*, pp. 15–21, also stress deleterious consequences of slow institutional (and market) change.

4

ARGENTINA: LIBERALISM IN A COUNTRY BORN LIBERAL

Tulio Halperín Donghi

The earliest articulation of a specifically Argentine version of Spanish American liberalism dates from the long years of conservative hegemony between the first liberal wave of the 1820s and the more vigorous and durable midcentury liberal renaissance. In the Argentine provinces that reaction had brought about Juan Manuel de Rosas's rise to power, but the political and administrative style of this formidable ruler was too idiosyncratic for his regime to be classified as one of the successful conservative experiments, among which Diego Portales's Chile took pride of place as the model country of Spanish American conservatism. The Rosas dictatorship (much like those of José Gaspar Francia in Paraguay and of Rafael Carrera in Guatemala) was instead considered exceptional and, after 1840, when he introduced terror for political control, as an indefensible political aberration. It was with this regime that the forerunners of the second liberal wave, who in 1838 had proclaimed themselves the Young Generation (Esteban Echeverría, Juan Bautista Alberdi, Juan María Gutiérrez, and Vicente Fidel López, among others), first tried unsuccessfully to come to terms and from which most of them were forced into exile since the early 1840s.

This national experience made the opposition between liberals and conservatives a less central feature of political life in Argentina than it was (or was soon to become) in most other Spanish American countries. The liberal-inspired contributions to social and historical analysis and criticism in Argentina during the middle years of the nineteenth century, not surprisingly, reflected this somewhat different background. Admittedly, Argentine writers were as eager as most other

Spanish American liberals to expose the many social, political, and cultural shortcomings inherited from the colonial past that still weighed heavily on their country. To mention the most obvious example, *Civilización y Barbarie* (1845), published by Domingo Faustino Sarmiento during his Chilean exile and the most durably successful of the works of this ideological persuasion in all of Spanish America, went further than most in stressing that it was in Argentina's past, and in its tainted legacy, that the causes of its current predicament were hidden.

Even at that early stage, however, a subtle difference could be detected between his depiction of that past and those found in Francisco Bilbao's *Sociabilidad chilena* or in J. V. Lastarria's thesis submitted to the University of Chile, *Investigaciones sobre la influencia social de la conquista y el sistema colonial de los españoles en Chile* (both works were published in 1844). In Sarmiento's view, Argentina's ills owed as much to its short revolutionary experience as to its colonial past, and as for the latter, what made its legacy so damning was not so much the influence of a stagnant and archaic metropolis as the legacy of three centuries of primitive frontier life, itself a consequence of a Spanish presence too tenuous to exert a decisive influence on the vast expanse of the pampas.

While Sarmiento was no more partial to the model on which Spain had tried to mold its overseas offspring than its liberal critics from Mexico to Chile, in his opinion its influence on postindependence Argentina was more limited than on other neo-Spanish countries. This partially different diagnosis was reflected in a different emphasis when Sarmiento proposed a cure for national ills: while Chile was crushed by the legacy of the past and desperately needed to eradicate it, Argentina was an almost empty historical stage; what it demanded from its political redeemers was the wholesale importation of all the elements of civilized life, starting with the population, whose sparseness was at the root of the country's predicament.

In the more optimistic climate created by the overthrow of Rosas in 1852, what had begun as a different emphasis soon developed into a claim to Argentine historical exceptionality: thus for Bartolomé Mitre—the political and ideological disciple of the *antirosista* exiles and the man who was to become the founding father of modern Argentina—the task of the Argentine liberals could not be that of cancelling the legacy of the past. On the contrary, their triumph reflected the ideological coming of age of a country finally ready to discover in the liberal creed the distillate of the spontaneous convictions developed in its collective wisdom during its whole historical experience.

Part of the explanation of this growing divergence from the Spanish American norm can be found in the ideological context in which the Argentine version of the liberal revival had developed. While in most of Spanish America it emerged under the stimulus of the revolutionary hopes of 1848, in the River Plate a revised liberalism had already surfaced ten years earlier, under the more ambiguous auspices of the 1830 revolution. That event had broken the hegemony of Restoration ideologies in continental Europe, without, however, offering any radical alternative to them. Equally important, when 1848 erupted, the members of the Argentine Young Generation were veterans of ten years of obstinate but hapless political struggle. True, they momentarily allowed themselves to be swept up by the wave of ideological radicalization that followed the European upheaval throughout Spanish America. But as soon as the 1848 revolutions ended in crushing defeats, they were to hasten back to moderate positions.

They were then better able to understand that in a world in which reaction was again triumphant, liberalism could not survive as a revolutionary creed of national death and transfiguration, but as the political expression of forces already dominant in society, whose aspirations it intended to fulfill. It was this that Mitre meant when he argued that in post-Rosas Argentina—a country that had finally discovered the hidden meaning of its whole historical experience and knew that it had been born liberal—liberalism was the only possible conservatism.[1]

The rise of an Argentine version of liberalism that diverged on essential points from the one preferred in most of Spanish America thus owes much to the circumstances of world politics and even something to opportunistic consider- ations. But it does not necessarily follow that the claim that Argentina is somehow different is only a convenient figment of the Argentines' ideological imagination, rooted in a systematic (if perhaps not totally willed) self-delusion. Even the most stylized and ideological images of the past incorporate recognizable features from that past. And if the concept of the nation's past that found in Mitre its ablest defender was so quickly incorporated into the conventional wisdom of his fellow Argentines, it was not only because it flattered their national pride, but also because they discovered in it a reasonably faithful description of the country they had learned to know by living in it; moreover, it offered a credible expla- nation of why it had come to be what it was.

This explanation was to be provided in careful detail in Mitre's historical writings. In his view, Argentina's historical experience diverged from that of the rest of Spanish America in that the lack of mineral resources and vast masses of sedentary Indians made it impossible to build on the banks of the River Plate the kind of "feudal" societies that emerged in Mexico and Peru (and even, thanks to a triumph of the will against unpropitious circumstances, in Chile). In the inhospitable Platine lands, universal destitution created a rough economic equality, and the instinctive democracy (*democracia genial*) of frontier life left its mark on both lifestyle and social relations. Thus, instead of the ruins of an obsolete social order, the Argentine past offered the spare but healthy foundations for the liberal civilization that it was the country's manifest destiny to build on the unpromising soil of Spanish America.

Again, it is not difficult to discover the ideological bias behind this stylized and simplified rendering of a complex and contradictory historical experience. Not a few among Mitre's contemporaries, and on occasion Mitre himself, de- nounced the land tenure regime in the pampas as at least partially "feudal," by which they meant essentially that too much land was in the hands of too few landowners. But in his evocation of the infancy of a nation born liberal, Mitre carefully avoided the question of how this deplorable situation could be part of the legacy of a colonial experience placed under the sign of social equality.

According to him, Argentina was at the same time blessed with a past untainted with feudal influences and yet suffering from the feudal residues inherited from that past: the conclusion is so clearly self-contradictory that the temptation is strong to dismiss it as mere nonsense. This would, however, be a mistake: if nothing else, it gives a precise indication of where, in the opinion of the protagonists of the Argentine liberal renaissance, lay the difference between their country and the rest of Spanish America.

That difference was not to be found in the Argentines' blueprint for social and political reform. As much as in Mexico or New Granada, its core element was a radical restructuring of rural society around a new class of independent freeholders, which would provide the social base for a truly liberal political order and one for the full integration of the national economy into the world market. In Argentina, the incorporation of this ideal into the conventional wisdom of the political class and of public opinion proceeded more smoothly than in most Spanish American countries. This fact was reflected in the frequent denunciations of the feudal remnants of the colonial past, as a corollary of the commitment to radical social change in the countryside.

Mitre was then right in arguing that Argentine liberalism's unexceptionably conservative inspiration didn't make it any less uncompromisingly liberal than its counterparts in other Spanish American countries, as far as its long-term objectives were concerned. But these objectives had a very peculiar place in the world of ideas of the midcentury liberals. They offered little more than a projection into a remote, utopian horizon of demands that, once implemented, were to achieve effects far short of the wholesale social redemption they prophesied. Seen in this light, the radical agrarian motif recalls the more utopian visions of the Bourbon reforms, in that in both cases it provides a lofty ideological justification for more self-serving and conceivably more easily achievable objectives: for the eighteenth century reformers such aims were the economic and social unification of the lands ruled by the Catholic King; for the nineteenth century liberals, as Joseph Love reminds us when defining the themes of this volume, they consisted in the freeing ''of economic activity from all constraints on the market'' and the promotion of ''the international division of labor through the alleged complementarity of parts of the world economy (given their differing factor endowments).''[2]

There was an additional element of continuity between the utopian horizons of the Bourbon reforms and those of mid-nineteenth-century liberalism, namely that the rural emphasis shared by both reflected a common conviction that the main stumbling block for Spanish American progress was to be found in the countryside, and more specifically in the control of land by ecclesiastic and secular corporations. First among the latter, of course, were the Indian peasant communities, those bulwarks of routine-bound agriculture and indifference to profit. While this liberal concern found its benevolent expression in an ideology of economic liberation and in legislation aiming at the metamorphosis of the routine-bound peasants into dynamic farmers,[3] the fact that it resulted mostly in a shift from peasant to hacienda commercial agriculture confirms that here again the main objective was to open yet another sector of the economy to the beneficent impact of market forces, much to the advantage of those who were assumed to be more alert than the traditional peasantry to the opportunities created by a quickening world economy.

On this point the really significant difference between Argentina and the rest of Spanish America does not lie in the fact that Argentina went farther in the implementation of some portions of the liberal agrarian program.[4] What was radically different about Argentina could instead already be found before that expansion had even started: if European immigrants were called to colonize the pampas under conditions that made this outcome possible, this fact in turn owed to the lack of a local peasantry whose dispossession might otherwise have offered both the land and the labor base for a different style of agricultural expansion, closer perhaps to that of the Chilean Central Valley.

Was this so because, as Sarmiento had stated in 1845, Argentina, far from being crushed by the heritage of the past, was an orphan of history, indeed little more than a void to be filled, or, to restate the argument in the more optimistic terms later preferred by Mitre, because Argentina had been liberal since its birth in the sixteenth century? Not quite: it was rather that, as Mitre was ready to recognize when following his historian's instincts rather than his ideological agenda, while there was no way of proving (or for that matter disproving) that an unconscious liberal influence had already been at work since the earliest stages in the history of the River Plate, the transformations that had prepared Argentina to identify so deeply with the liberal view of the world did in fact predate 1848 and even (if not by much) the struggle for independence.

The restructuring of the Spanish empire by the Bourbon reforms had created an administrative and military center in Buenos Aires in 1776 and had ensured its financial and mercantile supremacy over the heterogeneous territories included in the viceroyalty it governed. When the opening to foreign trade inaugurated a new economic era, the accumulation of resources in that center was to sustain the quick expansion of cattle raising in the Buenos Aires district: by 1830 that district, which of course included the port through which all the overseas trade of the country was transacted, also contributed more than two-thirds of the exports for that trade.

Despite these changes, as late as 1810 all of the riverine lands that could take advantage of the opportunities created by free trade harbored just a quarter of the population of the future country, while three-quarters lived in the interior, under conditions that had more in common with those of the "feudal" societies of much of Spanish America than with the rough-and-ready frontier life of the littoral.

But the economic marginalization of the interior (effected in some branches of its economy by the Bourbon reforms and generalized by 1809) led to political marginalization, finally achieved when the more powerful armies of relatively affluent Buenos Aires imposed a crushing defeat on the dissident anti-Rosas provincial movements of 1840–42. These events made the Argentine interior politically irrelevant, even if by the midcentury more than half of the scanty national population was still located there.

Revealingly, in the press campaign Florencio Varela launched in 1846, while in exile in Montevideo, to rally provincial opposition against the hegemony of *rosista* Buenos Aires, he called for free navigation of the rivers of the Plate system by foreign vessels. Yet he readily admitted that this salutary reform had nothing to offer to the interior provinces: "It is obvious," he tersely stated, "that no political and economic system can fully overcome the disadvantages born of nature. The provinces locked up in the heart of the Republic, like Catamarca, La Rioja and Santiago, no matter what concessions are granted them, can never progress in the same proportion as Buenos Aires, Santa Fé or Corrientes, situated on navigable rivers. But these differences are not offensive, because they are not the effect of the injustice of men, but rather the work of nature itself: It is not them of which we are speaking."[5] For all Varela's legendary intellectual integrity, his easy dismissal of the ambitions of the interior provinces also reflected his conviction that they had lost whatever ability to influence political developments they might have enjoyed in the past.

The Argentina that really counted was made up of Buenos Aires and the other riverine provinces (one of which, Entre Ríos, led the decisive attack against Rosas and the stifling Buenos Aires hegemony he had imposed, an enterprise that was by then clearly beyond the collective capabilities of the landlocked provinces). In this Argentina the liberal program, which proclaimed that nothing less than a social revolution was needed to achieve full integration into the world market, suffered not from any excessive audacity, but from its obvious irrelevance. In terms of per capita value of foreign trade, in 1825 Buenos Aires province was more closely integrated into the world market than the United Kingdom.[6] By 1850 the yearly volume of imports of the lowest quality of British cotton cloth amounted to a per capita consumption of forty yards for all Argentina (including the comparatively isolated interior); no doubt most of this avalanche of "cotton white and plain" found its outlets in the littoral.[7]

But even before this massive invasion of overseas goods started in 1809, the River Plate area already relied almost completely on long-distance trade, in which, to be sure, the intercolonial traffic in Andean textiles played the dominant role. On the eve of the opening to overseas imports, Hipólito Vieytes, a disciple of the new economic doctrines, remarked that rural wages in the River Plate countryside were double those in Chile. It was his opinion that this situation, which he believed made the development of a prosperous grain agriculture clearly impossible, could not be changed unless the wage worker learned to rely on the production of female family members for clothing and food, as was already the case in Chile, instead of turning to the marketplace. What interests us in this precocious and insightful discovery of the role of the "informal sector" in the Latin American economy is that it originated in an exploration of the consequences of the lack of such a sector in the frontier conditions of the pampas.

Not that these conditions did not leave much to be desired. Thus, it was not because the Porteño economy was more advanced than that of the United Kingdom that the value of per capita foreign trade was higher in Buenos Aires. Rather, it was the unilateral growth of a very dynamic export sector within an economic framework more rudimentary in many ways than what could be found in more "traditional" areas of Spanish America (and made even more primitive by the concentration of resources in the profitable export sector) that brought about this paradoxical result. How advanced could an economy be considered in which even the humblest and simplest products of manufacture, from furniture to beams and posts, and even tallow candles, had to be imported, if not from overseas, then from the more "backward" areas of the hinterland? How advanced could it be, if during the midst of the export boom, even in the most prosperous stock raising districts, the skulls of cows had to make do as chairs, and not only in the dwellings of the day laborers? Or, for that matter, how modern was a society that, while including a labor force that was undoubtedly free and made even more independent by its very scarcity,[8] shared some features of slave societies? Like these, it was at the same time primitive and emphatically not traditional; like these, it had been shaped by the needs of the export sector even in its demographic structure, and, as a consequence, the same imbalance between the sexes could be found in the pampas as in Brazilian or Cuban sugar districts.

In such a society, the agrarian utopia Argentine liberals shared with their Mexican comrades did not provide, as in Mexico, an ideological justification for the elimination of all barriers against market forces. On the contrary, it challenged the assumption that such an elimination was always and necessarily beneficial. From Vieytes to Sarmiento to the turn-of-the-century critics of the socioeconomic consequences of the grain boom, all those who condemned first the triumph of stock raising and later the pattern of concentrated landownership that was to be its legacy were very much aware that stock raising owed its victory to its superior suitability to local conditions characterized by the abundance of land and the scarcity of other factors of production. They knew as well that the durable land tenure pattern it left behind resulted also from the untrammeled action of economic forces. But this did not stop them from asking for legislative remedies such that, while economic laws would be respected, their effects would be channeled in directions more compatible with the national aspirations for social and economic equality, as well as for cultural sophistication.

Thus in Argentina the faith in the laws of the market appeared compatible with the recognition of a more complex policy role for the state than that of demolishing the legal barriers inherited from the past. Thanks to this circumstance, in post-Rosas Argentina economic debates achieved a sophistication, but also an imprecision, seldom matched elsewhere in Spanish America. These features in turn were due not only to the fact that most of the liberal agenda had already been implemented before its proclamation as such, thus removing much of the tension and urgency from economic discussions; it was equally important that in the riverine lands of Argentina, no social group of any consequence identified with antiliberal positions as firmly as did similar groups in most of Spanish America. Argentine society had already been fashioned by a half-century-long expansion of an open export economy. Those who had suffered from its rise had already found ways to adapt to it or otherwise had lost their economic and political influence. Not surprisingly, when free trade became again an issue, what brought it back to the fore was a common but short-lived readiness to try protectionist remedies when the export economy ran into bad times, rather than the newly acquired influence of any specific social group permanently identified with the cause of protection.

It is then not surprising that the search for the historical roots of the protectionism preached by the industrial interest in the 1920s, and the more extreme one implemented by the Peronist regime after World War II, led to disappointing results. A closer look at the first protectionist campaign in the late 1860s (an agitation for higher tariffs on imported woolens and the creation of a state-owned textile factory) reveals that it was essentially the answer of the sheep breeders (now the core of the landowning class) to the difficult situation created by lower world prices, higher import tariffs in the United States and France, and a de facto increase in Argentine export taxes, owing to the refusal of the government to revise downward the officially appraised price of wool while real prices fell. It did not of course imply a permanent change of heart on the part of the sheep breeders, who knew very well that their future depended on that of the export economy, and as soon as the emergency passed, they were happy to return to their orthodox convictions in matters of international trade. The crisis of the late 1870s, which originated in the financial sector and had a wider but more diffuse impact than that of the earlier decade, generated in turn an even larger but more fickle protectionist front than the sheep breeders' lobby of the late 1860s, and its fervor once again dissipated as soon as the economic weather improved in the 1880s.[9]

When the issue of protection and free trade emerged again, in the very last years of the century, it was in response to federal policies introduced under the influence of the very provinces whose prospects Varela had painted in so somber colors in the 1840s. The consolidation of a federal regime had allowed their ruling groups to regain part of the political power they had lost after their catastrophic defeats in the battlefields during the previous era of civil wars. In this new context, the Tucumán elite, during the twelve years in which two of its members (Nicolás Avellaneda and Julio Roca) successively occupied the national presidency (1874–86), was able to take advantage of the federal railway, credit, and tariff policies to develop sugar plantations in the estates that until then had harbored their not very prosperous stock raising *estancias*. With less active federal support, beginning in the 1890s, the incorporation of the Cuyo provinces into the national railway network made it possible for the wine growers in San Juan and Mendoza to take advantage of the high tariffs on wine and spirits—in force since the 1810s mainly for fiscal reasons—to enlarge their share of the now more accessible and rapidly expanding littoral markets. But these deviations from free trade principles, similar in inspiration to the ones Rosas introduced in the Buenos Aires tariff of 1835 (when he still felt that he needed to offer concessions to keep the allegiance of the interior provinces), were too inconsequential to generate the social conflicts that would have lent larger relevance to the frequent parliamentary and journalistic denunciations of their self-serving inspiration. Only in the twentieth century would the Socialist party, which had early given up any ambition to gain a foothold in the sugar belt, make a permanent electoral issue out of tariff protection for sugar.[10]

While, in a country that was so successfully riding the wave of world trade expansion, protection could not, for obvious reasons, become a crucial policy issue for very long, the agrarian component of the liberal program was a different matter: the very fact that the vertiginous expansion of pampean agriculture, after promising for a fleeting moment to realize the liberal utopia in riverine Argentina, took a quite different turn—precisely when Argentina emerged as one of the great exporters of grain in the world economy—was to lend to that program the permanent relevance of a disappointed hope. The memory of that hope was kept alive by a constant outpouring of critical literature dealing with the economic and social aspects of the agricultural expansion in the pampas.

That literature showed a remarkable continuity not only in its thematic approaches, but also when defining the central issues posed by the expansion; thus, the echoes of Mitre's denunciation of the ''feudal'' features in the pampas' social landscape could still be heard a century later. Given this continuity, and the lack of an equally vigorous countercurrent that would defend the socioeconomic aspects of that expansion, it might appear surprising that no serious attempts were made to correct shortcomings so universally condemned. Here again it would be useful to look at the concrete circumstances in which that critical literature flourished, an exercise that requires going beyond the basic contrast between the frontier society of riverine Argentina and the Indian peasant lands at the core of the Spanish empire in the New World: what lent such durability to the critical approach that inspires this literature was not so much the insights it offered on some lasting features of Argentine rural experience as its unobtrusive but continuous shifts in emphasis. These allowed it to adjust to parallel movements in the balance of social groups and forces in Argentine society. The resiliency of this ideological tradition starts to make sense only once it becomes clear that its remarkable continuity has accommodated not a little change.

We shall examine this complex counterpoint of continuity and change through three stages in its progress: the first is indeed just a fleeting moment and offers no more than a glimpse of the lines on which it might perhaps have developed, had the social background of the pampas been different from what it was in fact. In 1856 a press campaign in the city of Buenos Aires and a spate of agitation in Chivilcoy, then the most important wheat-growing district in the province, resulted in the transfer of the property of the agricultural land in the district from the landowners to their tenants. This episode is mostly remembered because of the opportunity it offered for some public figures to display a more militant agrarian radicalism than they were inclined to proclaim in more normal circumstances. It was then that Mitre, who usually described his own Party of Freedom as the legitimate political expression of, among others, the Buenos Aires landed classes, threw caution to the winds and condemned in harsh words the oppressive weight of the latifundia inherited from a feudal past. But his statements sounded cautious when compared with those of Sarmiento, who went as far as condemning a social system that denied shelter and livelihood to the gauchos and made them pariahs in their own land because, as in More's England, he claimed, in the pampas the flocks were eating the people, much to the advantage of landowners frequently less Argentine than their victims.

No doubt these statements reflected, albeit in atypically uncompromising language, convictions that Sarmiento held firmly during his entire career. Even before his visit to the United States in 1848 revealed to him the agrarian foundations of U.S. democracy, his roots in the interior of Argentina had made him more sensitive to the social conflicts that develop around land in more settled rural societies than that of the littoral. In the 1860s, in *Vida del Chacho*, which he wrote as an apologia for the savage war that ended with the execution of the caudillo from La Rioja, he commented in an aside that one of the victims of that barbarous creature belonged to a patrician family fated always to lose members to political strife. The reason was that the family had given free rein to its inordinate greed for the land and the water rights of the neighboring peasantry. Understandably, Sarmiento refrained from pursuing a line of discussion potentially damning to his main argument, but in less inopportune moments he was ready to reach the political conclusions suggested by this insight. Thus in 1869 he advised his friend José Posse: "Don't you have land in Tucumán to provide a home for those that have nothing? In your electoral labors don't abandon the people, which in truth is so ignorant, so unwashed. Alas, such is our Republic."[11]

But even if this was the case, it was but the exceptional context of the Chivilcoy conflict that brought forth such views and they were usually expressed in defiant language of this kind only through revealing non sequiturs or in private correspondence. What made the context so exceptional? There were no doubt political reasons for the atypical vulnerability of the Chivilcoy landowners: after the fall of Rosas, Buenos Aires refused to enter the federal constitutional structure created by its conqueror from Entre Ríos, Justo José Urquiza, and justified its secession by presenting itself as the bulwark of intransigent liberal *antirosismo* against a national leadership that included too many former supporters of Rosas. The legal fate of the Chivilcoy farm plots was then to be decided in a violently *antirosista* political climate. And it so happened that the Chivilcoy landowners had received their land grants from Rosas, as a reward for their political or military services; their blood-stained property deeds, *boletos de sangre*, far from strengthening their case, were used by their challengers as the most damning argument against them. It was the political dimension in the conflict that allowed attacks on these property rights without creating excessive alarm among the propertied classes. After all, the vast properties of Rosas, most of them acquired before his rise to power, had only recently been confiscated, also without protest from the landed interests. Both the Chivilcoy tenants (some of them already established on the land as squatters before the Rosas grants) and the city politicians who took up their cause wisely stressed the factional-political dimension of the conflict at least as much as its social aspects.

But, while the political climate did help, the main reasons why the episode could develop as it did arose from its social context. In Chivilcoy the liberal politicians who had taken power in Buenos Aires in 1852 had finally found what they had despaired of finding in the *campaña*: a sizeable social group ready to fight for its own goals of agrarian change. Sarmiento, for one, proclaimed in 1868 that a solid social base for the new political order would only be built if "a hundred Chivilcoys," a hundred farming centers, were created in the pampas. This social metamorphosis would change him, the recently elected president by the almost accidental decision of some fractions within the notoriously fickle elite, into a true popular leader; he would then be at last "the caudillo of the gauchos transformed into peaceful freeholders."[12] Wisely, Mitre never shared this illusion: what Sarmiento did not see was that, while the 1856 episode had been possible because there indeed was a Chivilcoy in the Buenos Aires countryside, the presence of many Chivilcoys would have made such a favorable outcome much less likely. As things stood, with only a few districts put under grain agriculture, the conflicts between tenants and the landowners—themselves not very affluent, and clearly marginal within the Buenos Aires propertied classes—did not threaten to subvert the much larger stock-raising areas of the countryside, where social conditions were vastly different and where any agitation against *estancieros* would have provoked a much less tolerant response.

Because there was just one Chivilcoy, what happened in 1856 was not a portent of things to come. But also because this was so, Sarmiento's candidacy for the presidency in 1868 could be received with enthusiasm by Eduardo Olivera, the most eminent "organic intellectual" of the Buenos Aires landed elite from the 1860s until his death in the next century: "The spirit of progressives is thrilled by the prospect of how much an intellect like that of Señor Sarmiento, endowed with the willpower we know so well, could do as a direct influence on the true progress of these lands."[13] Thus proclaimed Olivera when Sarmiento began to be mentioned as a possible presidential successor to Mitre.

But the new president, who in 1868 had promised to cover the pampas with as many Chivilcoys as necessary to eradicate the legacy of a barbarous past, by 1870 had already given up on the first province, "occupied by an old colonial society that owns the land and reserves for itself all positions of influence." He had now transferred his hopes to the vast areas opened to pioneer agriculture by the new railway line that connected Rosario, the port on the Paraná, with Córdoba. There, he believed, "the revolution that will make North Americans of us, that will dethrone the *estanciero* who in turn has given rise to the gaucho and the *montonera* [irregular army], is already under way. Here in this piece of the pampa that stretches to Córdoba, a new society will arise, a new nation, leaving the dead to bury the dead."[14]

The Buenos Aires landowners witnessed this revolution with remarkable sang-froid. They were no doubt aware of the rapid rise in the price of land that it was bringing about in Santa Fé. Colonization was indeed an excellent business for landowners used to buying and selling their land by the square league, who now found buyers ready to acquire it by the square *cuadra* at previously unheard-of prices. The circumstances in Buenos Aires (where prices were much higher to start with) were different, and the landowners there obviously did not find in the rise of a group of independent farmers in a neighboring section of the pampas much reason to fear that they themselves would soon be reduced to the funereal duties mentioned by Sarmiento. Yet neither did they find in the agricultural colonization in Santa Fé much valid inspiration when addressing their own concerns as a group.

It is therefore not surprising to find that, while the writings of the *hombres progresistas* gathered about the Sociedad Rural (Stockbreeders' Association) reflect general support for the creation of a new rural society organized around an expanding class of independent farmers, this was never to become a central concern for these spokesmen of the Buenos Aires landed interests. Their own version of the agrarian gospel dwelt on themes presenting the whole countryside as a homogeneous sector, firmly unified under the leadership of the landowning class. It was precisely in the late 1860s and 1870s when this view was most persuasively articulated, in the *Anales de la Sociedad Rural Argentina* no less than in José Hernández's immensely popular gaucho poem, *Martín Fierro*.

This successful formulation of a ruralist ideology at one stroke both legitimated the hegemony of the landowning class in rural society and described it as the productive class par excellence. Such a formulation not only reflected the over-whelming hegemony of that class in Buenos Aires society—which according to Sarmiento could not be effectively challenged—but was also an expression of the new intensity of some deeply rooted conflicts in which indeed the rural sector as a block opposed other segments of the Buenos Aires sociopolitical structure.

In Buenos Aires, as already noted, stock raising had developed vigorously in a context of chronic labor scarcity. To make things more difficult, the state had its own claims on the scarce rural population, from which it intended to recruit the troops required for the defense of the provincial territory against the Indians and, when needed, for interprovincial or international war. Already in the 1820s, an arrangement was found making it easier to reconcile the claims of the stock raisers with those of the state: the army was to serve as a penal institution for vagrants and, more exceptionally, for criminal or just unreliable rural workers. But for this arrangement to work effectively, the state's demand for recruits had to be kept within reasonable bounds, and this was of course not the case in times of foreign crisis. Something of this sort had been experienced in the 1840s, when the siege of Montevideo and the recurrence of military confrontations with other provinces intensified recruiting pressure, and Rosas's enemies had used the issue for what it was worth in their propaganda.

In the late 1860s the problem became even more acute; the Paraguayan war (1865–70) soon became the most bloody and costly in Argentine history, and to it was added a civil war in the interior in 1866. Moreover, the base for recruitment had been drastically narrowed by the influx into the countryside of immigrants exempt from the draft and by a less successful control of the territory by the provincial judiciary and police than in Rosas's time. This development placed many of the marginal elements (whom the recruitment laws designated as the main targets for the draft) beyond the reach of the authorities. Since wage workers in good standing were theoretically exempt from active service, the authorities were forced to turn to the independent stock raisers themselves; among them the landowners could afford to offer a *personero*, a stand-in paid by them to take their place. But affluent landowners ready to pay for substitutes were not numerous enough to solve the recruitment problem. This left only the much larger group of non-wage-earning rural workers, from small cattle raisers on rented land to shepherds remunerated with a share of the wool from the flocks they tended. The government overoptimistically and self-servingly included such men among the independent rural entrepreneurs assumed able to afford a *personero*. Thus the middle strata of the rural population became the main targets of the recruiting drive, and José Hernández chose one of its members, the owner of a herd of cattle that he raised on rented land, as the hero of his poetic complaint about the gauchos' martyrdom in the hellish frontier forts.

It is easy to understand why recruitment into the army and the frontier militia became the preferred issue with the defenders of the rural interest. It was made even more indefensible by its systematic brutality and arbitrariness, and its direct victims were mostly men of the people—even if, as the Sociedad Rural stressed, its indirect negative effects reached the landowners, who found it ever more difficult to recruit a stable labor force without paying money wages. But it was not the only issue in which the rural interest, as defined by the landed elite, could truthfully be described as identical with those of most, if not all, the inhabitants of the countryside. Thus the opposition to export taxes or the complaints over the excessively limited credit available through the state-owned Banco de la Provincia de Buenos Aires did reach beyond the upper strata of the landed classes.

This defense of rural interests was supported by ideological justifications fashioned in the liberal mold. Its liberalism, however, was less close to the Spanish American norm, which in the name of liberalism had demanded a ruthless use of state power to introduce radical changes in a society stagnant or worse, than to the version more popular in developed countries, wherein the social forces themselves could be trusted with the task of ensuring economic and social progress.

According to this version of the liberal creed, what Argentina needed was for the free institutions adopted in the constitution of 1853–60 to be really implemented and even modified further to emphasize decentralization and local self-determination. In this way, a countryside that, under the enlightened guidance of its landowning elite, was building one of the most successful export economies in the world, would finally be freed from the humiliating political oppression and the rudimentary, economically detrimental administration practiced by the parasitical political elite in Buenos Aires.

Thus the elimination of the barriers that the constitution—and, even more decisively, political practice—had erected against any further progress toward democratization and decentralization was not expected to bring about a more equal society. On the contrary, the consolidation of a de facto oligarchic regime would finally fulfill the political aspirations of a deferential society eager to follow the lead of its landed elite. José Hernández was to offer in his newspaper articles a systematic presentation and defense of this political program, for which he found inspiration in the ideas developed by an Uruguayan jurist, Gregorio Pérez Gomar, in his youthful *Idea de la perfección humana* (1863). In this scheme the social sphere is firmly isolated from the individual and the political ones and is characterized as a set of institutions organized according to the law of nature, for which the aspiration of individual liberty that rules the first sphere, and that of equality that defines the second, are equally irrelevant.

This version of the liberal program was undoubtedly better attuned to the balance of social forces emerging in Buenos Aires. Endowed with ideological complexity and sophistication, it could address very different constituencies in very different languages that reflected the program's various roots in society and strengthened its hold on public opinion.[15]

Yet, for all its popularity, the modified liberal program of the *ruralistas* was never to exert a significant influence on state policy. The issues that had helped it to attract such wide support lost much of their acuity when the end of the Paraguayan war alleviated the recruiting pressure on the countryside and provoked a temporary improvement in public finances that made it possible to lower export taxes. By the late 1870s the imminent conquest of the Indian territory completely dominated the landowners' agenda. They were readying themselves to share in the territorial booty soon to be opened to the political and military elite and its associates, and of course when the Indian territory was conquered in 1879, the greatest irritant in the relation between the state and rural society, namely the capricious conscription of the rural population, was finally eliminated.

Even before the complaints reflected in the ruralist campaign became a thing of the past, the campaign itself was failing its most crucial test: it was not winning the active support of the landowners as a group. Their spokesmen were well aware of this sorry state of affairs and deplored the passivity of the class whose defense they had shouldered. They accused the landholders of ignorance of their self-interest, as well as ideological and political timidity. Through these criticisms the spokesmen themselves implicitly admitted that their presentation of the landowning class as the acknowledged and respected leader of rural society included a significant element of wishful thinking, but this fact in their opinion did not diminish the validity of their approach, because the only thing that was needed for the landowners to assume that role was for them to wish to do so.

However, as not a few landowners understood better than their self-appointed spokesmen, this last assumption was also an exercise in wishful thinking. The *campaña* was anything but a deferential society, and the view that presented it as a homogeneous social bloc ready to follow the lead of the landed elite no doubt read too much into the universal recognition of that elite's dominant position, which went unchallenged but not necessarily unresented. It was difficult to believe that the ambivalent relations between the elite and the rest of rural society would not be affected if the elite were to challenge the control of the state by the political and military ruling circles. For all clashes with both circles, the elite's own rise to prominence had owed too much to the consolidation of state power in the countryside for its prominence not to suffer from the disappearance of that tense alliance. Thus, while the complaints about the self-serving and economically and socially destructive ways in which the state applied the draft were well founded, the landed interest still benefited from the role of army recruitment as an instrument of labor discipline, as some of its spokesmen were to recognize after its abolition.

When all this is taken into account, it is easier to understand why the modified version of liberalism offered as an ideological justification for the conquest of direct political power by the landowning class never achieved a discernible political impact, though it was able to inspire numerous and frequently insightful descriptions of the social and political conditions in the Buenos Aires countryside.

Thirty years later conditions in the pampas were again radically changed. The agricultural colonies, these first *focos* of the revolution that was to change Argentina into a Southern Hemisphere replica of the United States, had triumphantly invaded the pampas. After covering the whole territory on which Sarmiento had expected a new society and a new nation to rise, they were advancing into Buenos Aires province. As the 1914 national census was to reveal, the *primera provincia* was now the leading agricultural district in a country that since the 1890s had found a place among the major overseas exporters of grain to the European markets.

Yet this expansion followed lines very different from those anticipated by Sarmiento. Supported by an extreme abundance of land, which allowed a technologically backward grain agriculture to thrive and expand, it was soon to depend more and more on the labor of immigrant tenant farmers and sharecroppers. The financial crises of 1873 and 1890 had hastened a shift away from freeholding that was made more acceptable to the immigrants by their long-term objectives: most of them did not intend to settle permanently in the pampas; rather they wanted to win big in a speculative agricultural enterprise and retire to the more pleasant surroundings of their native lands, for which purpose it made more sense to rent as much land as possible than to buy on credit the smaller family plots available for immigrants with very limited or nonexistent resources.

After the expanding railway network reached the outer limits of the fertile pampas in 1905–12, the sudden closing of the frontier had as its consequence the rise in the price of land for purchase and rent. That change was made possible by the revival of massive immigration in the new century and the presence of new generations of farmers raised in the grain belt, processes that drastically expanded demand. Thus the abundance of labor made up for the end of the abundance of land. Rents did indeed rise dramatically, but by 1912, when after a series of bad harvests the return to normal agricultural conditions was followed by very depressed prices, the first organized movement of tenant farmers and sharecroppers imposed the principle of collective negotiations for tenancy contracts, within a legal framework created first under the informal sponsorship of provincial or federal authorities and soon through federal legislation.

The conflicts of 1912 did not take public opinion by surprise. By then the notion that something had gone radically wrong with agricultural expansion had achieved an almost universal consensus. The distance between the society that was emerging in the pampas and the one made up of affluent farmers and independent citizens of a regenerated republic that was projected by the liberal spokesmen of the mid–nineteenth century was recognized as the clearest sign of such failure.

Thus the liberal program, as defined in the primitive frontier society that Rosas had ruled with an iron hand, was still held relevant in very different circumstances. For one thing, the country was in the process of freely electing its first government by universal male franchise, and, for another, Argentina now had a durable representative association of tenant farmers, the Federación Agraria Argentina, which was soon to emerge as a permanent legacy of the conflict in the grain districts of the pampas.

But in such ideological continuity there is less than meets the eye and not only because different observers reached different conclusions from the comparison between the emerging rural society and the agrarian blueprint inherited from the previous century. Though some of them kept faith with the traditional approach that stressed the negative social and cultural consequences of the discrepancies between the two, others preferred to emphasize the dangers intrinsic in a system of agricultural enterprise without entrepreneurs, in which the landowner was just a *rentiste* and the tenant little more than a supplier of his own and his family's labor. In this view he was an indigent manager of assets that the valorization of land had made too substantial to be left to his incompetent and feeble hands. These observers further emphasized that nobody was taking care of the investments needed to make Argentine agriculture more productive and hence more competitive, now that the advantages it had derived in the past from the availability of cheap land had vanished forever.

Even more important, by now the imperative of successful integration into the world market (always less central to the aspirations for social change in rural Argentina than in other areas where that integration faced more serious obstacles) was still recognizable behind the growing concern about the competitiveness of Argentine agriculture. Yet its main effect was a further strengthening of the tendency, already present among Argentine thinkers since Vieytes, to turn to a more active version of social engineering than mainstream liberalism would have considered acceptable in order to channel the market forces toward objectives of social progress that they would not spontaneously foster.

This approach was, not surprisingly, the one preferred by Juan B. Justo, the founder of the Argentine Socialist party. For Justo the landowning class had proven unable to introduce agrarian capitalism in the pampas, and he advocated its replacement at the helm by forward-looking farmers recruited from among the tenants, whom he proposed to favor by a drastic increase in the land tax. Justo's conservative counterparts, who had not completely given up on the landowners, were also ready to propose schemes that assigned an equally active role to the state, in order to force them, albeit by less unfriendly means, to become the entrepreneurial class that Argentine agriculture needed to ensure its durable prosperity.

Yet there was also in this final triumph of a deeply rooted faith in social engineering less than met the eye. If the rural agitations of 1912 and the state's response to them taught anything, it was that the times in which an ideological or political elite could win control of the state and use it to refashion an essentially passive rural society were now closed forever. The relations between state and society, which had always included more give-and-take than the universal reliance on social engineering had acknowledged, was becoming more clearly interactive than in the past. The emergence of a new nation, so similar to and yet so different from the one announced by Sarmiento, brought to the fore issues and conflicts for which none of the successive versions of liberalism after 1837 could offer a valid orientation.

The agrarian conflict and its outcome thus offered one of the earliest signs that the sun was starting to set on liberal Argentina. Even though the economic policies with which Argentine liberalism had identified were still to hold their own for almost two decades and prosperity continued under their influence, the powerful myths that rejoiced in anticipation of the coming of age of a country born liberal started to dissipate at the very moment when this coming of age became imminent.

Why? Was it because the country that was finally emerging did not quite fulfill the historical promise discovered by Mitre in the dark travail of its early history? Could it be that in proposing the myth of a country born liberal, the shrewd and wise founder of modern Argentina was well aware that, to be effective, an ideology cannot be built on lies but on adroit manipulation of the truth and that he had found a flattering way of presenting a much less admirable historical legacy? And was it not the case that indeed Argentina had inherited from its idiosyncratic past a social and cultural structure as marred by inequality and oppression as those of its "feudal" neighbors, but better able than these to survive intact the assault of liberal reforms?

In the long half century since the nation's history took a route very different from the one that, according to Mitre's prophesies, was to continue to eternity its majestic progress to always loftier heights, this melancholy view of its past gradually won wider acceptance. By now it has probably replaced that of Mitre in the conventional wisdom of the country. Nothing less than this radical metamorphosis was needed to ensure the survival, in the somber landscape of the ruins of late-twentieth-century Argentina, of the faith in its exceptionality, which originally had reflected the euphoria of a frontier society on the verge of one of the most rapid expansions in modern history.

NOTES

1. The same point is found in "Ideas conservadoras de buena ley," *Los Debates*, Buenos Aires, 24 July 1857.

2. Personal communication, January 1987.

3. After all, even the Mexican Reform laws, so unpopular among twentieth-century scholars, rather than decreeing the dispossession of the peasants, intended to make freeholders out of them, whether they liked it or not.

4. Although in fact it did: in 1914, during the last stage in the expansion of grain agriculture in the pampas, the proportion of family farms cultivated by independent landholders fell to around 30 percent; while this result was considered wholly unsatisfactory, it was still far from negligible.

5. *El Comercio del Plata*, Montevideo, 19 March 1846, reproduced in Varela, *Rosas y sus opositores*.

6. A little more than one pound sterling in the United Kingdom as against £4.94 in Buenos Aires. Sources quoted in Halperín Donghi, *Guerra y finanzas*, p. 12.

7. Customs figures, in Public Records Office, London, Customs, series 6, year 1850.

8. Foreign observers used to complain that the attitude of the rural poor toward their social betters was not what could be found in a deferential society.

9. Both protectionist campaigns have been thoroughly studied by Chiaramonte, *Nacionalismo y liberalismo económicos*.

10. There is no reason to believe, however, that this firm antiprotectionist stance was an important factor in the unspectacular but steady growth of the Socialist vote in Buenos Aires.

11. D. F. Sarmiento to J. Posse, Buenos Aires, 15 Sept. 1869, in *Epistolario entre Sarmiento y Posse* 1: 274.

12. D. F. Sarmiento, "Discurso pronunciado en Chivilcoy en una fiesta dedicada al Presidente Electo," 3 Oct. 1868, in *Obras completas* 21: 237.

13. Eduardo Olivera, "La carta del señor Sarmiento," in *Miscelánea* 1: 211.

14. Sarmiento to Posse, Rosario, 24 Jan. 1870, in *Epistolario* 1: 283.

15. In the case of Hernández, these reached from the heady philosophical vocabulary borrowed from Pérez Gomar to the versified lamentations of Martín Fierro in the language of the country gauchos.

5

THE ECONOMIC ROLE OF THE STATE IN LIBERAL REGIMES: BRAZIL AND MEXICO COMPARED, 1888–1910

Steven Topik

Latin America's underdevelopment is largely a legacy of the nineteenth century. At the beginning of the century, Latin Americans optimistically looked forward to a glowing future once the shackles of Iberian colonialism were removed. With relatively large labor supplies and rich natural resources, they felt that they could match the prosperity of the United States and Europe. After all, there had been periods during the colonial era in which per capita wealth had surpassed that of their European colonizers; as late as 1800 Mexico was richer than some European nations and not far behind the United States. Yet these dreams were to be dashed; most Latin American economies, particularly those of the two largest nations, Brazil and Mexico, stagnated for most of the century.[1]

What explains this disappointing nineteenth century performance? Generally two answers are offered: the disruption caused by the independence process and the effects of neocolonialism. The former, while important in Mexico, played almost no role in Brazil, which experienced a peaceful transition to nationhood. Neocolonialism was of considerable importance in both countries, and indeed in all of Latin America. Economic liberalism has been seen as the ideological blueprint for the construction of neocolonial economies.

The object of this essay is first to examine the doctrine of economic liberalism in its pure form and then to establish the degree to which the "state" in Brazil and Mexico followed its precepts in the years of oligarchical rule and export-led growth, 1888–1910.[2] Finally I will suggest some reasons for their divergence from classical economics and their unique paths.

Economic liberalism arose in the last quarter of the eighteenth century, just as the industrial revolution was gaining steam. Its father, Adam Smith, based his ideas on the assumption that human beings acted rationally and that there were discoverable laws governing economic behavior. His guiding principle was that the marketplace, through the forces of supply and demand, created maximum productivity; that is, it most efficiently employed the factors of production (land, labor, and capital). This was only true, however, to the degree that there were no substantive impediments to the free flow of information and the factors of production. Thus the state was to interfere in the economy as little as possible. The state, Smith believed, based its involvement in the economy on political exigencies rather than economic efficiency and hence was economically counterproductive. State action was justified in four areas only: national defense, the maintenance of internal peace and the protection of private property, the establishment of public utilities too expensive or unprofitable for individual investors to undertake, and education. Aside from these areas, the state was to refrain from economic action or regulation. Since the marketplace, left unfettered, already enjoyed the self-regulating homeostatic device of supply and demand, there was no need for the interference. Nor was the state to lend moral guidance in economic affairs. The public good arose necessarily from the structure of the free market, even though individual participants might not realize it. As Smith observed: "Every individual is continually exerting himself to find out the most advantageous employment for whatever capital he can demand. It is his own advantage, indeed, and not that of society, which he has in view. But the study of his own advantage naturally or rather necessarily leads him to prefer that employment which is most advantageous to the society."[3]

Laissez-faire, in the late eighteenth century, implied not only that the state not intervene in the economy, but that it be forced out of the areas in which it already played a large role in the mercantilist system. In particular, land, water, and mineral rights should be freely tradable, individually owned commodities with no state or corporate privileges or restrictions. Individual laborers should be free to seek the best wage; they should not be bound by such institutions as slavery, debt peonage, or guilds (and later labor unions). Moreover, capital should be free to search out the most profitable opportunities. To insure that the state keep a low economic profile and to reserve resources for civil society, taxes should be kept at a minimum. To adapt Thomas Jefferson's famous dictum: that state governed best that taxed least. To make sure that the state did not find reason to require greater taxes and to keep the state treasurer's hand out of capital markets, the state should not incur debts. That, in turn, meant that it should balance its budget. If the state were diminished and restrained in these ways, the economy would thrive.

However, there was a problem with this formulation. As Thomas Malthus and David Ricardo noted, the growth of population and capital created stresses in the system. Even the full adoption of liberalism meant that the national economy would confront internal contradictions that would retard the pace of growth unless an international solution could be found. While the growth of capital and the labor force stimulated increasing returns for industry because of technological advances, economies of scale, and subsistence wages, agriculture and mines faced growing production costs and hence diminishing returns as ever more marginal lands and deposits were worked. Unfortunately, the decline of the primary sector eventually would inhibit industrial growth as well; despite a large surplus labor force, industrial wages rose with the cost of subsistence (food), and raw material prices also rose. The predicted result of the growth of population and capital within the national context that English economists were studying was wages at a subsistence level, a lowered rate of profit, and higher rents per acre. Thus some of the gains from expanding industrial productivity were ultimately transferred to the lagging agricultural sector.[4]

The escape from these constraints was to import food and raw materials from other countries. In Latin America, fertile unexploited lands were still abundant and labor was cheap; the latter was the case because of a lower subsistence level (which Ricardo pointed out was socially determined) and because of a lower general price level owing to capital scarcity and greater agricultural productivity. Thus economic liberals championed an international division of labor through free trade. Each country would produce those goods in which land, labor, capital, climate, and natural resources provided a comparative advantage. This global division would obviously benefit the industrial nations that received cheaper food and raw materials. Moreover, it would also benefit the agricultural nations. Indeed, Ricardo argued that because of diminishing productivity in agriculture, the terms of trade would favor the agricultural nations; they would be able to buy ever more industrial goods for the same quantum of agricultural exports. The agricultural nations would also prosper because capital from the capital-rich industrial nations would flow to the poorer agrarian ones until interest rates reached equilibrium.

It should be pointed out that free trade was based not only on the need to solve the problems of population pressure and rising agricultural costs. Primarily it was based on a redefinition of wealth. Echoing the physiocrats and denouncing mercantilists, Adam Smith announced: ''Wealth does not consist in money, or in gold and silver, but in what money purchases and is valuable only for purchasing.''[5] Thus rather than trying to hoard gold gained from a positive balance of trade in order to protect domestic industries from foreign imports, free traders called for a flow of trade that would capitalize on a country's comparative advantage. As a Brazilian minister of finance, Joaquim Murtinho, later argued: ''The economic ideal of a country should not be to import little, but to import and export much.''[6]

For the international division of labor to function successfully, states should not interfere in the international movement of the factors of production. This meant minimal customs and export duties, encouragement of immigration to equalize wage rates internationally, and unhindered movement of capital among nations. Convertible currency based on gold (and initially silver) was also essential for the health of the international system. Under a regime of convertible currency, the money supply and hence interest and wage rates of each country were determined by that country's international balance of payments. It was self-regulating. If a country had a trade deficit, money flowed abroad, causing wages to fall, which in turn improved the country's international competitive position and allowed it to balance its trade.

This system of interrelated principles that came to be known as economic liberalism was the child of political necessity as much as abstract economic reasoning. In Europe, it served to justify the supremacy of the industrial bourgeoisie in its struggle with the aristocracy and the commercial bourgeoisie. Latin America had no industrial bourgeoisie, but the doctrine of economic liberalism appealed to its export-oriented landowners and urban middle class for some of the same reasons that the European bourgeoisie embraced it.[7]

Moreover, liberalism made good political sense for one faction of the emerging national elites. This doctrine supplied potent ammunition for Latin American landlords who used the writings of Adam Smith to justify the dismantling of colonial corporate privileges of the church, indigenous communities, and guilds. By weakening the state's grasp on the economy, the new elites could lay hands on more resources. Free trade was also a useful solution to the economic dead end Latin Americans faced in their own underdeveloped domestic markets; it provided, through imports, cheaper goods than those that could be produced at home. By granting to individuals land taken from corporations, the liberal state bound the landowners to the regime.

Although economic liberalism eventually triumphed in Latin America, it manifested itself differently. This was to be expected; Arthur J. Taylor has pointed out that even in England laissez-faire was not completely adopted. But the essence of the doctrine was applied, and that is what we must consider. As the nineteenth-century British economist J. R. McCulloch observed: "To appeal to it [the doctrine of laissez-faire] on all occasions savors more of the policy of a parrot than a statesman or a philosopher."[8] As a result, the extent to which "pure" economic liberalism reigned varied. The range of the differences is not clear, because the doctrine has not been studied in a comparative context. It is also not clear to what degree the variation in the application of economic liberalism was a result of different preferences on the part of political society or of structural impediments that prevented its complete enactment. This study is a preliminary effort to consider these questions by examining economic liberalism in Brazil and Mexico in the period 1888–1910.

I have chosen to compare Latin America's two most populous nations for several reasons. The two states have come to play the largest public economic role in capitalist Latin American economies and they are frequently compared in economic and sociological literature. In the late nineteenth century, Brazil and Mexico shared enough characteristics to make comparison meaningful while manifesting some intriguing differences. Yet no one has attempted to compare the state's role in the process of export-led growth in the two nations.[9]

Both Brazil and Mexico were predominantly rural and underdeveloped raw material exporters. They both enjoyed substantial export-led growth in good part because of the vast sums of foreign capital invested in them. (They were the second and third largest recipients of foreign investment in Latin America in the 1888–1910 period). Capitalist labor relations were transforming both countries: Brazil abolished slavery in 1888, and Mexico appropriated indigenous community lands and thereby pulled native labor into the market. Moreover, both Brazil and Mexico were ruled by authoritarian, oligarchic regimes that followed, in principle at least, liberal economic policies.

The historical legacies and contemporary perceptions of the two states diverged markedly, however. The Brazilian Empire has been viewed as Latin America's most centralized, patrimonial regime.[10] The demise of this centralist tradition came with the Republican Revolution in 1889. Republicans set out to forge a decentralized, laissez-faire regime in order to unshackle the country's productive capacity.

The Mexican state had a different legacy and a different task. Having been torn asunder by internal civil wars between liberals and conservatives, robbed of half its national territory, invaded four times by foreign armies, and occupied for five years by the French, even liberals agreed that Mexico required more centralized authority. Both Presidents Benito Juárez and then Porfirio Díaz were bent upon subduing caudillos, sharply reducing regional autonomy, and harnessing the military. Díaz succeeded, becoming the *Jefe Máximo* and the *Gran Elector*. Thus the Mexican state was centralizing while the Brazilian state was decentralizing.

Despite their substantially different historical experiences with state building and their contrasting trajectories in the years after 1888, both states were primarily guided by the principles of economic liberalism. In Brazil, according to Celso Furtado, economic liberalism was applied dogmatically: "European economic science in Brazil . . . tended to become transformed into a body of doctrine which was accepted independent of any endeavor to compare it with reality. Where such reality was far removed from the ideal world of doctrine, this was felt to be a symptom of social pathology. Thus such statesmen passed directly from an idealistic interpretation of reality into the policy-making stage, to the exclusion of any critique of the doctrine in the light of reality."[11] In Mexico, says Pascal Arnaud, "the determination of the evolution [of the economy] seemed to be based on economic restrictions imposed by a blind respect for certain principles inevitably termed 'economic laws,' such as free enterprise, private property, and free trade."[12]

Furtado and Arnaud reflect the conventional views of the liberal regimes in Brazil and Mexico. We shall see that they are exaggerated. In order to determine the extent to which the Brazilian and Mexican federal regimes in fact adhered to laissez-faire strictures, I will sketch the state's participation in key economic areas during the 1888–1910 period. In particular, I will offer an overview of revenues, spending, debt, monetary policy, state enterprises, and land and labor policies.

REVENUE

Liberals should, in theory, seek to keep state revenues, and hence taxes, low. In both Brazil and Mexico, however, central government revenues calculated in current terms grew unsteadily but inexorably from independence to 1910. The Brazilian upsurge began at independence, while in Mexico the growth only started after the middle of the century. In both cases, the expansion of revenues was closely tied to demographic expansion and economic upturn. When government revenues are deflated and population growth is taken into account, swelling state revenues shrink. Brazil's per capita revenues mounted steadily from independence until 1865–69, then dropped off, bottoming out in 1896–1900. That decline in part derived from the fact that provinces were gaining a greater share of total revenues after the 1860s, a tendency that was sharply magnified after 1891, when the Republican Constitution ceded to the provinces many taxes that had formerly belonged to the central government. Thus total state revenues continued to grow even while central government income declined. From 1900 on, central government revenues rose (see Table 1), even though provincial revenues continued to rise more rapidly.[13] Mexican per capita revenues fell sharply with independence and then stagnated until at least 1856. They grew from at least 1877 to 1882, then leveled off until 1894, when they again rose until a downturn in the Porfiriato's last four years.[14]

Brazil's federal government was substantially more active in extracting wealth than was Mexico's, though the extent of Brazil's lead varied (see Table 2). At both the beginning and the end of the period Rio collected twice as much per capita as Mexico City. Throughout the period Brazil's advantage never fell below 50 percent, still a substantial edge.

In order to determine if greater federal revenues in Brazil meant larger total state revenues, we must ascertain the degree of fiscal centralization in both countries. Also, we must compare state revenues to the size of the economy as a whole. What percentage of available resources was captured?

Regarding the first matter, Brazil was granting more funds to the provinces while Mexico was steadily centralizing revenue. In Brazil, the provinces' and municipalities' portion of total revenues grew from 19 percent in 1863 to 27 percent in 1886 and then 39 percent under the republic in 1907–10.[15] Between 1895 and 1899 Mexican provinces and municipalities took in 38 percent of total revenues.[16] By 1903–6 the provinces' and muncipalities' share had fallen to 31 percent.[17] Although there was some variation, overall provincial and municipal revenues represented approximately the same proportion of total national revenues in both countries.

But how successful were the respective states in extracting resources from their economies? Two useful indicators are federal revenue as a share of total exports and of gross domestic product (GDP), all measured on a per capita basis. As Table 3 demonstrates, there was no clear pattern in the relationship of revenues to exports. At the beginning and end of the period, the Brazilian state clearly

Table 1
Federal Revenues and Spending of Brazil and Mexico 1890–1910

	1890	1895	1900	1905	1910
Federal Income:					
Mexico[a]	37,391	50,521	62,999	101,972	111,142
Brazil[b]	195,253	307,755	307,915	401,025	524,819
Federal Spending:					
Mexico[a]	39,087	45,102	59,423	79,470	100,913
Brazil[b]	220,646	344,767	433,555	374,868	623,536
Population:[c]					
Mexico	11,727	12,632	13,607	14,449	15,160
Brazil	14,334	15,755	17,318	19,988	23,151
p/c Income:[d]					
Mexico	2.67	2.14	2.26	3.53	3.65
Brazil	6.14	3.83	3.38	6.40	7.37
p/c Spending:[d]					
Mexico	2.79	1.91	2.13	2.75	3.31
Brazil	6.93	4.29	4.76	5.99	8.77
Deflated p/c Income:[e]					
Mexico	4.75	4.38	4.03	5.87	5.18
Brazil	10.92	7.85	6.02	10.65	10.47
Deflated p/c Spending:[e]					
Mexico	4.96	3.92	3.80	4.57	4.71
Brazil	12.34	8.79	8.48	9.97	12.46

Notes:

[a]In thousands of current pesos.   [b]In thousands of current milréis.
[c]In thousands.   [d]In current U.S. dollars.
[e]In U.S. dollars, deflated by U.S. wholesale commodities index.
p/c = per capita

Sources: Colegio de México, *Estadísticas económicas del Porfiriato: Fuerza de trabajo e actividad económica por sectores*, pp. 25, 153, 213; Brazil, Diretoria Geral de Estatística (DGE), *Anuário estatístico, 1939/1940*, pp. 1293, 1410; U.S. Department of Commerce, *Historical Statistics of the United States*, p. 117.

Table 2
The Ratio of Brazil's and Mexico's Per Capita Indexed Federal Revenues and Spending

Year	Brazilian Revenue / Mexican Revenue	Brazilian Spending / Mexican Spending
1890	2.30	2.49
1895	1.79	2.24
1900	1.49	2.23
1905	1.81	2.18
1910	2.02	2.64

Source: Table 1.

Table 3
Mexican and Brazilian Federal Revenues Divided by Exports

Year	Mexican p/c Exports[a]	Brazilian p/c Exports[a]	Mex. p/c Rev. / Mex. p/c Exps.	Bz. p/c Rev. / Bz.p/c Exps.
1885	3.80	5.63	-	-
1890	4.83	7.39	.55	.83
1895	4.64	10.03	.46	.38
1900	5.73	9.24	.39	.36
1905	7.75	10.83	.45	.59
1910	9.27	13.22	.39	.56

Note: [a]In current U.S. dollars.
   p/c = per capita.

Sources: Colegio de México, *Estadísticas económicas del Porfiriato: Fuerza de trabajo*, p. 25; *Comercio exterior*, pp. 155, 175; Brazil, DGE, *Anuário estatístico, 1939/1940*, pp. 1293, 1358.

had the higher ratio of revenues to export earnings. But in the late 1890s the Mexican state had the higher ratio.

By a more significant indicator, federal revenue as a share of GDP, the Brazilian central government manifested a marked lead (see Table 4). It often extracted a 50 percent greater share of national income than did the Mexican central government. Admittedly, these GDP estimates are only rough estimates. But the difference between the Brazilian and Mexican figures are large enough to indicate that it is most likely that state income was significantly larger as a share of economic activity in Brazil than in Mexico.[18]

To put the relative activity of both state central governments in a broader

Table 4
Brazilian and Mexican Per Capita Central Government Revenue as a Percentage of Per Capita GDP
(in current US dollars)

Year	Brazilian GDP		Mexican GDP[c]	Bz. Revenue as % of GDP		Mx. Revenue as % of GDP
	a	b		a	b	
1890	44.37	25.48	35.51	14	24	07
1895	64.29	38.58	34.19	06	10	06
1900	59.23	38.50	42.13	06	09	05
1905	69.42	51.57	44.28	09	12	08[d]
1910	84.74	69.58	52.97	09	11	07

Notes: [a]In current U.S. dollars, based on Nathaniel Leff's calculation that exports as a percentage of GDP in 1911–1913 was 15.6 percent and that it was unlikely that the percentage was higher in the nineteenth century. Thus per capita exports were divided by .156. My figures for Brazil are substantially above those employed by John Coatsworth in his pioneering effort to compare the GDPs of the two countries. In "Obstacles to Economic Growth," he puts Mexico's per capita GDP in 1910 at 50 percent above Brazil's. My figures show Brazil with the larger GDP. Since Coatsworth's estimate for Brazil was based on an earlier work of Leff, which Leff has since revised upward, my figures are more likely correct.

[b]Based on real product calculations made by Contador and Haddad and increased by 10 percent to account for the service, transport, and government sectors that were not included in their estimates. This figures exports in 1890 as 29 percent of GDP. Another estimate, by Buescu in *Brasil, disparidades de renda*, p. 16, puts exports in 1890 at 20 percent of GDP. It is most likely that the correct answer is somewhere between the [a] and [b] calculations.

[c]Based on Coatsworth's calculations that Mexican exports composed 9.3 percent of GDP in 1877, 13.6 percent in 1895 and 17.5 percent in 1910. I used 13.6 percent for 1890, 1895, and 1900, and 17.5 percent for 1905 and 1910. Coatsworth's estimate for 1910 is approximately the same as that of Nacional Financiera's *Statistics on the Mexican Economy*, p. 41, though substantially above that of Bulnes in *Whole Truth about Mexico*, pp. 9, 10.

[d]Randall, in *A Comparative Economic History* 1:178, estimates Mexican government spending as only 3 percent of GNP in 1906.

Sources: Leff, *Underdevelopment and Development* 1:21, 28; Contador and Haddad, Produção real," pp. 432–36; and Coatsworth, "The State and the External Sector."

context, I have compared them with nine other Western Hemisphere countries in Table 5. Brazil is close to the top of the list; Mexico, close to the bottom. In a broader sample of eighteen Latin American countries compiled in 1912, only six had greater per capita federal revenues than did Brazil and only six had less than Mexico.[19]

Brazil's place in total state revenue is even higher on the list than its ranking for federal income because it was one of the most decentralized regimes in Latin

Table 5
Central Government Revenues and National Exports of Selected Western Hemisphere Countries, 1912
(in Brazilian milréis of 16 English pence)

Country	Revenue p/c	Exports p/c	Revenue p/c / Exports p/c
Argentina	60.5	185.1	.33
BRAZIL[a]	21.0	45.5	.46
BRAZIL[b]	29.7	45.5	.65
Bolivia	9.1	48.7	.19
Canada	69.7	146.8	.47
Chile	65.0	123.0	.53
Costa Rica	32.9	77.0	.43
Cuba	47.8	205.8	.23
MEXICO	11.3	29.7	.38
Peru	11.2	24.4	.46
United States	31.6	76.0	.42
Uruguay	90.8	126.7	.72

Notes: [a]Federal revenues.
[b]Federal and provincial revenues.
p/c = per capita

Source: Brazil, DGE, *Anuário estatístico, 1908/1912*, vol. 2, pp. XL, LXXI.

America. Hence federal revenues constituted only 62 percent of total revenues while in other countries they often represented 80 percent.

As mentioned above, another way to evaluate the relative weight of state revenues is to divide real state income by exports (which are used as a proxy for GDP), all on a per capital basis. As Table 5 demonstrates, Brazil was surpassed in this measure only by Uruguay, Chile, and Canada (even if one takes the lower of the estimates for Brazil). Both Uruguay and Chile had quite centralized fiscal systems, so that their edge was not so great as the figures indicate. Certainly total Brazilian revenues consumed a greater share of GDP than did those in Argentina, Great Britain, and the United States, and about the same share as did those in Cuba.[20] Thus, in terms of revenue extraction, the Brazilian state strayed a good deal further from the limited state preferred by economic liberals than did the Mexican.

Of course the total amount of revenue collected measures only one aspect of the impact of revenues. The sources of the income are important in determining if the state remained relatively neutral, as most economic liberals believed it should, or played an active part in the accumulation or redistribution process. The bulk of income in both countries long came from indirect taxes (see Table 6).[21] There were no appreciable wealth, income, or land taxes at the federal level. (Some Brazilian provinces, such as Rio Grande do Sul, did tax land, but even there it was a secondary source of income.) Nor were state enterprises, sales or rentals of state lands, or state monopolies of much importance in raising revenue. While both countries gathered close to half or more of their funds from taxes on international commerce, Brazil's reliance was a good deal stronger. By 1910 it was far more dependent on import duties (65 percent of total revenues) than was Mexico (44 percent). This reflected in good part Brazil's more dynamic export sector and coastal settlement pattern, both of which made imports a target for heavy taxation. (Brazil's per capita imports were generally 50 to 100 percent higher than Mexico's.) The same tendency was noticeable in the provinces. In Brazil most provinces earned over half and often two-thirds of their income through taxes on exports from and imports into the province.[22] It is impossible to determine what percentage of these were produced abroad or to be shipped abroad or just sent to a neighboring province. No doubt the mix differed from province to province. Nonetheless, it is fair to assume that a considerable share of the goods were internationally linked. Mexico's provinces did not depend much on taxes on international commerce. The central government abolished the interstate *alcabala* (a colonial sales tax) on national goods in 1895 and on foreign goods in 1902.[23]

A close examination of the distributional effects of tax collecting would require a large study and is outside the scope of this essay. But one can venture several hypotheses: There were no efforts in either country to force the landlord class to become capitalist investors by seizing or taxing land, as was done in Meiji Japan. Instead, Brazil, and to a lesser extent Mexico, relied on export taxes. This meant that the more productive, capitalistic landlord paid higher taxes. The rentier did not face appreciable tax rates. Instead public land and mineral policies encouraged land speculation and concentration.

The import tax obviously did benefit some domestic producers when it provided protection against imports. A U.S. congressional investigator concluded in 1915 that Brazil had the highest customs duties in the Western Hemisphere on many consumer goods such as textiles and hats. Indeed, the levels of protection were higher than in Germany and France at the time. While such tariffs were in good part intended to raise revenue, politicians left little doubt that they also aimed to protect domestic producers.[24] Mexican duties, while a good deal lower on many consumer goods, were sufficiently high to afford protection, a conscious goal of Mexican politicians.[25]

The emphasis on import and sales taxes meant that the urban population most involved in the money economy paid a disproportionately high amount. Since they also generally received more economic benefits from the state, it is not clear whether these taxes were redistributive. In Brazil, import duties were fairly

Table 6
Source of Brazilian and Mexican Central Government Revenues
(in percentages)

	1890	1895	1900	1905	1910
Indirect taxes:					
Brazil	74.8	83.9	82.5	85.8	88.0
Mexico	76.4	76.1	76.0	73.2	70.0
Direct taxes:					
Brazil	9.2	.1	1.7	1.3	.9
Mexico	5.0	6.6	4.4	5.4	7.8
Other sources:					
Brazil	16.0	16.0	15.8	12.9	11.1
Mexico	19.6	17.3	19.6	21.4	22.2
Total:					
Brazil	100	100	100	100	100
Mexico	100	100	100	100	100
Specific Indirect Taxes as a Share of Total Revenues					
Import duties:					
Brazil	52.3	53.1	56.0	61.9	64.8
Mexico	55.0	44.1	45.7	50.9	43.7
Internal sales:					
Brazil	0	.2	12.5	9.7	12.3
Mexico	19.1	17.3	18.7	15.7	15.3
Industry and Professions:					
Brazil	2.6	.1	.9	.8	.8
Mexico	0	5.3	6.4	8.5	5.5

Sources: Brazil, DGE, *Anuário estatístico,1939/1940*, pp. 1410, 1411; Villela and
Suzigan, *Política do governo*, pp. 419–21; and Colegio de México,
*Estadísticas económicas del Porfiriato: Fuerza de trabajo e actividad
económica*, pp. 199, 220, 221.

regressive. The proximity of its largest cities to the ports meant that the urban working class consumed a substantial portion of imports, especially foodstuffs. Import duties were probably more progressive in Mexico because the upper and middle classes consumed far more imported goods than did the working class and rural peasantry. In both countries reliance on import duties was regionally progressive in the sense that the federal and, to a lesser extent, provincial capitals, which received the bulk of state expenditures, also purchased most of the imports.[26]

EXPENDITURES

The gulf in federal spending between the two countries was significantly larger than that of revenues. In some years, Brazilian per capita spending almost tripled Mexican outlays (see Table 1). The discrepancy between the two lay in Brazil's inability to balance the budget as it should have, according to economic liberalism. In the twenty-one years between 1890 and 1910, the Brazilian central government ran fourteen deficits. The Mexican government, on the other hand, balanced every budget from 1894 on, running deficits in only four of the twenty-one years.[27]

In many ways the distribution of outlays differed little. Were the state following closely the precepts of economic liberalism, one would expect most of the expenditures to go toward national defense, internal security, public works, and education. This was in fact the case, particularly for the first two categories. The Brazilian central government spent a great deal on repression. The military averaged over 40 percent of spending until 1870 and then fell to 23.7 percent by 1910. This decline was offset somewhat by rapidly growing state police forces in some provinces.[28]

The Mexican military consumed the largest part of the budget in the early years after independence and continued to use more than one-third of the budget until 1891. Then the percentage dropped rather steadily, reaching 20 percent in 1910 (see Table 7). But while their relative share fell, absolute expenditures on the armed forces grew, especially after the early 1890s, this despite the fact that the size of the army declined, the state was supposedly consolidated, the country was at peace, and the railroads had increased repressive efficiency. Even at the end of the Porfiriato, the military received more funds than all social services combined and more than the rest of government administration. Indeed, soldiers constituted almost half of the public bureaucracy. The army remained important for external reasons as well as internal ones. As the *New York Times* remarked, "The Government considers it to be the best proof of its desire to guarantee foreign investment to maintain forces for the preservation of order."[29]

The two countries differed in direct government investments in public works, though in both cases capital improvements received less than the armed forces and police. It was in investment and transfer payments that the most noticeable difference in aggregate spending appeared. The Brazilian federal government

Table 7
Brazilian and Mexican Central Government Spending by Category
(in percentages)

	Administrative	Investment	Transfer Payments	Debt
1890:				
Brazil	60.8	10.8	3.7	24.7
Mexico	68.7	4.6	16.1	10.6
1895:				
Brazil	72.8	6.2	3.5	17.5
Mexico	54.6	7.2	4.4	34.4
1900:				
Brazil	52.7	2.5	5.8	41.5
Mexico	56.8	7.8	7.1	28.3
1905:				
Brazil	55.1	14.2	4.8	25.9
Mexico	55.3	9.9	8.2	26.6
1910:				
Brazil	51.3	18.2	3.4	27.1
Mexico	62.0	9.2	5.5	23.4

Sources: Calculated from Villela and Suzigan, *Política do governo*, p. 414; Colegio de México, *Estadísticas económicas del Porfiriato: Fuerza de trabajo*, pp. 305, 311, 323.

generally spent a good deal more proportionately—often twice as much—for capital improvements, and in absolute terms it invested three to four times as much per capita (see Table 7). The difference results largely from Brazil's greater reliance on state enterprise (discussed below), while Mexico preferred to offer private firms subsidies, which showed up as transfer payments. Consequently, Mexico devoted a much bigger part of the budget to transfers. It should be noted, however, that both governments included subsidies to foreign railroads for construction under the rubric "foreign debt," not "capital investment," and often borrowed abroad to finance construction projects. Thus the investment figure of Table 7 substantially underrepresents actual outlays for capital improvements. On the other hand, many of the improvements were more cosmetic than developmental. Officials of both states also sought to impress foreign investors with the prosperity and high level of civilization of their countries by investing huge sums in monumental building in the capitals. Hence much of the capital investments went into building such showpieces as the Paseo de la Reforma in Mexico City and the Avenida Central in Rio de Janeiro.

Education, the fourth area of state activity sanctioned by Adam Smith, was largely ignored, though both states did make advances. In Brazil, education and justice combined received at most 9.2 percent of the federal budget. The Brazilian provinces, on the other hand, spent 14 percent of their budgets on education. Municipalities varied in their contributions to education. Though São Paulo dedicated over 20 percent of its expenditures to education, poorer cities contributed much less.[30] Brazil's literacy rate was only 26 percent in 1900, which was nonetheless 11 percent better than at the onset of the republic.[31] The Mexican central government devoted 3.1 percent of its budget to education in 1877, 6.7 percent in 1910. This low figure was in part because the provinces were responsible for schools. The provinces and municipalities (the latter contributing very little) spent 10.5 percent of their budgets on education in 1878 and fully 23.1 percent in 1910.[32] Nonetheless, education was woefully lacking. Less than 20 percent of the adult population was literate in 1910. Interestingly, Mary Kay Vaughn attributes this failure largely to "the relative financial scarcity in which the neocolonial state operated. Priority expenditures, within the dominant ideology, had to be those judged most necessary for the process of private accumulation."[33] While this is true in the sense that little attention was paid to the social infrastructure, this judgment ignores the possibility of garnering more revenue. As already noted, the Mexican state collected and spent a considerably smaller proportion of national wealth than did Brazil or, say, Cuba, Chile, or Uruguay. Even within the restricted resource base Mexican politicians allowed themselves, there was room for more social spending, since the country ran up surpluses 50 percent larger than total federal spending on education. An acceptance of a limited social role for the state and insufficient popular pressure for reform, as much as fiscal stringencies, explain the backward education system. The same was true for public health and pension programs, which received even less than education.

In both countries the two major expenses, in addition to military outlays, were administrative overhead and the public debt. These three categories consumed at least two-thirds of the budget. Brazil spent twice as much per capita on the machinery of government as did Mexico. This was reflected in the fact that Brazil had a public bureaucracy (civil and military, national, state, and local) twice as large as Mexico's. In 1900, I have calculated, Mexico's *fuerza pública* and *administración pública* stood at 64,000 people. Brazil's, in the same year, was about 129,000. By 1910 Mexico's public work force remained around 64,000 while Brazil's public sector grew 18 percent to about 152,000.[34] Brazilian critics continually complained about what they perceived to be the bloated size of the bureaucracy. It was seen by many as an employment office for the friends of the influential. In the size of the public bureaucracy also, the Brazilian state departed further from orthodox liberal economics than did the Mexican.

Moreover, Brazil outraged the sensibilities of economic liberals with the size of its public debt. As Table 7 illustrates, debt servicing regularly consumed one-quarter of the budget. This debt was incurred increasingly abroad. While in 1890 about 60 percent of the federal debt was internal, by 1910 about two-thirds was foreign.[35] Brazil's foreign debt was by far the largest in all Latin America, equaling in 1912 over 40 percent of the debt of all South America. European obligations weighed ever more heavily on the country's foreign exchange, as Table 8 illustrates. From consuming about 6 percent of exports in 1890, foreign debt servicing rose to 20 percent by 1910. The total international outflow was even greater, since most of the internal debt was probably held by foreigners.[36] (This large debt servicing charge combined with imports led Brazil to current account deficits in the balance of payments almost continuously.) Brazil's foreign debt was two to three times greater than Mexico's, though both consumed a similar share of the budget by the end of the period. Mexico's internal debt servicing, even more than Brazil's, also left the country.[37]

Liberals would have been somewhat appeased if state officials had directed the loans to capital improvements that repaid the investment. However, a substantial, but indeterminate, portion of the debts were dedicated to financing deficits, repaying earlier foreign loans, or urban beautification. It is unclear how much of the loans were actually invested in ports, public works, and railroads because often, even if the loan was earmarked for such ends, such as the 1893 Brazilian loan for the Oeste de Minas railroad, the funds were in fact used by the government to cover current costs. Certainly much of the loans were used for covering such costs, as government critics pointed out.

One of the centerpieces of the liberal economic system was convertible, gold-backed currency. Neither country complied faithfully, but Brazil strayed farther from liberal orthodoxy on this point as well. Brazil had traditionally used un-backed paper currency. There was an effort in 1889–90 to retire that currency and replace it with gold-backed private bank notes, but this failed. The experiments with returning to convertibility and private banknotes of the early 1890s caused a precipitous fall in the value of the milréis. To halt the slide, the government prohibited new private unbacked issues in 1893, ceased issuing new treasury notes in 1898 and began, in fact, retiring those that existed. Treasury notes, backed only by faith in the government, were the only legal currency from 1898 until 1906. In that year the federal Caixa de Conversão was created. Its task was to issue notes in exchange for convertible foreign currency. Unlike Mexico's tight money policy, Brazil expanded the money supply at the same time that it moved to the gold standard.

Mexico had long had bimetallic currency, backed by silver and gold; the ratio in value between the two was 16 to 1. Until the price of silver began to slip in the 1870s, this policy overvalued gold and made the Mexican peso one of the

Table 8
Foreign Debt and Debt Servicing as a Percentage of Exports

	Foreign Debt (in 1,000 U.S.$)	Debt Payment as % of Exports
1890		
Brazil	149,000	5.8
Mexico	51,000	6.2
1895		
Brazil	193,000	9.5
Mexico	93,000	3.3
1900		
Brazil	221,000	3.5
Mexico	111,000	8.0
1905		
Brazil	383,000	10.8
Mexico	---	8.3
1910		
Brazil	627,000	20.3
Mexico	219,000[a]	7.3

Note: [a]Mexican figure for 1911.

Sources: Villela and Suzigan, *Política do governo*, pp. 368, 451; Bazant, *Historia de la deuda exterior*, pp. 107, 135, 145, 154, 155, 168, 169, and tables 6 and 7; Colegio de México, *Estadísticas económicas del Porfiriato: Fuerza de trabajo*, pp. 321–22, and *Estadísticas: Comercio externo*, p. 456.

world's most dependable and widely traded currencies. Indeed, it was legal tender in the United States until 1856. After 1876 when the United States began to produce massive amounts of silver and numerous countries demonetarized silver, the white ore's value plunged, and with it fell the value of the peso. This movement became pronounced in the 1890s. In 1902 the peso, traditionally valued at one U.S. dollar, hit its low mark, 40 cents. The depreciation of the peso in fact helped Mexican exporters and protected Mexican industry. It was also a boon to people with internal debts. On the other hand, the national treasury was hurt, because it owed gold abroad and found the real value of tax receipts reduced (though customs duties were put on a sliding scale in 1902 to compensate for the fall of silver). Importers and foreign investors who wanted to repatriate profits were also adversely affected. The opponents of the silver standard prevailed. To halt the peso's fall, the minting of new silver coins was ended in 1905, the peso was pegged exclusively to gold, and its value was fixed at 50 U.S. cents, half the historic par level. The Money and Exchange Commission was created to maintain the peso at par; for the last six years of the period, the peso was stable. To stabilize the peso, however, the money supply had to be restricted.[38] This was acceptable to Mexican financial specialists who, quoting the French economist Leroy Beaulieu, agreed that banks of issue must be very conservative.[39]

There were other differences between the mechanisms for issuing convertible currency in the two countries. Mexican banks and mints issued first according to the amount of gold and silver and, after 1905, only according to the gold they had. They responded simply to economic stimuli. The Brazilian treasury in the 1890s issued currency to cover budget deficits or repay the floating debt.

The countries' exchange institutions also diverged. The Caixa de Conversão was created to prevent the value of the milréis from rising to the level of par, because that event would have hurt indebted coffee planters. Indeed, the Caixa was the key institution to the Treaty of Taubaté, which planned Brazil's first valorization of coffee. It signaled a victory for Brazil's principal exporters. The Mexican Comisión de Cambios, on the other hand, sought to prevent the peso from falling below par. The reform represented a defeat for Mexico's main exporters, silver miners, who now found one of their primary markets, government mints, closed.

The greater monetary orthodoxy of Mexicans was also manifested in the size of the money supply. According to the Comisión Monetaria's upper bound estimate of Mexico's money supply in 1903, it was the equivalent of U.S. $3.32 per capita. Brazil's money supply in the same year was more than twice that, U.S. $8.10. In 1910, Brazil's per capita total was U.S. $12.12, while Mexico's lagged behind at U.S. $3.73, according to other estimates.[40] It is noteworthy that Brazil had a per capita money supply more than three times greater than Mexico with largely inconvertible currency, and yet the value of that currency suffered no more than did Mexico's.

Part of the reason that the milréis was able to fare fairly well despite its apparent oversupply is that Brazil's GDP per capita may well have been larger than Mexico's. The per capita estimate for 1910 was fully 58 percent above Mexico's. But that only explains a portion of the divergence. Monetary conservatism on the part of the Mexicans, intended to reassure and attract foreign investors, is also relevant. Ironically, as Laura Randall has pointed out, in spite of the fact that Mexico enforced greater fiscal and monetary orthodoxy than Brazil or even Argentina, it did not attract a greater share of foreign capital. However, it constricted the domestic economy and made it more susceptible to international crises, such as the panic of 1907.[41]

The means both states employed to expand the money supply reflect their diverging views on state enterprise. In Mexico, one national private bank, and after 1897 provincial private banks as well, issued banknotes. There were no state-owned banks of any sort. Even the much applauded Caja de Préstamos para Obras de Irrigación y Fomento de la Agricultura, formed in 1908, was only one-quarter state owned.[42]

The Banco Central in Mexico City, which served as a currency exchange and bankers' bank, belonged to private, largely foreign capitalists.[43] Mexico did not entirely hand over the right of issue to private capitalists, because mints followed a different trajectory. In the early years of the Porfiriato they were leased to private concerns, but gradually, under Ministers of Finance Matías Romero and José Yves Limantour, the federal government reclaimed them. By 1895 they were all back in state hands. Coins lost relative importance, however, over the course of the Porfiriato as bank notes grew. By 1910, minted coins had fallen to one-ninth their 1893 level and represented only 3 percent of the money in circulation.[44] Thus here, too, the Mexican state was removing itself from direct participation in the economy. In Brazil, on the other hand, the treasury controlled the issue of currency after 1893. In 1906 the Caixa de Conversão, a state institution, joined in the issuance of legal tender. Such institutions were, of course, not strictly speaking state enterprises. But the Brazilian state did own some very important enterprises, an activity that the Mexican state shunned. In 1905 the federal government took over one-third of the stock in the Banco do Brasil, the country's largest bank. It also appointed the bank's president and exercised, thereby, veto power over the bank's actions. The Banco do Brasil held one-quarter to one-third of the deposits of the entire banking system between 1907 and 1910. It was also the country's single largest lender and together with the Caixa de Conversão was the preponderant power in the exchange market.[45] In addition to the Banco do Brasil, the federal government inherited the Empire's state savings banks, the *caixas econômicas* of the provinces, which held about 10 percent of national deposits. The provinces of São Paulo and Minas Gerais also held interests in mortgage banks, and São Paulo established small rural savings banks.

The other major area in which Brazil had important state enterprises was railroads. The Empire had initiated the practice of state ownership of vital lines, so that in 1889 the republican central government inherited 3,200 kilometers of track, 34 percent of the national system. In the course of the republic, state ownership greatly expanded. By 1914 the central government and provinces owned 13,552 kilometers, 52 percent of the national system. Much of this was leased out to foreign investors; nonetheless, the union and provinces operated 20 percent of the network. The impact of the state-owned lines was even greater than those numbers imply, because the Central do Brasil railroad that ran from Rio de Janeiro to Minas Gerais and São Paulo often carried one-third of the national passenger traffic and one-quarter of the freight.[46] As with the Banco do Brasil, these state-owned railroads were nationalized more as rescue operations to bail out bankrupt private firms or to reduce government subsidy outlays, than as entrepreneurial state capitalist developmentalist endeavors. Nonetheless, once government property, the lines did serve developmentalist aims, particularly by offering fare reductions for strategic goods.

The Mexican government, while quite active in subsidizing private railroads, did not really engage in state enterprise. At the most, it preferred mixed enterprises such as the Tehuantepec railroad. Between 1903 and 1908 the federal government purchased a majority share in railroads that represented 64 percent of the total national track. The purpose of the purchases is disputed: the Minister of Finance, José Yves Limantour, asserted that the government feared that the Harriman-Rockefeller trust would capture the country's key lines and therefore, in the interest of national defense, the government took them over. Critics argued that the takeovers were aimed at helping the hopelessly indebted railroads avoid bankruptcy, thereby averting damage to Mexico's credit. Judging from Limantour's willingness to allow the supervision of the state railroads to remain in North American hands, Limantour's critics were probably correct.[47]

So far the discussion has shown that in terms of revenues, spending, debt, monetary policy, and state enterprises, the Mexican state complied more closely with the principles of economic liberalism. The Brazilian state was far more economically active. Yet, we must agree with observations of contemporaries and scholars that the Porfirian state exerted a great deal of influence in the economy. Pascal Arnaud, for example, notes that the Porfirian state's paradoxical role lay in the "importance of its influence over markets, national supply and demand, and the distribution of income, while it was promoting the absence of all interference with the forces of the market."[48] The resolution of the apparent contradiction comes from examining the Mexican state's role in regulating economic activity. Theoretically, the liberal state was to regulate minimally. Its main concern was supposedly to free the flow of goods, capital, labor, and land and to protect the sanctity of private property, so that the most economically efficient could benefit the most. Two areas of particular concern were assuring that land, mineral, and water resources, as well as labor, were freely traded commodities.

The drive to end corporate land ownership and establish title in order to encourage immigration had been under way since the middle of the nineteenth century. The nationalization of church lands and privatization of indigenous community and state lands caused vast tracts to change hands or receive official title. In some provinces, such as Chiapas and Tabasco, over 40 percent of the land was conferred on private owners between 1867 and 1910. In this period, one-fifth of the nation's area was alienated.[49] Government land was sold very cheaply, for only about two pesos an acre, and frequently in large lots. Between 1889 and 1903 the average title was for over six thousand acres.[50] Government land was given to the surveying companies that charted the *tierras baldías* (public domain) and sold them to influential Mexicans and foreigners. Similarly, the wealthy were generally the victors in court battles over title; the poor rarely had proper title and fared badly in court. Thus the verification of title, an apparently neutral "modern" impulse, in fact led to the despoiling of the true owner who had worked the land; instead speculators accumulated the land. The state's use of eminent domain was also used to benefit private individuals. When landowners refused to sell to foreign companies deemed important to the economy by authorities, the state forced the sale.[51]

The Mexican state also sought to make mineral rights a component of property rights by abolishing the traditional state monopoly on the subsoil. This decision led to a massive alienation of mines, and, as a consequence, foreigners owned over 90 percent of the mines by the end of the period. At the same time that miners and petroleum producers won a clear title to natural resources, taxes on them declined steadily. Silver, which had paid as much as 30 percent in total fees and taxes during the colonial period and 15 to 26 percent after independence, fell to 20 percent in 1886 and even to 5 percent by 1905. Moreover, though mining companies formerly had to work their mines to maintain their claims, after 1905 they only had to pay taxes on the site, which fact encouraged speculation by the large companies.[52]

Water rights, of tremendous importance in the arid North, also became commodities. A law in 1888 authorized the president to grant water concessions to private individuals or companies who wanted it for irrigation purposes or for hydraulic power. They also received the right to expropriate "any lands belonging to private parties, indemnification being . . . made on the same basis as that governing railroads."[53] This was clearly not a neutral state. As Clifton Kroeber has observed: "Beginning in the 1880s the central government played a much more active part in arbitrating and mediating among property owners who were contending for scarce resources." In particular, "President Díaz's irrigation and waters policies reflected the regime's strong bias in favor of development by rich investors with undertakings of large scale."[54] Between 1896 and 1910, the federal government offered 373 such contracts. This practice often gave large companies virtual local monopolies.[55]

The Mexican state clearly took a partisan stand in labor disputes as well. Liberalism held that individuals in the marketplace should establish wages. The employer should not use extraeconomic coercion, and the employee should not resort to collective action. The Mexican government was adept at insuring that unions did not become significant. Leaders were arrested and strikes brutally broken. Yet, nothing was done about coercion of workers. Indeed, officials in many provinces enforced the debt peonage contracted at the *tiendas de raya* (company stores). They also made de facto slaves of prisoners or recently conquered Yaqui Indians shipped to the plantations of Yucatan or Oaxaca. Even in the wage-earning sector, the federal government had a hand. It counseled northern mine owners, for example, not to pay higher wages than were paid in other parts of the country. Efforts at securing an even larger work force through immigration failed, however.[56]

The Mexican state also intervened by granting some companies special local privileges. The most famous case was the Mexican National Dynamite Company, which received the monopoly for importing and producing all dynamite, a lucrative award in a mining economy.[57] More common were local monopolies, such as state banks, railroads with monopoly routes, and water rights to rivers.

The Brazilian state was less active in directly intervening in the accumulation process. It did try to regularize land titles, but a national registry failed. The central government ceded most of its land to the provinces, which were to stimulate orderly development. Generally, however, land on the frontiers was simply seized by individuals without state authorization, and property rights were sometimes regularized decades later. Legislation over mineral rights became the domain of the provinces, which in turn granted the rights to the land owners. But because of an absence of precious minerals and copper, this did not lead to a land rush. Water rights were not very important in most of Brazil, because most land received sufficient rainfall. The federal government did intercede in labor markets by subsidizing the trans-Atlantic passage of immigrants in the 1890s. Thereafter the province of São Paulo took over the program. Over 95 percent of the arriving immigrants in São Paulo in the 1890s had been subsidized; during the next decade the share fell to about 60 percent.[58] But there is no evidence that the state was active in the enforcement of slavery after abolition in 1888 and there was relatively little debt peonage.

I know of no monopoly concession similar to the Mexican dynamite company. The closest analogue was with the monzonite sand concession granted to a German exporter. This, however, was of far less significance for the national economy.

CONCLUSION

In conclusion, both the Brazilian and Mexican states generally sought to follow the principles of economic liberalism in the period 1888–1910. As the countries' economies and populations grew, so did the resources and scope of activity of the states. But there were no fundamental changes in the nature of their activities. Neither lower-class pressures for social reform nor nationalist cries for protection from foreigners or greater state guidance of the economy were sufficient to transform state policy.

But while both states were guided by a similar vision of the state's proper economic role, there were nonetheless substantial differences in their activities. The Brazilian government's economic policy strayed further from the principles of economic liberalism than did the Mexican. The Brazilian state spent far more and recorded constant deficits, while the Mexicans balanced every budget after 1894. Brazil allowed its currency to remain inconvertible for most of the period, while Mexico maintained the silver and then the gold standard. Brazil contracted twice as large a public debt and had far more public enterprises and capital investments. The greater activism of the Brazilian state is perhaps surprising in light of the popular image of the Porfirian state as robust and centralized and the republican state in Brazil as weak and splintered into semiautonomous cantons.

What explains the difference? It is clear to me, after an extensive study of newspapers, congressional debates, and ministerial and presidential reports, that both nations were fundamentally guided by the same ideology. But they were flexible—particularly the Brazilians. Indeed, Brazilian politicians were forced to be innovative, because the Brazilian economy, for most of the period, was more dependent on the world economy. Brazilian exports at the beginning of the period constituted twice as large a share of GDP as Mexico's. And Brazil's exports were concentrated in two commodities, coffee and rubber, which were responsible for as much as 80 percent of all exports. Mexican exports were more diversified, precious metals constituting under half of the total.

Not only was the Brazilian economy more dependent on the world economy, but so was the Brazilian state. It relied upon taxes on international trade for a substantially larger share of its income than its Mexican counterpart. And foreign exchange was a more pressing concern, since Brazil had twice as large a foreign debt. This debt consumed one-quarter of the budget. The dependency in Brazil was exacerbated for much of the period by an inconvertible currency that oscillated with trade balances. The result was that Brazil's ability to service its foreign debt also fluctuated.

In short, the Brazilian economy and state were much more dependent on the world economy and especially on one export commodity, coffee. Coffee was extremely vulnerable to dramatic cyclical fluctuations in price. The cycles forced state responses to rescue essential companies—especially ones in debt to the treasury, such as the Banco do Brasil and some railroads—in order to protect the country's foreign credit. Furthermore, Brazilian coffee dominated world production. It supplied as much as 80 percent of the world's coffee output. This meant that the state could induce changes in world prices by intervening in the coffee market. Mexico, on the other hand, supplied only one-third of the world's silver, and the commodity was experiencing a secular decline in demand.

The differences in state economic activities are explained by political considerations, as well as by differing relations to the world economy. The state in Brazil was internally strong and internationally respected, while the Mexican state was fragmented internally and internationally dependent. The republicans who took power in Brazil in 1889 inherited a fairly well institutionalized national state that had elite support. Brazil's path toward independence had been smooth. A weak church, relative ethnic homogeneity, and the social cement of slavery tended to convince the country's ruling class of the necessity to maintain a united front. Arguably, a nation was built and a state formed earlier in Brazil than anywhere else in Latin America. The Republican Revolution of 1889 reshaped regional power relations but kept the essence of the state intact.

The Brazilian state was strong relative to foreign investors and nations as well. Brazil had a dynamic national bourgeoisie that gave the state the political will to enact policies that occasionally clashed with the desires of foreigners. Brazil's coffee and sugar planters, cattle raisers, and rubber and maté growers were overwhelmingly nationals. The national bourgeoisie's strength was particularly apparent in the country's most prosperous and populous center-south, especially São Paulo. Although Brazil had about $1.65 billion of foreign investment by 1910, it was generally placed in areas complementary to the export economy. Of the European and North American capital, 40 percent was in the form of government loans, which strengthened the hand of the state, for the loans were used to nationalize railroads and control coffee prices. The political strength of the state and its long nineteenth-century history of punctually repaying loans made it a good investment for foreign bankers.

The state that Porfirio Díaz seized was less secure. Mexico before Díaz had been wracked by civil wars, regional rivalries, and foreign invasions. The treasury was plundered, foreign credit scant, power splintered, and sovereignty mocked. Internal peace and external pressures were constant preoccupations of Díaz.

Despite the regime's claim that it had brought peace, the reality was closer to the title of a recent study by Paul Vanderwood: "Disorder and Progress." It is clear from the Díaz archive that Mexico was constantly threatened by rebellious peasants, hostile indigenous groups, and disgruntled caudillos. Yet at the beginning of the Porfiriato, the regime lacked the funds to buy off important caudillos and caciques. Hence it awarded concessions and privileges that won the allegiance of the elite without directly burdening the treasury.

The Mexican regime was also much more concerned about foreign invasion. Its experiences with Texas, the Mexican-American War, and the Maximilian episode made Mexicans supremely suspicious of foreigners. This concern was heightened by the enormous economic and hence political influence that foreigners enjoyed in the country. Foreign investment was perhaps 25 percent greater than in Brazil in absolute terms, and more than twice as large as a percentage of annual GDP; 85 percent of it was in direct investments, not loans. Foreigners, moreover, dominated the major exports: mining, rubber, tobacco, cattle, railroads, and banks. By 1910 they even owned one-fifth of the national territory.

At the same time, the Mexican national bourgeoisie was relatively weak and usually dependent on its relations with foreigners. The strongest, in the North, were greatly dependent on U.S. capital and markets. The same was true of Yucatan's henequen growers. Mark Wasserman has observed that there was a division of labor in Mexico, in which Mexicans controlled the government and resources while foreigners controlled capital and technology. Most Mexicans served as intermediaries, "using their ownership or control of land and other natural resources [often gained through the action of the state] or their political influence to obtain financial rewards."[59] The weaker position of Mexico's capitalist class may explain why the Mexican state was more directly active in the accumulation process—for example, through land and labor policies—rather than concentrating on the economic infrastructure as the Brazilian state did. To create the necessary internal peace to attract foreign investment, Díaz essentially granted the Mexican elite an economic hunting license with a perpetual open season. To have the *pan* to distribute in his *pan o palo* (bread or the club) policy, Díaz needed the foreigners. In order to attract them, the Mexican regime strengthened the army, balanced the budget, punctually repaid its debt, established the gold standard, refrained from setting up state enterprises, and treated its own citizens as stepchildren.

Economic liberalism, then, was the prevailing ideology in both Brazil and Mexico during the apogee of the export economy, but not simply because it was fashionable in Europe. Rather, the doctrine was adopted and adapted because it appealed to the needs of the export oligarchy, foreign investors and state officials. Economic liberalism offered both the possibility of growth in poor, sparsely populated agricultural countries and a vehicle for nation building in states still struggling to assert their sovereignty domestically and internationally.

NOTES

Research for this essay was funded in part by grants from the American Council of Learned Societies/Social Science Research Council (ACLS/SSRC) and National Endowment for the Humanities (NEH).

1. Buescu, *Brasil*, pp. 15–33; Rodríguez, *Down from Colonialism*, p. 7; Haddad, *Crescimento*, pp. 13–19; and Coatsworth, "Obstacles to Growth," pp. 81–83. It should be noted that slow growth was not inevitable, because in the twentieth century the national product of Brazil and probably Mexico have been growing faster than that of the United States.

2. I use the term *state* to refer to the complex of public institutions that have a monopoly on the legitimate use of coercion within national boundaries. The state includes public bureaucracies, armed forces, public education personnel, and state enterprises. When referring to specific levels of the state I use either *federal*, *provincial* (even though Brazilians and Mexicans called provinces states), or *municipal*.

3. Smith, *Wealth of Nations*, p. 26.

4. Ricardo, *On the Principles of Political Economy*, pp. 93–109.

5. Smith, *Wealth of Nations*, p. 10.

6. Brazil, Fazenda, *Relatório 1899*, p. XIII.

7. Economic liberalism has often been viewed as inappropriate for Latin America, an "idea out of place", because few contemporaries could distinguish it from political liberalism. Schwartz, in "As idéias fora do lugar" points out the contradiction in Brazil, where planters accepted this doctrine based on the theoretical equality of all individuals before the law and at the same time owned slaves. The paradox is solved when one views slaves as property rather than people.

8. Quoted in Taylor, *Laissez-faire*, p. 16.

9. Indeed, the only historical comparison of the states' economies is Randall's *Comparative Economic History*, which dedicates a volume each to Mexico and Brazil and does some comparison. The state is not her major concern. Barbara Butler Page's "Legitimacy and Revolution" discusses the process of state building in the two countries.

10. Marchant, *Viscount Mauá*, p. 209. See also Faoro, *Donos do poder*.

11. Furtado, *Economic Growth*, p. 176.

12. Arnaud, *Estado y capitalismo*, p. 231.

13. See Love, *São Paulo*, p. 265.

14. Brazilian data can be seen in table 1 of Topik, "State and Economy," p. 22. The sources for the table are: Brazil, Diretoria Geral de Estatística (DGE), *Anuário estatístico, 1939–1940*, pp. 1293, 1353, 1359, 1410, 1412; Carreira, *História financeira*, passim; Villela and Suzigan, *Política do governo*, pp. 418–21; and Contador and Haddad, "Produção real," pp. 432–35. Mexican data are from Colegio de México, *Estadísticas económicas del Porfiriato: Fuerza de trabajo*, p. 323; and Tenenbaum, *Politics of Penury*, pp. 182–83.

15. Nery, *Brésil en 1889*, p. 450; and Brazil, DGE, *Anuário estatístico, 1939–1940*, pp. 1409, 1412, 1418.

16. México, Secretaría de Fomento, *Cuadro sinóptico, año de 1900*, pp. 70–73.

17. Ibid., pp. 70–71; and México, Secretaría de Fomento, *Anuario estadístico, 1906*, pp. 221, 222.

18. This conclusion is reinforced by the previously mentioned fact that in the last years of the period the Brazilian federal figure represented a smaller portion of total government revenues than did the Mexican (61 percent to 68 percent).

19. Brazil, DGE, *Anuário estatístico, 1908–1912*, 2:XI, LXXI.

20. Smith, *Politics and Beef*, p. 17. Deane and Cole, *British Economic Growth*, p. 333; and U.S. Department of Commerce, *Historical Statistics*, pp. 141, 711. Domínguez, *Cuba*, p. 32.

21. Tenenbaum, *Politics of Penury*, pp. 178, 179; and Topik, "State and Economy," p. 22.

22. Wileman, *Brazilian Yearbook 1909*, pp. 371–95 and passim. The provinces were prohibited by the constitution from taxing imports from other provinces or from abroad, but they did so anyway.

23. Villers, *Hacienda pública* 2:405–642, passim; and México, Secretaría de Hacienda, *Memoria, 1899–1900*, passim.

24. U.S. Federal Trade Commission, *Report on Trade*, p. 57.

25. Cosío Villegas, *Cuestión arancelaria* 3: 64–67, 80, 95. Servín G., "Nuestra política tributaria," p. 436, shows that the value of Mexican import charges as a percentage of the value of all taxed imports fell steadily from a high of 90 percent in 1891–92 to 30 percent in 1910. Tenenbaum, however, in "Planning for Mexican Industrial Development," p. 11, points out that the 1887 tariff and subsequent revisions did help factories in Mexico. Fiscal interests certainly partially explained the protective levels. Díaz said in September of 1891 (in México, Secretaría de Hacienda, *Hacienda a través los informes presidenciales*, p. 235), that he would "continue liberal reforms" and "provide commerce with all tax exemptions compatible with the fiscal interest [of the state]."

26. Topik, "Domination of Capitals."

27. The Mexican budget surpluses were not actually as great as they appeared to contemporaries, because Minister of Finance Limantour failed to deduct extraordinary expenses from revenues in his calculations. The extraordinary expenses were often considerable. See Rieloff to Buelow, Mexico, 24 Dec. 1907 and 8 Jan. 1909, Auswärtiges Amt des Deutschen Reiches (AA) 1741.

28. Topik, "State and Economy," p. 22.

29. *New York Times*, Aug. 3, 1892; Tenenbaum, *Politics of Penury*, p. 183; San Juan Victoria and Velázquez Ramírez, "Estado y las políticas económicas," p. 308; Colegio de México, *Estadísticas económicas: Fuerza de trabajo*, pp. 305, 311, 323.

30. Wileman, *Brazil Yearbook*, n.p. The Federal District spent 18 percent of its

ordinary expenditures on education, but when debt payments are included, education falls to 10 percent.

31. See Ludwig, *Brazil: A Handbook of Historical Statistics*, p. 132 (no figure for 1910).

32. González Navarro, et al., *Estadísticas sociales del porfiriato*, pp. 36–38, 237.

33. Vaughn, *Estado, clases sociales y educación* 1: 72, 73.

34. México, *Resumen del censo de 1900*, p. 61; San Juan Victoria and Velázquez Ramírez, "Estado y las políticas económicas," p. 308; Brazil, Contadoria Geral da República, *Resumo do orçamento . . . 1893*; Estrada de Ferro Central do Brasil, *Relatório, 1893*, table D1; Brazil, Contadoria Geral da República, *Tabela explicativa . . . 1912*, passim; and Topik, *Political Economy*, p. 21.

35. Brazil, Ministério da Fazenda, *Contas . . . 1925*, pp. 245, 246; Wileman, *Brazil Yearbook*, n.p.

36. Rui Barbosa to Rothschild, Rio de Janeiro, 13 June 1890, Doc. XI–65–78, N.M. Rothschild and Sons Archive, London.

37. The Mexican Comisión Monetaria estimated in 1903 that 90 percent of internal bonds were held abroad. See its *Actas de las juntas*, p. 154.

38. México, Comisión Monetaria, *Datos*, p. 2, table 34.

39. Casasús, *Reformas*, pp. 51–53.

40. Colegio de México, *Estadísticas económicas, Fuerza de trabajo*, p. 25; Brazil, DGE, *Anuário estatístico, 1939–1940*, p. 1353. Conant, *Banking System of Mexico*, p. 40, estimated that the money supply in 1908 was 96.1 million pesos, which agrees with the figures for bank notes and monetarized coin in *Estadísticas económicas*.

41. Randall, *Comparative Economic History* 1: 178–80.

42. Díaz Dufoó, *Limantour*, pp. 90, 212–15. Díaz Dufoó says the reason for the creation of state banks of issue was to keep the banks "absolutely independent of public powers." Bulnes argued that the purpose of the Caja was not to finance irrigation projects, but to bail out overextended landlords and thereby aid the banks who would otherwise have had to write off those bad loans; see Archivo General de la Nación (henceforth AGN), Bulnes Archive, caja 9 exp. 10.

43. Gurza, *Nuestros bancos*, pp. 49–51.

44. Colegio de México, *Estadísticas económicas: Fuerza de trabajo*, pp. 173, 186.

45. Brazil, Ministério da Fazenda, *Relatório, 1905*, pp. 74, 98; Brazil, DGE, *Anuário estatístico 1908–1912*, pp. 2, 213; and Banco do Brasil, *Relatório, 1924*, n.p., anexo.

46. Duncan, *Public and Private Operation of Railways*, p. 87; also see Topik, *Political Economy*, ch. 4.

47. *New York Times*, Aug. 20, 1908, Feb. 23, 1909; México, Secretaría de Hacienda, *Memoria, 1909–1910*, I, pp. 275–279; González Roa, *Problema ferrocarrilero*, pp. 140–88.

48. Arnaud, *Estado y capitalismo*, p. 150.

49. Calculated from González Navarro et al., *Estadísticas sociales del porfiriato*, pp. 88, 89, 223.

50. *Patria, el florecimiento de México*, April 2, 1906, p. 143; Pan American Bulletin, Feb. 1905, p. 376, gives varying prices for public land ranging from 6.1 pesos per hectare in the Federal District to 0.5 pesos in Quintana Roo. All of these prices are ridiculously low.

51. See the letter from Porfirio Díaz to Teodoro A. Delhesa, Veracruz, 7 Mar. 1890, in which Díaz tells the governor that he should intervene and force the sale of land to

the Interoceanic Railroad of Colis P. Huntington, ''because no injury to the company can be ignored by the government since that would injure all of the industrial interests of the country . . . the government should offer every sort of aid.'' Díaz Archive, copiador 17, Universidad Iberoamericana, Mexico City. Not only the poor were despoiled of land. See *New York Times*, 27 Feb. 1888, for an account of a U.S. woman fighting for eighteen years to regain title to her land.

52. México, Comisión Monetaria, *Actas de las juntas*, p. 81.

53. *Patria*, 2 Apr. 1906, p. 112. Francisco Bulnes claimed that this law and a similar one in 1894 were unconstitutional because they were using eminent domain to expropriate for private persons, not for public utility, as the constitution called for. AGN, Bulnes Archive, caja 12, exp. 2.

54. Kroeber, *Man, Land and Water*, p. 219, 220.

55. AGN, Bulnes Archive, caja 12, exp. 8; Kerig, ''The Colorado River Land Company,'' describes the U.S. company that dominated the Mexicali Valley.

56. Turner, *Barbarous Mexico*; Wells, *Yucatan's Golden Age*, pp. 151–82; *New York Times*, 6 Dec. 1903.

57. *The Mexican Investor*, 6 Jan. 1906, p. 2.

58. Holloway, *Immigrants on the Land*, p. 86, 87.

59. Wasserman, *Capitalists, Caciques and Revolution*, p. 85.

6

FREE TRADE, REGIONAL ELITES, AND THE INTERNAL MARKET IN SOUTHERN PERU, 1895–1932

Nils Jacobsen

Peru is usually considered a country in which the liberal tradition of economic policy making has been particularly strong and more enduring than in most other large Latin American nations. The Peruvian economist Gonzalo Portocarrero has recently written that the economic thought of the Peruvian oligarchy until 1930 was marked by a "liberal and evolutionist essence" with no particular vision of the future society or economy. In this ideal typical body of thought "the destiny of society is fundamentally decided on the level of the individual, and the state is only an orienting factor which has neither the means nor the responsibilities to predetermine, much less to realize, a particular type of society."[1] Rosemary Thorp and Geoffrey Bertram, in the most thorough study of the economy and policy–making in post–War of the Pacific Peru to date, observe a decline in the potential for autonomous development between the late 1890s and 1930. In essence, they argue that the oligarchy sold out key sectors of the Peruvian economy to foreign capital, that the same national groups that were involved in manufacturing had stronger interests in export activities, that export bonanzas prior to and during World War I prevented profits from being reinvested in industry, and that—more generally—since 1897 relative prices moved against import-substituting activities. In this climate there did not exist sufficiently strong interests to call for the type of state intervention deemed necessary by the authors for industrialization and the strengthening of a national market. Only with the tariff laws of 1926 and 1928 was the long-term trend of declining effective protection (begun ca. 1900) reversed, but even then the authors see no "determined policy of industrial promotion."[2]

There are two serious flaws in this notion of an all-powerful liberal impulse among the Peruvian elites during the four decades preceding the Great Depression. First, the expectation of "radical and coherent changes" of economic policies,[3] derived from a presumed model of Western European or North American bourgeois capitalists eager to develop their domestic markets, blocks our view for the subtle changes that *did* occur. It obscures our understanding of multifaceted mixes of liberal and interventionist planks in the spectrum of economic and social policy issues—from property rights to tariff questions, taxation, infrastructure investments, labor regulation, and education. It neglects the fact that a given economic policy, such as industrial protectionism, could have different meanings in two distinct economies. Lastly, it downplays the analytical problems raised by a nonintegrated and structurally heterogeneous economy such as Peru's during the early twentieth century.

After a vociferous debate about trade policy in the late 1890s, hardly any Peruvian espoused free trade principles pure and simple.[4] In a work published in 1913, Carlos Rey de Castro (a Limeño journalist and diplomat) rejected the "extreme" positions of free trade and protectionism, arriving at an intermediate stance according to which trade policy had to be adjusted to the peculiar "material and moral" circumstances in a given nation as well as to the economic policies prevailing among the trading nations.[5] The impact of the German historical school, both in economics and in law, as well as that of U.S. pragmatism, had freed Peru's thinkers and politicians from the need to derive their policies from inherently consistent economic models. It also made a virtue of a common inclination in Latin America to eclectically conjoin disparate social and economic axioms as long as they seemed to fit national reality. Thus, in 1899 J. Gubbins had warned against the debilitating effects of foreign investments for national capitalists, while still espousing the concept of comparative advantage.[6] Francisco García Calderón, one of Peru's most penetrating oligarchic intellectuals during the early twentieth century, similarly saw the country's progress depending, for the immediate future, on agriculture and mining, while warning against U.S. economic expansionism and contrasting the individualistic concept of the state in the United States with the Latin American nations' need for a "protective state," limiting the rights of individuals and ending traditional anarchy.[7] The historian Jorge Basadre has also pointed to the continuity in Agusto Leguía's drive to increase the role of the state in the economy through expansion of state finances after becoming José Pardo's finance minister in 1904.[8] Finally it should be noted that a deliberate protectionism to foster nascent industries in Peru was seen by men like García Calderón as raising the danger of a few monopoly companies dominating the nation's fragmented markets, more of a throwback to Bourbon times or to the 1830s and 1840s than a tool for creating a modern market society.[9]

The second objection to the notion of a pervasive liberalism in the Peru of the early twentieth century concerns the underlying assumptions about the nature of Peru's political regime that are made by many students of economic policy making during the Aristocratic Republic (1895–1919) and, with some modifications, during Leguía's Oncenio (1919–30). The prevailing paradigm has it that the Peruvian government until 1919 was dominated by the export-oriented *civilista* oligarchy, an elitist, self-serving group with no ''national project.'' Because the coastal oligarchs were incapable of establishing their hegemony, they entered into an alliance with foreign capitalists and the traditional hacendados of the sierra. This class alliance had a common interest in favoring the export and import trades and securing monetary stability. It considered foreign investment beneficial and wanted a state that was weak except in its capacity to control social movements and to provide economic infrastructure.[10]

A few years ago Rory Miller summed up the doubts that have arisen about this model of oligarchic rule in Peru: (1) Many leading members of the political elite between 1895 and 1919 did not belong to the coastal oligarchy. (2) Rather than combining interests in various sectors of the economy, it may have been much more common for oligarchic families to rely predominantly on income from one type of activity, and this often was not export agriculture. (3) Representatives of export agriculture were often deeply divided among themselves and at key junctures could not control government economic policy in their favor. (4) Rather than casting the Peruvian political process in terms of class alliances, a more promising approach would be to speak of clientelistic networks linking politicians representing specific groups within the coastal oligarchy with those representing regional hacendados from the sierra. In this environment economic decision making was more particularistic and patrimonial than universalistic and class oriented. (5) The Peruvian economy underwent significant changes between 1895 and 1919, and with it the economic issues debated and the political configuration of groups in the debate also had to undergo shifts.[11]

The consequences of this more fragmented vision of the Peruvian political process for our understanding of economic policy making and thought seem clear enough. We need to analyze economic interests, sociocultural ideologies, and resulting policy initiatives of specific regional and social groups in order to find out what type of particular negotiations and accommodations shaped national political decisions on economic and social issues.[12]

The main part of the present paper discusses the economic interests and socioeconomic thought and policy initiatives of southern Peru's elites between Nicolás de Piérola's rise to power in 1895 and the political and economic crisis of the early 1930s. For reasons of history, social structure and economic interests, this southern oligarchy, as it has been called, tended to view itself as distinct from the interrelated oligarchy composed of merchants and bankers from Lima, sugar and cotton planters from the central and north coast, and latifundists and miners from the central highlands. Due to the peculiar electoral system—based on provincial representation rather than on size of the electorate—the southern departments (Apurímac, Arequipa, Cuzco, Moquegua, Puno, and Tacna) had a strong congressional representation: 35 of the 126 deputies to the Congress of 1915 came from the south, and both Cuzco and Puno sent more deputies than Lima.[13] I shall argue that in spite of important internal cleavages, the economic interests of the region's elites were relatively cohesive, although they increasingly frayed during the 1920s as commercial conjunctures for the region's primary commodities became unstable.

Southern Peru's regional elite showed an instinctive free trade orientation and considered it crucial that the regional import and export business remain strong and autonomous. Here we have the "liberal impulse," tied to and arising from very specific regional economic interests. If such analysis was carried out for other regional or sectoral interest groups in Peru, similar policy orientations might be discovered. This exercise might render the construct of a national oligarchy useless, because it would provide a more precise instrument for analyzing why Peruvian national governments chose during the early twentieth century to pursue an export-oriented economic policy. This is not necessarily to deny that a national oligarchy existed as a social group—identifiable in the membership lists of the Club Nacional, income levels, and the like. What is in doubt, however, is whether there ever existed a tightly knit network of rich men in republican Peru, with the same interests and ideological orientations, who exercised exclusionary control over national politics. If we could get away from this image, we might see more clearly which social forces in Lima attempted to unite the nation, economically and socially, against the interests of regional power blocs such as southern Peru's.

I shall divide my observations into two parts, the first dealing with the period between the 1890s and 1919, the second encompassing the difficult 1920s and the early 1930s. For each period I shall present a brief overview of salient economic trends before discussing the economic thought and policy initiatives of the regional elite. I shall focus on the three large southern departments: Arequipa, Cuzco, and Puno.

1895–1919: THE ERA OF PROSPERITY AND RELATIVE CONSENSUS

By the 1890s southern Peru was quite integrated economically. All three core departments exported wool and other livestock products, linked by an as yet incomplete transportation funnel through the entrepôt Arequipa and the port Mollendo. Although this export-oriented southern economy began to emerge during the middle decades of the nineteenth century, the railroad strengthened such integration, particularly in the late 1880s and early 1890s, and heightened the dependence of many producers on the large export houses. As a consequence of the Grace contract of 1889 settling Peru's foreign debt, the railroad, as well as the Lake Titicaca steamers linking Puno with Bolivia, passed into the hands of the English-controlled Peruvian Corporation, a fact that was to be the cause of considerable friction in subsequent decades.[14]

But regional economic integration was much older than the rise of the export economy in the south. The starkly diversified ecology of the southern Andes had been utilized to build complementarity exchanges since the pre-Incaic kingdoms. During the colonial period the rapid rise of Potosí as the strongest pole for commodity and labor demand had created a fairly intensive internal trade in which the valleys around Arequipa and Cuzco became important suppliers of a great variety of agricultural and processed goods and Puno, supplier of livestock products since ancient times, became the *espacio de trajín*, the obligatory transit space for much of the supplies of the mining centers in Alto Peru.[15] In the century following the Bourbon reforms and the Tupac Amaru rebellion these trade links between southern Peru and Alto Peru/Bolivia had undergone successive crises and an overall decline. But in 1889 Peru still exported goods valued at 594,000 soles to the Altiplano republic, and most of these came from the south. Total wool exports through Mollendo, the port absorbing some 90 percent of regional maritime trade, in 1890 amounted to 1,483,000 soles (FOB).[16] While trade with Bolivia had declined, sales of goods such as cane and grape alcohol, sugar, maize, coca leaves, dried meat, livestock, hides, and tallow *within* the region had been increasing since midcentury, as the population grew and peasants in the Altiplano and the adjacent provinces in Arequipa and Cuzco were increasingly drawn into commercial transactions through their involvement in the exportation of wool. Although the south is generally portrayed as the region par excellence in which backwardness and exploitation coincided with an extreme degree of monocultural export dependence, in fact the share of per capita income generated by production and sales for the domestic market was greater here than for Peru as a whole during the first third of this century.[17]

The southern Peruvian economy by the late nineteenth century had two legs to stand on: exports of wool and a few other commodities of shorter cyclical duration, and a much more diversified circuit of exchanges within the region and with Bolivia. While the growth of foreign trade favored some local areas and hurt others, particularly through changing relative transport costs and the impact of imports, it seems unlikely that for the region as a whole growth of foreign and domestic trades were inimical to each other.

Although Arequipa was the greatest beneficiary of the commercial shifts in the wake of the growing wool export business and the construction of the railroad after 1871, members of the city's patriarchal families frequently voiced a sense of decline until the end of the nineteenth century.[18] This city expressed more than any other in the south the ambivalence between production for the regional southern market and the potentials of the export trade. The majority of the city's patriarchal families of colonial origin, such as the Goyeneche, Bustamante, Belaúnde, Paz-Soldán, Polar, Ugarteche, Tristán, Piérola, and López de Romaña, had their primary economic base in landholding and agriculture in Arequipa's *campiña* and the adjacent valleys of Majes, Siguas, Vitor, and Tambo, and secondarily depended on church and government employment and professional activities. The owners of estates in the valleys in the vicinity of Arequipa faced difficult times since the post–War of the Pacific recovery. Their grape-based alcohols could not compete any more with the *aguardiente de caña* that the modernizing sugar plantations of the north coast began to market throughout southern Peru, as the railroad line diminished transport cost advantages of the Arequipeños. After 1880 much land in the Majes and Tambo valleys was switched to sugarcane. Their market remained limited to the departments of the south and Bolivia.[19] But in spite of competition by northern sugar plantations, many Arequipeño hacendados managed to prosper during the first decades of the twentieth century, especially when they conjoined modernized agriculture around Arequipa with participation in the expanding trade with the highlands.

Hegemony over southern Peru's export trade and the incipient industrial activities was exercised by a distinct group in Arequipa, immigrant merchants, as well as upwardly mobile Peruvian entrepreneurs who came from the ranks of artisans, muleteers, and middling landholders.[20] The period between 1895 and World War I was the golden age for the large wholesale merchant houses in the city, such as Gibson, Stafford, Ricketts, Braillard, Emmel, Forga, Iriberry, and Rey de Castro. They exported *productos del país*—from wool and hides to gold and rubber; imported consumer goods as well as capital goods, such as iron plough tips and engines; distributed regional goods such as textiles, coffee, and cacao from Cuzco; and extended credit to producers and commercial agents. With this multifaceted activity they "constructed" the regional market, as Luis Ricketts wrote in 1917, by establishing ties with literally thousands of commercial agents, urban wholesalers and retailers, and various types of itinerant traders throughout southern Peru. In spite of fierce competition among themselves— often aimed at attaining a monopoly over specific local markets—their advantages in terms of capital and knowledge of international prices allowed them to maintain profit margins above those of traders in the interior and, more often than not, to impose their conditions on retailers and producers. The limits to this regional market were imposed by the relations of production in the interior, characterized by low productivity, low remuneration of labor, a low elasticity of labor supply, insignificant capital accumulation, and neocolonial sociopolitical structures that, through extraeconomic mechanisms, constantly reproduced unequal returns to factors of production (e.g., land rents, commodity prices, and wages received by Indian peasants were considerably lower than those received by mestizos). Arequipa's merchant elite, before 1919 in any event, saw no possibility of changing this situation and thus entered into an uneasy partnership with the beneficiaries of these traditional relations of production and structures of authority, the hacendados and traders of the interior.[21]

Industrialization proceeded slowly in Arequipa during the Aristocratic Republic. Until World War I, the merchants preferred investments in urban real estate and construction, agriculture, and mining to industrial ventures. Nevertheless, by 1922 the city boasted seventeen foundries, fifteen soap factories, eleven tanneries, four wheat flour mills, four textile factories, and eleven other enterprises, including a brewery. Most of these establishments were small, and many operated in niches in which competition from imported goods was minimal. They catered to traditional regional tastes (e.g., tanneries) and manufactured pieces of special design with small runs (foundries). They worked in sectors where regionally produced raw materials and cheap labor could still offset productivity advantages of foreign factories (soaps, candles, sweets) or produced wage goods for which transport costs still constituted effective protection against foreign competitors (the brewery and possibly the textile factories). Many factories depended on the merchants for credit and marketing. Such dependency on merchants at one and the same time assured them of the sale of their commodities, as long as the merchants found this relationship profitable, and limited their possibilities of growth and diversification, as the merchants continued to be strongly interested in import trades. In the crucial regional market for cheap cottons and woolens no major friction developed before the end of World War I between the southern factories and the stronger, foreign-owned factories in Lima. What mattered for the merchant houses of Arequipa was their exclusive control of the southern markets, and they did not care much whether the commodities they sold were imported, came from other parts of Peru, or were produced in the region.[22]

Puno and the adjacent livestock zones in southern Cuzco and highland Arequipa constituted the core space of southern Peru's commercial circuit. This was a vital trading zone for the producers of foodstuffs and stimulants from Cuzco and Arequipa as well as for the exporters and importers from the entrepôt city. Puno was simultaneously the area that was most perfectly attuned to the new regional commercial circuits flowing into Arequipa's export funnel and the one that underwent the fewest changes in its relations of production. There were no major shifts in the range of commodities produced in the countryside; methods of exploitation on the estates only changed minimally; and no modern industries developed in the small towns.[23] In a way, all that had happened in the nineteenth century was that Arequipa and Liverpool had supplanted Cuzco and Potosí as major destinations of the northern Altiplano's livestock products. However, this shift was accompanied by two processes of great consequence for income distribution. Associated with the changing transportation system (the railroad and the steamer services across Lake Titicaca), the export and import business, particularly after 1890, had given rise to a large number of merchants, shopkeepers, and traders, thereby stimulating urban growth and strengthening middle strata. Producers felt increasingly dependent on the Arequipa merchant houses and their local representatives, who did not only purchase their commodities. The Arequipeño merchants also served as purveyors of all imported commodities—the Norwegian beer and the Spanish canned sardines that hacendados preferred for their celebrations, and also the scissors, wire, and other equipment needed for estate operations—and were the major providers of credit, as bank loans remained nearly unattainable for Puno's hacendados until the 1920s. While this sense of dependence was somewhat attenuated through the competition among Arequipa houses in the wool production zones—most effective during expansionary phases of the trade cycle—hacendados still felt that they were getting less than their fair share of the final value of their commodities. But before 1920, as most estate owners were basking in their unprecedented earnings from wool sales, there was only grumbling by individuals and no organized effort to redress the perceived imbalance.[24]

In the countryside the wool export boom led to an unprecedented cycle of encroachments upon the lands of the Indian community peasantry by old and new hispanicized landholding families, a cycle that reached frenetic proportions in the first two decades of this century. In most parts of the Altiplano, where Indians had still held more than half of the crop and pasture land during the early republican period, the growing community population was reduced by 1920 to less than one-third of the land. The land tenure pattern that resulted from this massive process of land transfers, accompanied by violence, fraud, and deceit, was characterized by an enormously widening gap between the few very large haciendas and the overwhelming majority of small peasant holdings. At the same time the number of small, marginal estates increased, and the minority of affluent peasants—not a new phenomenon in itself—grew.[25]

Between the mid–1890s and the heady days of heightened demand for wool between 1916 and 1919, most social groups in the Peruvian Altiplano participated, albeit highly unevenly, in the growth of the pastoral economy. The growing prosperity of the region was accentuated by brief gold and rubber booms in Puno's montaña, exploited primarily by foreign capitalists and adventurers, but providing additional demand for labor, transport services, and supplies (foodstuffs, sacks, leather, etc.) from the Altiplano.

In the Puno of the Aristocratic Republic, then, the interests of all elite sectors were tied up with the wool export economy. Cleavages, however, could and did arise over income and property distribution, both between producers and merchants and between hacendados and peasants.

When, in 1895, the citizens of Cuzco enthusiastically joined the revolution that removed War of the Pacific hero Andrés Avelino Cáceres from power in Lima and terminated a repressive local administration, the city appeared to awake from a century of somnambulance. During this period its urban population had declined by more than half, and it found itself marginalized by the reconstituted trade circuits that had shifted regional hegemony to Arequipa. With its highly diversified productive base, ranging from high altitude livestock zones to temperate cereal-producing valleys and to rich subtropical and tropical valleys in the montaña, the department exported agricultural and mineral products overseas and supplied regional markets, as well as northern Bolivia and Chile, with maize, alcohol, coca leaves, and textiles.[26] What the department urgently needed and what, at the same time, some sectors of the elite feared was to be connected to the railroad line from Mollendo to Puno to have a better vent for its commodities in regional as well as foreign markets.[27] By 1908 the railroad reached Cuzco, bringing with it a veritable avalanche of goods that saturated the small urban market. Local cane alcohol producers (Apurímac and La Convención valleys) faced increasing competition from the more efficient north coast producers, and some traditional urban crafts were seriously affected by new styles and fashions introduced with luxury imports.[28] With the closer integration of the department into the regional commercial circuits, Cuzco's economy began to experience more acutely the rhythms of export conjunctures. Demand for its maize, coca leaves, sugar, and alcohol in neighboring departments and northern Bolivia was highly correlated with the ups and downs of southern Peru's wool exports. Their buoyancy in most years between 1895 and 1919 also led to rising demand for these Cuzqueño products. During the height of the export boom in the last years of World War I, cereal purchases in the wool-producing area had climbed so much that maize prices in Cuzco skyrocketed. Food riots in the city followed, prompting the city council to forbid maize and other basic foodstuffs to be sold outside the department.[29]

The first two decades of the twentieth century saw a rapid growth of output in Cuzco's Oriente, stretching from the montaña valleys of Lares and La Convención further down into the Amazon basin. The region became one of the major sites of Peru's rubber export boom until it was cut short by Asian plantations in 1912. Growth of coffee, cacao, tea, and sugar production was more continuous, based both on foreign and regional demand, the incorporation of new lands into vast estates, and the establishment of what Eric Hobsbawm has called neofeudal relations of production.[30] Paradoxically, although all of Cuzco's external markets were articulated through communication with the neighboring departments to the south and west (Apurímac, Puno, Arequipa), the fear of outside competition and the lure of multifaceted progress and dynamic markets in Europe created something like an eastward-looking chimera of riches in the imperial city. As unrealistic as it may seem today, many members of Cuzco's elite were hoping—even after the collapse of rubber exports in 1912—to export directly to Europe via a railroad link to an Amazon basin river navigable by ocean steamers.[31] This dream was actively stimulated by the powerful estate owners of La Convención, notably Benjamín de la Torre, heir to the largest haciendas in the province and longtime deputy and senator in Congress. Construction of a railroad line from Cuzco was finally begun in 1913, but its advance was extremely slow. It reached Machu Picchu, the entry to the montaña, only in 1928, and another fifty years would pass before the first train arrived at Quillabamba, capital of La Convención province.[32]

Nevertheless, the dream reflected at least a bit of Cuzco's economic reality during the early decades of the twentieth century. The city was located in a cul-de-sac of the regional commercial circuit. Farthest removed from the point of entry for imports and from the hegemonic regional entrepôt, Arequipa, it was an active center of exchange for a diversified provincial production and a growing, albeit still small, urban market. This location offered both effective protection and favorable conditions for the supply of raw materials, allowing the city to develop a stronger industrial sector than that of Arequipa until 1920. By 1915 the city had four textile factories (three of which processed regionally produced wools), a number of modern flour mills, a sizable brewery, and a small hydroelectric plant built by local private capital, along with a number of smaller, more traditional establishments.[33] The textile mills were founded by immigrant entrepreneurs and merchants as well as by some of the wealthiest landholders of the department.[34] In a way Cuzco's early twentieth century industrial experience was a repetition of its *obrajes'* experience during the eighteenth century, albeit with more advanced technology. It was able to flourish briefly in spite of disadvantages concerning access to capital, skilled labor, and advanced technology, until a fairly sharp reduction in transport costs owing to truck transport eliminated much of the effective protection for the industry.[35]

This ambiguous development of Cuzco's economy between the 1890s and 1919, namely the growth through closer integration into the regional trade circuits dominated by Arequipa's export and import merchants, combined with a certain degree of autonomy within those circuits, was reflected in the composition of the department's elite. Large landholders, particularly the newly wealthy owners of estates in the montaña and the large ranchers, dominated society. In contrast to Puno's hacendados, they maintained a considerable degree of autonomy vis-à-vis the wholesale merchants. Although far from becoming impoverished, the owners of cereal estates had lost importance compared with these newly rising large landholders. While less prominent socially and politically, the large wholesale merchants controlled as much or more capital than did the wealthiest landholding families. All of the leading merchant houses belonged to European immigrants; some were merely subsidiaries of Arequipa firms, while others had their center of operation in Cuzco.[36]

Cuzco's elite then contained an array of social groups among whom there was cause for mutual resentments and recriminations, as the integration into the regional market favored some groups more than others and hacendados—with the apparent exception of the large sugar cane growers of La Convención—became increasingly dependent on the merchants' credit. But it is difficult to pinpoint any group whose interests might have been damaged by the integration into the regional market under the hegemony of Arequipa. The most likely candidates, industrialists, were either merchants themselves or depended on the merchants for the sale of their goods outside of Cuzco town, in markets as distant as Puno, Bolivia, or Arequipa.

What type of economic initiatives did these southern elites develop during the Aristocratic Republic, and what type of economic and social ideas informed such initiatives? The large landholders of the south had a definite interest in protection during the early years of this century. However, they were thinking of protection from producers in other parts of Peru rather than from foreign competitors. When in late 1903 President Candamo's minister of finance, Augusto Leguía, introduced in Congress his package of excise taxes, the stiffest opposition came from representatives of the southern departments of Arequipa, Cuzco, and Apurímac.[37] Claiming that Leguía's proposals would deliver their traditional markets to the large sugar and alcohol producers from the north coast and thus spell the death sentence for the *cañaverales* of the south, the representatives advocated differential rates that strongly favored *serrano* producers. They argued that the principle of equitable legislation called for differential treatment of distinct groups in accordance with their varying chances from the outset—an idea that was gaining currency at the same time with regard to the "Indian problem." They freely admitted that the southern producers operated "anemic industries" with outmoded machinery of considerably lower productivity than that of modern north coast refineries. Apurímac's Senator Leoncio Samánez estimated the northerners' cost advantage in the elaboration of alcohol at 50 percent. But they blamed the central government for the backwardness of the *serrano* industry, because the lack of good roads and of an adequate railroad network made it impossible to install modern processing machines in the isolated *cañaverales* of the interior and increased the costs of marketing. In the words of Cuzco's senator Teófilo Luna, "National progress does not only depend on the progress of the coast, but also on the progress of the sierra, which is destined to make living on the coast inexpensive in exchange for the means which the latter should extend [to the sierra] for its material progress." The dire predictions of the death of southern industries, then, were strangely mixed with the optimistic view that the region could even extend its markets to the coast, if only it were given the proper support. Arequipa's Senator Moscoso Melgar even went further in his justification of protection. He proclaimed that "we cannot proceed in the laws guided only by a certain spirit of protection for the powerful, to the extreme of oppressing those who most need some help to lift themselves up." If some protection would aid an "anemic industry" to get on its feet, it would be unjust not to grant it, because "it is the duty of the law to attend to [the need of] all to the extent that they defend their own interests, their development or their very life."[38]

Leguía's most emphatic response chastised the southerners' ideas as "monstrous," "a return to the fourteenth century," and as "transgression against the principles of modern economy." Exalting the principle of competition, he denied that any industry had a preordained right to survive. If inefficient *trapiches* with equipment from the last century could not withstand competition, they had to go, and the owners had to look for another line of business or thoroughly modernize their operation, as the *cañaverales* of the valley of Tambo (Arequipa) had already done. He explicitly blamed regional interests for Peru's lag in elevating excise taxes on alcohol compared with other nations. In other words, Leguía's defense of the north coast sugar and alcohol producers here coincided with the push for the creation of an integrated national market, the very thing southern hacendados feared most, wishful declarations to the contrary notwithstanding.[39]

It is important to reemphasize that the protectionist arguments proffered by southern politicians in the tax debates of 1903–4 only referred to protection against rival Peruvian producers. For the period up to 1919, there is little evidence that the southern elites applied protectionist ideas to foreign trade. Indeed, the same idea espoused by the southerners in the excise tax debate, namely that the principle of equality in the laws could require differential treatment, was at times employed to argue against increased tariffs. Thus the deputy for Arequipa province, Víctor Pacheco Benavides, in 1915 opposed a 10 percent duty on a range of hitherto free imports, including agricultural implements. He argued that while the large agricultural enterprises of the north coast could easily sustain the resulting increased costs for tools, the small family farmers of Arequipa's *campiña* could not. He suggested that they should pay a lower rate.[40]

To be sure, there were a few calls for industrial protection in the south during these decades, but they remained vague or came from groups that did not represent the region's elites. In 1898, at the height of the debate between free traders and protectionists in Lima, the prefect of the department of Puno, Fernando Elías, advocated the establishment of processing plants in the Altiplano for the area's raw materials, including woolen textile mills, that were to be granted "decided and open protection." He suggested, as one of Puno's advantages for such projects, that the Indian peasants already were expert weavers.[41] But his call found no echo among Puno's large landholders and traders.

A socially more relevant call for industrial protection came from the Partido Liberal Independiente in Arequipa during the first years of this century. Not unlike its contemporary Mexican namesake, this was a movement of intellectuals and professionals. It rejected the stodgy clericalism of Arequipa's patriarchal families and their self-righteous defense of a preordained, hierarchically ordered society. On the basis of a somewhat vague and rather contradictory ideology containing anticlerical, utopian socialist and anarchist elements, the group developed a discourse of redemption through revolution directed toward Arequipa's artisans, farmers, and small groups of workers. While in their day-to-day political work the group was primarily concerned with advancing workers' rights and diminishing the role of the church in the city, their program of 1903 also contained the following plank:

To achieve industrial development, bringing into play all measures that would stimulate it. To remove the obstacles that impede the founding and flourishing of industrial companies, regardless of whether they are nationally or foreign, individually or collectively [owned], and to provide these companies with guarantees that protect them from burdensome taxes and allow them to develop steadily.

It is evident that the liberals were not concerned with protecting specific, existing industrial interests. Rather, they were calling for a program of industrialization toward which they hoped to push Arequipa and the nation. In the words of Francisco Mostajo, longtime leader of Arequipa's liberals, "every factory that is installed is a battle silently won against obscurantism."[42] But in any case, during 1900–1910 Arequipa's liberals opposed the city's oligarchy. When in the following decade some of the intellectuals of the considerably weakened liberal movement began to rally around the issue of decentralization in closer proximity to reformist sectors of southern elites, they were less interested in economic issues.

In Cuzco, with its not inconsiderable manufacturing sector during the early twentieth century and its long tradition of processing industries since the colonial period, we might have expected a relatively pronounced protectionist sentiment. But the scant expressions of protectionism there confirm the lack of concern about foreign competition in the region. Between 1897 and 1907 the body that concerned itself most with economic and cultural development was the Centro Científico del Cusco, which brought together the more enlightened men and women among Cuzco's professionals (judges, physicians, lawyers, professors, even clerics) and also landholders. Writing in the *Boletín* of the organization in 1907, Jacinto Castañeda declared it to be a duty of the state to protect the "Andean industries." What he meant by industries was primarily agricultural production, and he found it "repugnant to patriotism" that Peru was importing wheat, maize, and potatoes from Chile and California (for consumption in Lima). But what was the solution? The state should build railroads connecting the sierra with the centers of consumption on the coast, providing a multiplier effect for local economic growth.[43] Another measure demanded in Cuzco (as in Arequipa) under the heading of protection for industries was the reduction or abolition of certain municipal taxes and fees imposed on the output of manufacturing enterprises (for example, Cuzco's beer tax). Since the incidence of such fees varied from town to town, they were thought to hinder the competitiveness of specific establishments in the regional markets. In more general terms, for Hildebrando Fuentes, prefect of Cuzco in 1905, the development of industries "primarily requires active and honorable municipalities."[44]

For the young Luis Valcárcel, son of a modest Cuzco merchant and soon to become a leading spokesman of the *indigenistas*, "state protectionism" should not "disturb foreign commerce," as he wrote in 1914. Permissible protective measures included differential railroad tariffs, state interest guarantees on certain types of investment, and temporary tax exemptions. The goal was to strengthen private economic initiatives, as he found "nothing more enervating than to expect everything from the action of governments."[45]

The notion of protection evident in most of these proposals was a vague one that owed more to early and mid-nineteenth-century concepts of state privileges and *fomento* than to any modern concept of state intervention to protect the creation or growth of specific branches of industry deemed important for the development of a national economy. Most members of southern Peru's elite could probably agree with Arequipa-born Carlos Paz Soldán when, in 1915, he asserted that "truly national [industries] subsist unaided." National textile factories, such as the Lucre woolen mill in Cuzco, did not need high duties on competing imports, he continued, "because everything in these factories is national—the wool, the cotton, etc.; only the machines are imported and a large number of our fellow citizens find work in these factories."[46] He thus accepted a corollary of David Ricardo's theory of comparative advantage, namely, that there are natural and artificial industries.

Southern Peru's elites continued to view infrastructure investments as the crucial field of activity of the state in the economy. But here the range of demands was rapidly growing. As we have seen, foremost among elite concerns continued to be the extension of railroads, feeder roads, and, more generally, means of communication. It is somewhat surprising that more than thirty years after the opening of the railroad line from the coast to Puno in 1873, trains could still be praised as the virtual panacea, the key to the magic kingdom of economic progress. But in good measure the ornate language used in such declarations was merely the inevitable, idiosyncratic Andean means for advancing concrete, particularistic material interests. The greatest political commotion in Cuzco during the quarter century under consideration concerned the routing of the rail line into the montaña. In 1910 and 1911 the issue deeply divided the city's elite between the cereal growers of the Valle Sagrado de los Incas (middle section of the Urubamba river) and the sugarcane growers of La Convención in alliance with the city's merchants. The conflict, overcome only after the personal intervention of President Leguía's minister of finance, was settled, predictably, in favor of the sugarcane growers and merchants.[47]

More frequently, however, the efficacy of the state was gauged by its capacity to provide much smaller infrastructure investments. The trustworthiness of congressional deputies from the southern sierra was measured, among their small electoral base of provincial notables, by success in channelling funds from the central government to various local projects: 7,000 soles for construction of schools in Sandia and Azángaro, 5,000 soles for a dam to protect Sandia against floods, 11,000 soles for potable water in Azángaro, 200 rails for construction of a telegraph line, and so on.[48] The very fact that after 1895 such projects became so much more important a part of the work of Congress and a significant aspect of the redistributive mechanisms of the central state meant that in the minds of provincial elites the provision of locally tangible material progress became a key function of the state. But this expectation of disbursements from the central government also constituted a slowly advancing threat to the aspirations of regional or local self-determination, so dear to southern hacendados. In 1905 Hildebrando Fuentes warned the federalists, who became more vociferous in the south over the following two decades, not to forget that nearly two-thirds of the outlays for Cuzco's departmental administration came from the central government.[49]

Southern elites began to place greater emphasis on the type of obligations of the central government that previously had been considered an exclusive domain of private capital, municipal governments, or the church: provision of credit, especially mortgage banks, that could free hacendados from dependence on merchant credit; veterinary services and experimental farms and ranches that would extend the results of their work to the practical farmer and rancher; a "rural code that guarantees investments and industries"; a net of rural police posts; and finally a whole gamut of educational institutions, all to be oriented toward "practical teaching."[50] Many hacer.dados, traders, professionals, and officeholders were forced to define their positions on such issues for the first time, as the central government was extending its power into the provinces and was investigating abuses of Indian labor and illegal appropriation of peasant lands. Indians themselves began to resist abuses more actively, and a few of the notables' sons were turning *indigenista*, denouncing what they deemed to be the feudalism of the region's traditional society.[51] As a consequence, traditional society was gradually pushed into a hitherto unknown level of ideologization.

Those imbued with positivist ideas, penetrating the south from Lima between the 1890s and 1910s, called for authoritarian, centralist models of instructing the Indian that would temporarily remove him from the putatively deleterious milieu of his family and community.[52] But the positivists' faith in instruction to "civilize" and "make useful" the "degenerate" Indian population was by no means shared by all hacendados in the south. Traditionalists feared that any schooling, even that proferred to Indian recruits in the reorganized military, might teach community peasants insubordination and even anarchism[!]. In more than a few instances, thugs of local hacendados destroyed rural schools.[53] For the same reasons other hacendados advocated a minimum of institutionalized instruction with itinerant teachers briefly giving lessons in the peasant hamlets. Estate owners themselves were to be responsible for schooling the children of their *colonos* (labor tenants).[54]

Ideological currents from Lima affected consideration of issues that lay at the heart of southern Peru's agrarian elites' self-perception. In 1911, in a congressional speech, Senator Mariano H. Cornejo, eminent Peruvian diplomat and sociologist and the most influential member of Puno's congressional delegation, explained his concept of property. As with other major institutions and values, Cornejo viewed the notion of property within the framework of the evolution of human societies. Property as *señorío* (implying dominion over people), and as "simple source of rent," had lost legitimacy in the modern age. "In the light of modern legal conceptions," property was only justifiable "as instrument of labor."[55]

Cornejo's notion of property goes considerably beyond that of classical liberalism, getting close to the idea of the social responsibility of property, already embraced by Arequipa's radical liberals nearly ten years earlier.[56] By espousing an evolutionary scheme of the property concept based on contemporary European notions of social evolution since feudalism, Cornejo could effectively criticize the *serrano* hacienda as an institution still enshrining *seigneurie*. There is little doubt that his views were shared, in theory, by the more enlightened members of southern Peru's elite. They could embrace the notion that the estate was an enterprise like any other modern capitalist firm rather than a source of rent and that the relation with the Indian *colono* was based on free contract. But on a practical level this could not change the conduct of affairs on their own estates, because in their view they had always approached estate operations in this manner.[57] The *gamonal,* the exploitative rural boss of the Peruvian Andes, was always somebody else.

For many traditional hacendados, however, the positivists' subversion of the seigneurial aspects of their estate ownership and their paternalistic, personal, almost "natural" authority over their colonos was a real threat. Some called upon Catholicism to supply the hierarchical order that could put the endangered preideological, traditional order on a new footing. They were aided by a Catholic clergy on which the social theory of Rerum Novarum (1890) had as yet little impact. In a fascinating pamphlet that expresses this new Catholic conservatism, José Angelino Lizares Quiñones, an infamous *gamonal* and deputy from Azángaro (department of Puno), lashed out against the "despotic unitarians of the capital," the "directing magnates of centralism," and proposed a slapdash federal constitution for Peru that eclectically incorporated many elements of the Tahuantinsuyo (the Inca empire). For him it was absolutely essential that religion permeate every facet of society. He wanted provosts to teach Indians in each and every hamlet ("casi en todas las aldeas hay capillas") and insisted on the overriding importance of religion for every soldier:

We know very well that the great progress of the century in the most civilized centers tends toward atheism which has provoked the ire of heaven; . . . such ideas . . . among us, who are still believers, have produced the horror of witnessing murder and suicide among the officers. . . . The Peruvian soldier used to have "Dios y la Patria" as his motto; he had his religious and military exercises; now they have taken from him the former . . . and with them the fear of his superiors.[58]

Insubordination, Indian rebellions, and even the weakness of Peru's national defense were for Lizares all consequences of the irreligiosity of the times. The dilemma for many of the more traditionalist members of southern Peru's elite was to develop an effective new formulation of hierarchical authority. For men like Lizares Quiñones this became crucial, once they believed that their traditional, largely preideological authority over *colonos* and peasants had been undermined by the extension of centralized state power and the growing ideological ferment and unruliness in their provinces. They were between the devil and the deep blue sea. Increasingly vilified as exploitative feudal latifundists, they were loath to grant the measure of authority to the central government that they deemed necessary for social order, as long as they perceived that they could not control it. Even such a relatively enlightened positivist like Hildebrando Fuentes was aware of this conflict and was convinced of the necessity of maintaining the pervasive traditional social authoritarianism in the southern sierra. Measures by the central government to achieve respect for the Indians' "freedom of action," so that they could not be "forced to work," were merely "beautiful theories," lacking knowledge of local conditions. In undermining the authoritarian means of labor recruitment, such measures "decreed the ruin of agriculture, of industry and of the progress of the department."[59]

The economic and social ideas of southern Peru's elite during the early decades of this century lacked internal consistency and were a patchwork of concepts derived from economic liberalism, ultramontane Catholicism, Incaic notions of a just and moral order, and mere affirmation of the traditional paternalistic order. Many hacendados, merchants, and traders felt profoundly ambivalent toward the idea of material progress. Attracted by the multifaceted lures of improving income, infrastructure, and "civilization" in the region, at the same time they were frightened by the perceived threat of loss of control and the specter of godless social anarchy. In a first optimistic moment their formulations stressed the future affluence of the region without giving much thought to social order. In a second moment, beginning no later than 1913–14, the mood turned more somber, even pessimistic, and now the demands for measures of social control became more urgent and authoritarianism more ideologized.

But throughout the life of the Aristocratic Republic, landholders and merchants in the south remained distrustful of the central government. They expected more from it, slowly extending the scope of what they considered legitimate state intervention in the economy and society. However, this was not an organic vision of a bourgeois national government with a legitimate mission to impose universalistic laws and social relations and an integrated national market in every corner of the republic. Rather, the right to define the agenda, to decide how the government was to intervene, was thought to rest with the "civilized" strata in each town, province, or department, who, by dint of their property, instruction, or even their birth into positions of authority, were the only ones capable of exercising power in the best interest of their local or regional society. For the southern elite, this meant most of all the right to protection against stronger competitors from other parts of the republic, the right to exchange regional goods freely in foreign markets, the right to receive infrastructure investments from Lima, and the right to protection of property against social disorder.

1920–31: ECONOMIC CRISES AND A RETROGRADE RECOVERY OF INTEREST COHESION

The economy of southern Peru underwent two serious crises and intermittent instability during a period of no more than twelve years that threatened to tear asunder the relative cohesion of the various sectors of the regional elite. The crises were essentially induced from abroad through enormous fluctuations in demand for the region's major export commodity, wool. As a consequence of the postwar readjustments in Europe, prices for Peruvian wools fell by more than 50 percent in England (and up to 80 percent in Arequipa) between their peak in 1918 and their nadir in 1921. In late 1920 and 1921, wool purchases by the Arequipa merchants nearly came to a standstill. The repercussions were felt deeply throughout the region. Encroachments of estates on peasant lands came to a halt. Unable to repay their debts, quite a few livestock hacendados were forced to sell their land to Arequipa merchants. The years of recuperating wool prices between 1923 and 1929 saw attempts both by export merchants and by foreign capitalists to form huge modern wool-producing enterprises and sales cartels that briefly threatened to shatter the tenuous coalition of merchants and landholders. Hurt by the completion of the rail line La Paz–Arica in 1914, the British-owned railroad company, the Peruvian Corporation, sought to offset the loss of its revenues by two means: First, the company increased transport tariffs by 41 percent to 274 percent between 1919 and 1923. This produced a xenophobic outcry among all sectors of southern Peruvian society, orchestrated by Arequipa's Chamber of Commerce, which demanded the nationalization of the company. Secondly, the Peruvian Corporation sought to increase southern Peru's agricultural production for export. Allied with and in part instigated by the British manager of the state-financed experimental sheep ranch in Puno, the Peruvian Corporation in 1923 sought to attract a large foreign sheep-breeding company, the Compañía Río Negro of Argentina, with the aim of buying up huge tracts of pasture land. When the Río Negro Company, in spite of guarantees by President Leguía, became aware that this project would involve serious conflicts with the Altiplano's communal peasantry over land rights and the implantation of wage labor, it withdrew, and the plan came to naught. In 1929, when a shadowy foreign company (possibly from the United States) applied to the Peruvian government for the right to hold a monopoly on alpaca wool purchases, certain sectors of southern Peru's elite again mounted a nationalistic campaign to block this project, claiming to speak for peasants, merchants, and estate owners alike, "in defense of the Peruvian sierra, bulwark of nationality." The project was abandoned after the fall of Leguía in early 1930.

In part as a reaction to these developments, but also because of the growing indebtedness of many hacendados, the largest export house, Enrique W. Gibson y Compañia combined with various hacendados from Puno in 1926 to form a very large ranching corporation, the Sociedad Ganadera del Sur. While these hacendados were hoping to see their estates thoroughly modernized through the infusion of merchant capital, the Gibsons primarily saw the company as a means to increase their share of the wool market. The Gibsons' failure to invest in the modernization of the estates led to a legal battle and the ultimate withdrawal of the hacendados from the company, leaving the Sociedad Ganadera del Sur totally in the possession of the merchant house by 1933. Other merchants and hacendados also incorporated estates as shareholding companies, albeit on a smaller scale, and at least some of them attempted to introduce a more capital-intensive type of ranching, with investments into fencing, improved breeds and pastures, and so on.

But for most hacendados this was not an option, since they lacked capital and perceived their own social position as inextricably intertwined with the control over traditional service tenants, who, in turn, resisted attempts at any transformation toward a wage labor regime. By the end of the decade there had evolved a three-cornered stalemate between a minority of modernizing haciendas, a majority of estates that were becoming increasingly archaic and were unable to resist the advance of the "internal peasant economy," and a communal peasantry whose land base now stabilized but who suffered the effects of demographic growth on their shrunken domain. This precarious balance was to hold until the Agrarian Reform of 1969.

The world depression hit southern Peru's wool exports hard, as prices and total sales in 1931 plummeted to the lowest level since the early 1850s. Prices did not recover to the level of the mid–1920s until the end of the decade. Unemployment was recognized as a serious problem in southern Peru for the first time between late 1930 and 1933, as impoverished and unemployed people from throughout the region swelled the cities. Peasants from the interior, released Peruvian nitrate workers from northern Chile, and Peruvians who had worked in the *yungas* of La Paz and now fled conscription into the Bolivian army after the outbreak of the Chaco War all hoped to find shelter and food in the cities.

After the slump of 1920–21 the number of wool exporters had grown significantly, as some large hacendados entered the business in response to the ruthless pricing policies of the Arequipa merchant houses during the early 1920s. But after 1929 this trend was reversed: several merchants failed or withdrew from the export business (bringing down with them numerous retailers and small wool bulkers), and during the 1930s the control over wool exports underwent a process of concentration among a new group of merchants. While in the central highlands during the 1940s and later the larger share of wools were sold to the Lima textile factories, in the south they continued to be destined predominantly for exports. Upwards of 80 percent of the alpaca wool clip and 50 percent of the sheep wool clip from the south were exported between 1939 and 1941. Even during the period of stagnation, then, the southern regional economy remained tied to the export funnel through Arequipa.[60]

It is more difficult to draw a clear picture of other aspects of the regional economy during the 1920s. Evidence suggests a limited decoupling of export cycles and regional markets after the slump of the early 1920s. Probably the most important stimulus for this change came from accelerated demographic growth and, in particular, the increase of urban populations. Arequipa's growth rose from 1.24 percent annually between 1876 and 1917 to 3.9 percent annually between 1917 and 1940. Urban agglomerations in the south were more considerable during this period than on the north coast with its more advanced productive structure.[61] This created favorable conditions for the regional producers of foodstuffs, while imports of agricultural implements seem to have grown in spite of the instability of the wool market. For some of the merchant houses, especially those in Arequipa, supplying the regional market increased in importance vis-à-vis their wool export business.[62] It is much less clear, however, whether there existed propitious conditions for the expansion of processing industries in the south during the 1920s.

The following development seems plausible: In Cuzco, industries such as textiles and beer brewing and some of the artisanal trades seem to have weathered the slump of 1920–21 relatively well.[63] Some factories in fields like textiles, beverages, shoes, leather, and clothing were still opened during the 1920s in both Cuzco and Arequipa. But according to one source for Arequipa the founding of new industrial companies fell below that of 1915–19.[64] Between 1921 and 1926 competitive pressures on southern Peru's cotton mills, but possibly also on its woolen mills, lessened as the foreign corporations operating the largest and most capitalized mills in Lima (Grace and Duncan Fox) decreased their national production in order to take advantage of the favorable export conjuncture, especially for raw cotton. But this changed drastically after 1926, when protective tariffs were imposed on cotton textiles and the government ceased to intervene in the money market, allowing the sol to depreciate. In the following years the Lima factories increased their output and tried to strengthen their market share in the south. Arequipa's largest textile factory, La Industrial de Huaico, succumbed in the price war in 1929 when, after the bankruptcy of its owners, the Forga family, it was sold to Duncan Fox. The strongest cotton mill in Cuzco, El Huáscar, was stunted in its growth.[65] It is not clear whether in the late 1920s Limeño companies in other industrial sectors began to displace their southern competitors. But in the case of the cotton factories we can say that it was the environment of national protection and not a free trade regime that favored the centralization of industrial production in Lima by the 1920s and that disrupted industrial growth in the south. The defeat of Arequipa's El Industrial de Huaico at the hands of larger and more productive mills such as Vitarte and El Inca (Grace) and Progreso and La Unión (Duncan Fox) constitutes an early example of "transnational corporations" displacing national competitors under the utilization of protective barriers. It had been the foreign companies who had pushed for higher import duties on cotton textiles.[66]

Squeezed in the middle were the regional import and export merchants. As Lima's industrialists pushed into southern Peru's markets, the merchants became their agents in order to maintain their share of the regional market. But, although the Arequipa merchants had originally scrambled to represent Lima factories, during the 1920s their relationship again and again turned conflictive. Grace and Duncan Fox employed varying strategies to expand their marketing shares in the south: competitive sales to numerous wholesalers, exclusive agencies for certain areas, and fierce price competition. While the Lima factories temporarily granted favorable conditions to the southern wholesalers, in the long run they imposed much tighter control on their marketing and credit arrangements than had ever been done by the distant overseas manufacturing partners of the merchants. The factories from the capital also left the Arequipeños with narrower profit margins, especially during the difficult trading climate of the late 1920s. The southern wholesalers lived under the constant fear that exclusive agencies of the Limeño factories would sell directly to retailers, ultimately causing the wholesalers to lose control over their regional market.

By the late 1920s it was obvious that the Limeño textile factories had become a strong, permanent element in southern Peru's markets, a fact that the merchants could ill afford to ignore. But it was just as obvious that the more lucrative business, guaranteeing them a greater degree of autonomy, consisted of their old lines of imports from Europe. And even here they faced new competition: several new import houses representing U.S. machinery and consumer goods manufactures (especially automobiles), to whom the older immigrant merchant houses had no access, established themselves in the city. It was probably these new importers, such as the Arequipa Agencies, who profited from the growing share of machinery and vehicles among the total imports through Mollendo.[67]

At the end of the period under consideration, then, the autonomy of southern Peru's regional market showed major fissures. Those that had benefited most from it during the Aristocratic Republic, the exporters and wholesalers and the large landholders, faced powerful competition from several sectors. Foreign industrialists were building a national market; foreign capital attempted to transform the agrarian structure of the region; and, lastly, a new group of import interests arose. But before trucks plied the coastal highway linking Arequipa (and thus the rest of the south) with Lima in the 1940s, autonomy had not completely disappeared. During the severe crisis of the early 1930s the regional elites that had come into their own during the Aristocratic Republic responded to these challenges in a retrograde manner: they defended the old patterns of regional interchange and production against the new competitors. Merchants clung to the measure of control left to them over the import and export trades and continued to distribute regional and national products in the south. After the turbulent 1920s they mostly had to retrench from their hopes of transforming the relations of production in the countryside by themselves, and they reasserted their assymetrical relations to hacendados, peasants, and the myriad of retailers and itinerant traders. While a few progressive hacendados with enough capital began to modernize their estates, most of their confreres contented themselves with stagnating incomes, authority—only slightly tempered—over their service tenantry, and the prestige they inherited as a birthright in their province. From the 1920s onward a growing number of their sons and daughters sought to achieve middle-class positions in the cities.

Jolted by the severe crises of the regional economy and widespread Indian uprisings and influenced by a bewildering array of new political, social, and economic currents from Bolshevism to fascism, southern Peru's elites underwent a process of ideological definition and differentiation during the 1920s. This process, still insufficiently understood, can only be outlined in broad terms here. State intervention played a growing role in the socioeconomic thought of most regional elite sectors, but the specifics of desirable state action proved divisive. Since the increasingly centralist Leguía regime failed to satisfy most demands of southern elites, and after 1923 tended to neglect the region's interests altogether, such divisions never led to a complete rupture between traditional hacendados, mercantile interests, and incipient industrialists. Aided by the inactivity of the central government, southern elite groups could plaster over their divergent ideologies by rallying around the defense of common regional interests. The cleavage between ideal theoretical positions and successful policy initiatives with significant social backing widened. Broadly speaking, one can discern five ideological groups among southern Peru's elites in this period:

1. Intransigent authoritarian traditionalists, who only expected increased state repression of Indian uprisings and infrastructure investments in their region. During the severe crisis of the early 1920s, this was a position held by the great majority of hacendados in Cuzco and Puno and seconded by some of their commercial partners in Arequipa.[67] But during the following decade this position lost strength, as hacendados espoused more encompassing and less traditional authoritarian positions and others paid at least lip service to the need for reforms.

2. New conservative reformists, who envisioned a much expanded, authoritarian role of the state in such fields as education, population and "family policy" (a new import from Europe designed to "optimize" the population "quantitatively and qualitatively"), the "militarization" of society, and a paternalistic social policy through which the state guaranteed that every family was provided with essentials. There was relatively little concern among proponents of these ideas about direct state intervention in key sectors of the economy beyond vigorous population and infrastructure policies. While granting the need for protection of Indian communities, they were cool to the mounting calls for an agrarian reform directed against the "inefficient, feudal latifundia" and continued to believe that economic growth and progress would come as an automatic consequence of population growth and an adequate transportation system.[69] Such ideas were increasingly expressed during the 1920s by less wealthy hacendados in Puno and Cuzco, as well as among the older generation of professionals and bureaucrats in those departments. In their quest for an austere, moralizing state and a precarious balance between authoritarianism and a free civil society, they echoed Incaic principles of social order but also seemed to incorporate certain elements of European fascist thought.

3. Proponents of Catholic social thought. This position slowly gained adherents after the foundation of the Catholic University in Lima in 1917 and encountered some of its eminent spokesmen among Arequipa's elite intellectuals, notably Víctor Andrés Belaúnde. In 1930, in his response to José Carlos Mariátegui's "Seven Interpretive Essays on Peruvian Reality," Belaúnde called for protection of the Indian communities and their property, expropriation of the unproductive latifundia, a whole range of further economic and social legislation protecting small rural and urban producers and workers, and, "as culmination and capstone of this whole system, substitution of the pseudo-democratic-liberal parliament with a representative body of all living organisms [of society], in which the laboring masses would have a large majority."[70] Belaúnde hastened to add that this was a long-term program that could only be realized gradually. Indeed, during the debates of the Constituent Congress of 1931, he opposed the outright socialization of haciendas and the reorganization of Indian communities as cooperatives demanded by Socialists and radical *indigenistas*. Rather, he merely called for state authority to expropriate specific backward estates with compen-

sation, if and only if it had been determined that particular Indian communities held insufficient land for its members' livelihood.[71] Belaúnde's Catholic reformism remained weak politically for lack of a firm constituency. Among southern elites it shaded imperceptibly into more conservative Catholic positions, such as that of Benjamín Chirinos Pacheco. Railing both against "Yanqui imperialism" and the threat of "Bolshevik dictatorship" in Latin America, he embraced the Catholic church as "the spiritual home of man." As late as 1929 Chirinos still proclaimed the sanctity of private property and viewed "the current political evolution" as "directed by democracy and liberalism." Protective legislation for workers or Indians had no place in this type of spiritual Catholicism, and for him the "Industrial Protector State" was synonymous with bolshevism.[72]

4. The Decentralists. By the late 1920s, southern Peru's old regionalist sentiments became converted into a cohesive political stance, culminating with the founding of the Decentralist party in Arequipa in January 1931 during the tumultuous crisis after the overthrow of Leguía. The southern Decentralists were reacting to Leguía's centralism in administrative and fiscal matters, but many of the movement's leading spokesmen, especially Puneños like Emilio Romero and Cuzqueños like Felix Cosío, had been influenced by Andeanist and indigenist thought during the preceding decade. The Decentralists' social base was fairly broad and diffuse: sons of *serrano* hacendados, shopkeepers, small industrialists, professionals, and intellectuals, but also middling wool merchants and even one of Arequipa's wealthiest landholders, Guillermo Lira, owner of the modern sugar estate Pampa Blanca. This social base, more middle class than elite, tends to account for the quite advanced positions of the Decentralists. They emphasized the need for political reorganization, with newly defined regional entities that would hold considerable power in fiscal and educational matters, with autonomous municipalities, and with strong regional influence on national legislation. In economic and social matters they called for a moratorium on payments of the foreign debt, nationalization of subsoil rights, and, most importantly, protective legislation for Indian communities, expropriation of latifundia without compensation, and a minimum wage for hacienda *colonos*.[73]

5. The heirs to the region's earlier elite-oriented liberalism were to be found primarily among Arequipa's wholesale merchants and allied professionals. By 1930 they espoused a constitutional order based upon liberal parliamentarism with a modest strengthening of regional jurisdictions that would prevent the type of authoritarian centralism exemplified by Leguía's regime. They favored parsimony in national expenditures and reductions of property taxes and duties on foreign trade. But reformist liberals, notably the influential cousins José Luis Bustamante y Rivero and Manuel José Bustamante de la Fuente, also admitted the social responsibility of property. A better economic situation for Indian peasants and service tenants on *serrano* estates and improved productivity of these estates in their view constituted preconditions for the expansion of the market economy.[74]

Through the 1920s, therefore, ideological cleavages between various sectors of the southern elite had deepened on some key issues. This division primarily focused on the questions of Indian communities and *serrano* estates, where opinions now ranged from a laissez-faire regime of individual property to calls for the inalienability of community lands and expropriations of inefficient estates without compensation. Important divisions had also surfaced about the basic nature of the state by this time, as proponents of a liberal parliamentary regime were increasingly challenged by corporatists and adherents of authoritarian notions of a "protector state." At the same time, however, the whole political spectrum of the southern elites found a few key issues around which they could reconstruct a united political front when their region was facing both increasing economic penetration by national and foreign entrepreneurs and the depression of the early 1930s. These were a staunch opposition to administrative and fiscal centralism, a tempered version of economic nationalism, and a renewed emphasis on an open export economy.

At the height of the depression and less than a year after the south as a region had shaped Peruvian national politics probably for the last time (first by supporting Sánchez Cerro's barracks revolt against Leguía and then by forcing the former's resignation through the decentralist movement), the new accommodation received its formal baptism at the Conferencia Económica del Sur, which met in Arequipa in February 1932 under the auspices of that city's Chamber of Commerce. The conference brought together delegates from all departments in the south, representing all major interest groups of the region (agriculture and ranching, industry, commerce, and mining). If one may believe the mood of success expressed in the congratulatory telegrams sent to the conference's president afterwards, the event was marked by a high degree of solidarity in spite of the clearly divergent proposals submitted by individual delegates.

The resolutions adopted by the delegates are an impressive testimony to the basic continuity of economic policies on which southern Peru's business elites could agree.[75] They demanded the extension of state and private banking facilities (in the wake of the collapse of the Banco del Perú y Londres). They rejected the recently passed banking laws, based on the Kemmerer commission report, for being deflationary and too restrictive in credit operations and for punishing the producer while favoring the "capitalist" with liquid funds. The resolutions on agriculture underlined the importance of rural credit, excluded any discussion of agrarian reform (or the return of hacienda lands to peasant communities), but did concede a need for state intervention to limit lease fees in Arequipa's *campiña*. In what was probably the conference's major departure from economic positions of the southern elite in the past, it approved a motion granting the state the right to expropriate private property. But this remained abstract, without any suggestion as to where or how it was to be applied. (Rather than in the section on agriculture, it appeared at the end of the report under "miscellaneous motions approved.") The delegates demanded the rapid completion of various road-building projects, all obviously important for intraregional commerce and communication. Although a commission on industry was established at the conference and entertained a few proposals, no corresponding resolutions were passed.

Economic nationalism was evident in many of the resolutions. The conference called for a reduction of the transport rates of the Peruvian Corporation (seen as a measure to avoid the drain of profits out of the country) and for the imposition of taxes on capital expatriation and, perhaps most tellingly, it voiced strong resentment against U.S. financial and commercial penetration. This resulted in a resolution suggesting that southern merchants and businessmen should buy from those foreign nations who bought from them, a clear pitch for strengthening the commercial ties with old trading partners in England and continental Europe. Resolutions calling for protection against imports were conspicuous for their absence. Rather the conference called for the abolition of export duties, the reduction of import duties on wage goods (an indicaton that the swelling urban population had exceeded Arequipa's capacity to feed itself), and the reduction of taxes on urban and rural properties.

In short, the conference passed a carefully balanced program that broadened the rights of the state so as not to interfere with the interests of any of the south's major elite groups. Even though some of the new themes, such as the recognition of limits on property rights and a mild economic nationalism, portended a significant shift in economic thinking, they were either of limited concrete importance or fitted nicely with the current interests of the southern elites, as seen in their critique of the Peruvian Corporation and of U.S. financial and commercial interests. But what is most striking about the resolutions is the continued desire to strengthen intraregional economic exchanges, a basic free trade orientation, and the high priority given to increasing government infrastructure investments (especially transport and banking).

The conference expressed the shared desire of all major elite groups in the south to improve the functioning of the regional economy along its old lines of integration, a *continuismo* with the minimal adjustments deemed necessary to overcome the present crisis. As the writer of the prologue to the official report on the conference wrote, "within a noble nationalism [the south] has reaffirmed its personality as a region."[76] Whatever their ideologies, the peculiar defensive position in which the southern elites found themselves after the onset of the depression allowed no single group to impose its designs on the others without endangering the renewed, if retrograde, accommodation.

CONCLUSION

Let us briefly summarize some of the main propositions of this essay. During the Aristocratic Republic there existed no basic contradiction between southern Peru's export orientation and the development of the regional market. The stimulus of export earnings had ripple effects throughout most areas in the region and most economic sectors, including manufacturing. This notwithstanding, the export orientation exacerbated geographic and social income inequalities within the region.[77] Despite the open-economy orientation, the major competition for southern Peru's economy was not foreign imports. On the contrary, national producers—first sugar and alcohol producers in the early years of the Aristocratic Republic and then, during the Oncenio, textiles—threatened the southern economy. A consequence of the greater capital accumulation and higher productivity in certain sectors of the coastal economy, this competition became a serious threat for southern producers and merchants when transport costs were reduced beyond a certain threshold and/or protective tariffs were imposed.

This was the reason why southern Peruvian elites maintained an ''instinctive'' free trade orientation. Nevertheless, southerners pragmatically rejected free trade in favor of protection, usually against other national producers, whenever it was convenient. But in the end it was a protective environment, not the earlier, more free-trade-oriented environment, that by the late 1920s began to favor the most efficient industries. These were located largely in Lima. The protectionism that helped them seriously hampered southern regional industrial growth.

Before 1919 the southern elites combined their liberal outlook on trade and their noninterventionist views on matters of property and taxation with an authoritarian position on most social issues. However, this was no coherent authoritarianism, and on specific issues different elite groups and different individuals held widely diverging views, derived from contrasting ideologies or fragments thereof. Positivism was viewed by many of the more traditionalist hacendados as a dangerous, subversive force that threatened the natural order of things.

But in spite of widely varying ideological positions, southern elites shared a nearly automatic distrust of the central government, a distrust that was perhaps the expression of a whole range of cultural, economic, and political interests and of regional identities. It thus seems meaningless, at least for southern Peru, to speak of a class alliance between the national oligarchy and the *serrano gamonales*, or regional oligarchies. This is not to say that the southern elites did not expect a growing range of services or investments from the central government. But these were expected on the basis of particularistic deals, involving complex negotiations in Congress that have as yet to be studied. Never did this type of personal alliance between a southern politician and a congressional leader or, more typically, a government minister imply any concession of legitimate authority to the central government over the provinces.

During the 1920s the southern regional economy lost its dynamism, as wool exports began to stagnate and the markets became unstable. In this difficult environment several new economic interest groups attempted to expand their market shares in the south or to transform the region's relations of production. This weakened the cohesion between the economically vulnerable older elite groups. The high degree of regional economic autonomy that had characterized the era of prosperity was seriously compromised, never to return. By the early 1930s, however, there was a reaccommodation between regional elite groups, who sought to continue the established import and export trades and regional interchange.

The peculiar constellation of southern Peru's regional economy during the early twentieth century can be expressed, as Baltasar Caravedo has observed, as the paradox between a "backward" agrarian structure and a relatively well developed regional market.[78] But this paradox dissolves when one considers the social forces that lay behind it: during the early twentieth century the fundamental cleavage of the south consisted of a strong, independent Indian peasantry and a more powerful "seigneurial" hacendado sector. In spite of (or perhaps because of) the differences in income, power, and prestige and their antagonistic clashes over the distribution of resources, both groups were part and parcel of an integrated society (and probably had more in common than anybody would care to admit) in which property—and possibly income—were distributed more evenly than in most regions of Peru. This, on top of old patterns of social adjustment to a diverse environment, was the basis for relatively intense regional interchanges. The Arequipa merchant, whatever his power vis-à-vis these other groups, had to "construct" his market accordingly. It was essentially a stalemated economy in which each of the dyadic elements, peasants and hacendados, knew that they could not totally dislodge the other or bring about a complete transformation of economy and society in their favor. *For this very reason* they were willing to employ whatever extraeconomic pressure was at their disposal to increase their share of the pie. But it is also this stalemated economy, this tug-of-war without conclusive victors, that, although allowing spurts of growth, placed narrow limits on the expansion of the internal market, as it made any structural transformation toward more intensive forms of agriculture (either under the control of the peasantry or of large landholders) incredibly difficult.

NOTES

I would like to thank John Coatsworth, Magnus Mörner, Vincent Peloso, and members of the University of Illinois Social History Group for thoughtful and very helpful comments on earlier drafts of this paper.

1. Portocarrero, *Ideologías*, p. 2.

2. Thorp and Bertram, *Peru*, pp. 32–37, 129–130, 378, n. 42. A student of Thorp has recently demonstrated that as early as 1923 effective protection again reached the levels prevailing before 1900; see Boloña, "Tariff Policies," ch. 2.

3. The words are Rosemary Thorp's, underscoring the basic continuity of Latin American economic policies before 1930; see Thorp, "Latin America," pp. 74–81; see also Joseph Love's essay in this volume for an explanation of this continuity.

4. For a brief overview of the debate see Cotler, *Clases*, pp. 135–137; see also Revilla, "Industrialización temprana," 19–28.

5. Rey de Castro, *Antagonismos económicos*, pp. 113f. and passim. Six years earlier, Francisco García Calderón (born in 1883) came to much the same conclusion. He warned that protectionism as the "recent tendency of our economic policy" did not "harmonize

with the facts" in Peru, while at the same time renouncing an "abstract policy" of "absolute free trade." See García Calderón, *Le Pérou*, pp. 267–68.

6. Cotler, *Clases*, p. 236.

7. García Calderón, *Pérou*, pp. 244–49, 268.

8. Basadre, *Historia de la República*, 11:178.

9. García Calderón, *Pérou*, p. 269.

10. See Cotler, *Clases*, ch. 3; Madalengoitia, "El estado oligárquico," pp. 285–89; Burga and Flores Galindo, *Apogeo y crisis*, pp. 88–94; Caravedo Molinari, "Economía" 8:203–5; Yepes del Castillo, "Los inicios" 7:305–10; Gorman, "The State"; and López J., "El estado."

11. Miller, "The Coastal Elite."

12. Indeed, the regions are at the very core of the political economy of Peru throughout the nineteenth and early twentieth centuries, because any transition toward capitalism or, put differently, toward the constitution of a domestic market necessarily required profound shifts in the configuration of regional market circuits and the type of power sharing between national and regional elites. See Colmenares, "La nación y la historia regional."

13. Miller, "The Coastal Elite," p. 116; and Ismael R. Echegaray C., *La Cámara de Diputados y las Constituyentes del Perú, 1822–1965* ([Lima]: Ministerio de Hacienda y Comercio, [1965]), pp. 669–79.

14. For an overview of southern Peru's export complex, see Orlove, *Alpacas*; Appleby, "Exportation," ch. 2; Burga and Reátegui, *Lanas y capital mercantil*, passim; and Jacobsen, "Landtenure and Society," ch. 4.

15. Glave, "Trajines."

16. Ministerio de Hacienda y Comercio. *Memoria de Hacienda y Comercio presentado al Congreso Constitucional de 1890 por el Ministro del ramo [Eulogio Delgado]* (Lima: Impr. de "El Nacional", 1890), pp. 44–45; and Bonilla, comp., *Gran Bretaña y el Perú* 4:19. For an analysis stressing the continued importance of cross-national trade, see Langer, "Espacios coloniales."

17. The ratio of per capita exports of the south relative to the nation as a whole amounted to .505 in 1910 and only .139 in 1935. The mean for the period was .252. That is to say, proportional to its population southern Peru only exported, on the average, one-fourth of what Peru as a whole exported. Data derived from Bertram, "Modernización y cambio," p. 18, table 2. Only part of this smaller per capita export value was due to smaller per capita incomes. In 1961 the mean per capita income for Apurímac, Arequipa, Cuzco, and Puno was 74.3 percent of the national per capita income. See Romero and Levano, *Regionalismo*, p. 42.

18. For a late jeremiad of Arequipa's presumed agricultural *and* commercial decline, see Polar, *Arequipa*, pp. 288–93, 300–302. For a midcentury lament, see Paz-Soldán, *Geografía*, p. 464.

19. Belaúnde, *Arequipa*, pp. 33–45; Polar, *Arequipa*, pp. 288–93, 300–302; and Flores Galindo, *Arequipa y el sur andino*, pp. 106–9.

20. Flores Galindo, Plaza, and Oré, "Oligarquía y capital comercial," pp. 65–66; and Villena, "Sociedad Arequipeña," p. 90.

21. Burga and Reátegui, *Lanas y capital mercantil*, pp. 74–110, 131–32, 150; Flores Galindo, Plaza, and Oré, "Oligarquía y capital comercial," p. 62; and Bertram, "Modernización," pp. 3–22.

22. Of 88 newly incorporated companies registered in Arequipa between 1870 and 1929 only 16, roughly one-sixth, were manufacturing concerns, and 12 of these were

founded since 1915. See Burga and Flores Galindo, *Apogeo y crisis*, pp. 36–37; Flores Galindo, Plaza, and Oré, "Oligarquía y capital comercial," pp. 65–66; and Burga and Reátegui, *Lanas y capital mercantil*, pp. 131–43.

23. See Jacobsen, "Wool Export Economy."

24. Appleby, "Exportation and Its Aftermath," ch. 2; and Burga and Reátegui, *Lanas y capital mercantil*, pp. 80–81, 106–10.

25. Jacobsen, "Cycles and Booms."

26. Mörner, *Notas sobre el comercio*, p. 27; Tamayo Herrera, *Historia social*, p. 84; and Fuentes, *Cuzco*, p. 119.

27. Hildebrando Fuentes, the department's perfect, reported that in 1905 the department's imports exceeded its exports and that nevertheless the trade deficit was paid in specie, something that he could not explain; see Fuentes, *Cuzco*, p. 119; and Tamayo Herrera, *Historia social*, pp. 84–85.

28. Fuentes, *Cuzco*, p. 121; and Valcárcel, *Memorias*, p. 35.

29. Burga and Reátegui, *Lanas y capital mercantil*, p. 37; and Dunn, *Peru*, p. 24.

30. Hobsbawm, "La Convencion."

31. Deustua and Rénique, *Intelectuales*, pp. 61–66; and Mörner, *Notas sobre el comercio*, p. 17.

32. Tamayo Herrera, *Historia social*, pp. 87–94, 100–101; and Baca Tupayachi, *Cusco*, pp. 6–10.

33. Fuentes, *Cuzco*, pp. 34–35, 119–120; Flores Galindo, *Arequipa y el sur andino*, pp. 111–12; Wright, *The Old and the New Peru*, p. 448; and Tamayo Herrera, *Historia social*, pp. 107–110.

34. Tamayo Herrera, in *Historia Social*, pp. 107–110, claims that by about 1920 Cuzco had "a small but vigorous industrial bourgeoisie." This assertion neglects the fact that the city's industrialists were first of all merchants and hacendados.

35. Concerning the decline of Cuzco's textile industry since about 1940, see Lovón Zavala, *Investigación*, p. 7. In the late eighteenth century Cuzco's textile industry had begun its long phase of decline as a consequence of growing contraband of European cloth and the Ordinance of Free Trade.

36. Valcárcel, *Memorias*, pp. 83 ff; and Mörner, *Notas sobre el comercio*, pp. 18–24. Mörner, "The extent and limitation," pp. 12–13 stresses the dominance and autonomy of Cuzco's large landholders.

37. Basadre, *Historia de la República*, 11:178–83.

38. Peru, Tercer Congreso Extraordinario de 1903, *Diario de los debates de la H. Camara de Senadores* (Lima: "El Comercio," 1904), pp. 64 ff. and 303 ff. [sessions of 6, 8, and 23 Feb. 1904].

39. Ibid. The laws that were finally passed by Congress (16 March 1904, alcohol; March 26, 1904, sugar) contained a moderately lesser rate for *serrano* producers, as planned in Leguía's original bill on alcohol and as a concession in the parliamentary negotiations in the case of sugar. See Basadre, *Historia de la República* 11:178–183.

40. Peru, Legislatura Extraordinaria de 1915, *Diario de los Debates de la H. Camara de Diputados* (Lima: "La Prensa," 1915), pp. 87 ff. [session of Nov. 5, 1915].

41. *Memoria del Sr. Prefecto de Puno [Fernando Elías], 1898* (Lima: "El País", 1898), p. 30.

42. Villena, "Sociedad," p. 105. Arequipa's liberals also warned that industrialization should not lead to monopolies and privileges prejudicial to the interests of the working class, an idea similar to and possibly derived from the rejection of protectionism by

European labor movements; see ibid., p. 104. For the German Social Democratic Party's rejection of protectionism prior to 1914, see Gerschenkron, *Bread and Democracy*, pp. 33–36. A fascinating glimpse into Arequipa's society during the early twentieth century and the work of the Partido Liberal in particular is contained in Peralta Vásquez, *Faz oculta*. Peralta was one of the earliest Aprista organizers in the city during the 1920s.

43. As quoted by Deustua and Rénique, *Intelectuales*, p. 65.

44. Fuentes, *Cuzco*, p. 119–121; for Arequipa see Polar, *Arequipa*, p. 302.

45. Valcárcel, "Cuestión agraria, " pp. 36–37.

46. Peru, Segundo Congreso Extraordinario de 1915, *Diario de los Debates de la H. Camara de Senadores* (Lima: "El Comercio', 1915), p. 45 [session of 15 Dec. 1915].

47. Tamayo Herrera, *Historia social*, pp. 100–101; and Deustua and Rénique, *Intelectuales*, pp. 57–68.

48. Entry "Luis Felipe Luna" in Juan Pedro Paz-Soldán, *Diccionario biográfico de peruanos contemporáneos* (Lima: Gil, 1917), pp. 253–54; and Lizares Quiñones, *Carta política del Sr. Coronel J. A. Lizares Quiñones*, pp. 9–12.

49. Fuentes, *Cuzco*, p. 102.

50. [Molina], *Discurso académico*, pp. 18–19 (Wenceslao Molina was heir to a large livestock estate in the Altiplano); Fuentes, *Cuzco*, pp. 238–39.

51. In Puno, major exponents of this early home-brewed critique were Frisancho, *Algunas vistas fiscales*, and Quiroga, *La evolución jurídica*. In Cuzco it was the "generation of 1909" in the university that began to formulate a thorough and intellectually broader-based critique of contemporary society and economy in the department; see Tamayo Herrera, *Historia del indigenismo cuzqueño*, pp. 174–83.

52. Fuentes, *Cuzco*, pp. 111–14.

53. Hazen, "The Awakening of Puno," pp. 36–41. The powerful Cuzqueño Benjamin de la Torre did not want Indians to be taught to read and write; see Mörner, "The Extent and Limitation," p. 15.

54. Urquiaga, *Sublevaciones de indígenas*, pp. 43–44.

55. Cornejo, *Discursos políticos*, p. 235. For a brief portrait of life and work of Cornejo, see Jorge Basadre, *Peruanos del siglo XX* (Lima: "Rikchay Perú," 1981), pp. 23–25; for similar views on property see Valcárcel, "La cuestión agraria," p. 35.

56. See Peralta Vásquez, *Arequipa*, pp. 165–66.

57. Perhaps the best example for this type of pseudo-progressive apologia is Urquiaga, *Sublevaciones*.

58. Lizares Quiñones, *Problemas*, pp. 28–29, 45, and passim; for the ultramontane position of Puno's bishop Valentín Ampuero and parish priests around 1910, see Hazen, "The Awakening of Puno," pp. 36–41.

59. Fuentes, *Cuzco*, p. 39.

60. The preceding section based on Bertram, "Modernización y cambio," passim; Burga and Reátegui, *Lanas y capital mercantil*, pp. 43–67; Jacobsen, "Landtenure and Society," ch. 7; and Bedoya, *Estadística de exportación*; and *Memoria . . . Junta Nacional*.

61. Caravedo, "Poder central," pp. 116–17.

62. Burga and Reátegui, *Lanas y capital mercantil*, p. 59.

63. Nominal wages seem to have risen faster in Cuzco's industries and artisanal trades than in the city's commercial sector between 1917 and 1921. See Roca, *Estudio económico*, pp. 110 and 126.

64. Burga and Flores Galindo report 3 new manufacturing companies in Arequipa

between 1900 and 1909, 2 for 1910–14, 5 for 1915–19, 2 for 1920–24 and 3 for 1925–29; see their *Apogeo y crisis*, pp. 36–37. In contrast, Caravedo, "Poder central," p. 117, speaks of 23 new foundations during the Oncenio. For new companies in Cuzco, see Tamayo Herrera, *Historia social*, pp. 107–10; and Roca, *Estudio económico*, pp. 66–72.

65. Burga and Reátegui, *Lanas y capital mercantil*, pp. 146–148; and Thorp and Bertram, *Peru*, p. 130.

66. Ibid. The process of industrial concentration in Lima is analyzed in López Más, "La gran industria."

67. Caravedo, "Poder central," p. 117.

68. Sociedad Ganadera, *Memorial*; and Drapognie, *La verdad*.

69. See the fascinating but forgotten work by Gamarra, *Orientación y organización*, passim; see also Lizares Quiñones' legislative record in *Carta política*.

70. Belaúnde, *Realidad*, p. 37.

71. Davies, *Indian Integration*, p. 116. For details of this debate in the Constituent Congress, see Lynch, *Pensamiento social*.

72. Chirinos Pacheco, *Imperialismo yanqui*, pp. 199–202 and passim.

73. Deustua and Rénique, *Intelectuales*, pp. 98–103; Lynch, *Pensamiento social*, pp. XXI-XXII, 79–91; Caravedo, "Poder central," pp. 119–21.

74. Ibid.; and More, *Zoocracia*, pp. 26–33.

75. For an opposing reading of the conference resolutions, see Caravedo, "Poder central," passim.

76. *Conferencia Económica del Sur*, p. 8.

77. For the specific case of Cuzco, Mörner comes to a similar conclusion; see his "The Extent and Limitation," p. 16.

78. Caravedo, "Poder central," p. 117.

7

ECONOMIC LIBERALISM: WHERE WE ARE AND WHERE WE NEED TO GO

Florencia E. Mallon

Since the 1940s and 1950s, when CEPAL structuralists first formulated their critiques of Latin American development, the importance of economic liberalism in Latin American history has become an increasingly controverted topic. Especially in the 1960s, Latin Americans and, later, foreign scholars sought to understand how and why Latin America underdeveloped economically. As they chronicled the ups and downs of export booms, showing how none brought more than fleeting prosperity, many became increasingly convinced that integration into the international market had impoverished Latin America and prevented its political and economic unification into modern nation-states. Here the role of economic liberalism in the nineteenth century, and especially of free trade policy, quickly became central.

After independence, *dependentistas* reasoned, dominant classes in Latin America were eager for the wealth they thought would flow from trade with newly capitalist northern Europe. Opening up their countries to European capital and goods, however, did not bring Latin American elites the prosperity they so ardently desired. Instead, it ruined local artisans and impoverished peasants involved in market relations, leaving only meager profits in return. By the second half of the century the continent's export orientation was firmly in place, bringing with it weak and dependent national states, huge chasms between rich and poor, and stubborn structural limitations to integrated economic growth. Here, then, was defined Latin America's modern heritage of underdevelopment, social conflict, and political strife.[1]

Dependentista perspectives were slow to permeate the historical literature on Latin America, particularly the work produced in the United States. Historians working on the nineteenth century, moreover, were among the slowest to incorporate the newer wisdoms. Through the mid–1970s some continued to accept, in a relatively uncritical fashion, the version of history presented in the writings of nineteenth-century liberal historians, who did not question the effect of liberal policy on Latin American development but were concerned instead with the struggle between ''civilization'' (liberal elites) and ''barbarism'' (conservative masses) and with the triumph of the former over the latter.[2] Some of the best work on the period dealt with other issues or took such an original perspective on the issues that dependency theory became, for all intents and purposes, irrelevant.[3] And especially among British historians, influenced by their own debates on British informal empire, a significant school developed by mid-decade that attempted to minimize the role of British capital and of international trade on Latin American development.[4]

By the second half of the 1970s, those historians of the nineteenth century who incorporated the *dependentista* perspective did so with a vengeance. Through the early 1980s, they traced a common theme across the variegated and conflictual Latin American landscape: liberal elites, eager to participate in the export of marketable commodities, in essence sold their countries out to foreign capital. There was often resistance, sometimes from more nationally minded factions of the dominant classes, usually from suffering artisans and peasants. In some places, these efforts delayed the inevitable a decade or two longer. But the end result was always, tragically, the same.[5]

An interesting wrinkle on this perspective as it developed was the occasional glorification of countries or periods in nineteenth-century history that appeared to go against the grain. By the early 1980s, there developed quite a sizable revisionist literature on Francia's Paraguay, as well as an occasional essay on Rafael Carrera's Guatemala. The message in the revisionist approach was clearly *dependentista*. The authors argued that previous historical analyses of these cases had made them out to be violent and bloodthirsty dictatorships precisely because they attempted to maintain autonomy vis-à-vis the international market and to redistribute the fruits of production more equitably.[6] The end result was a reversal of heroes and villains for nineteenth-century Latin America. Whereas for pre-*dependentista* historians, elite liberals had been the ''good guys'' and home-grown dictators, caudillos, and the masses more generally the ''bad guys,'' for the revisionist literature at its most extreme, Europeanized liberal intellectuals were the villains, while local dictators, caudillos, and the long-suffering folk became the heroes.

I use the language of heroes and villains deliberately, for as the *dependentista* historical literature developed, it defined an often conspiratorial undercurrent in its treatment of the nineteenth-century dominant classes. In its efforts to overcome the positivistic perspective of historians who catalogued the inevitable progress of liberalism and civilization, this new generation of scholars fell into a positivism of its own: inevitably, almost conspiratorially, Latin American elites were bound to sell out their continent to the world system. If that was the case, then it was less important to study the process by which free trade policy was adopted than it was simply to narrate a predictable and unchanging reality. Not surprisingly, the studies done in this period tended to be national-level and macroeconomic and to contain little information about regional diversity or intraelite differences.[7]

By the late 1970s, however, a new trend began to take shape in the historical literature. Some of the researchers trained in the dependency-oriented debates of mid-decade began returning from the field with the kind of empirically rich, regionally specific data that made untenable the new determinism implicit in the *dependentista*-influenced view of the nineteenth century. By the early 1980s, even as the most extreme versions of revisionist history continued to appear in print, a more measured school began to emphasize local diversity and internal class relations, arguing that dependence on the international market was a backdrop against which to understand the effect of local struggles on historical development.[8]

The essays in this volume demonstrate how this latest trend in the historiography can be applied to the study of economic liberalism. The pivotal question, as Gootenberg calls it, is to identify specific free trade liberal interests and to analyze, historically and empirically, how and why they became powerful. How did liberalism, in other words, become a prominent discourse in Latin America? Was it automatically imposed? What struggles preceded its hegemony? Why did liberalism take such a hegemonic role, or did it? When and how was it reversed?

Overall, then, the common purpose of the articles in this book is to expand our historical and empirical understanding of the process of economic underdevelopment. The authors uniformly accept the broad contributions of dependency theory—whether the nineteenth century was a central period or the integration of countries into the newly capitalist international market the common parameter are no longer at issue. Instead, most essays are case studies of specific instances in which liberal policies and ideals were implemented in different Latin American countries. The one exception is the Love article, which also criticizes the determinism of previous scholars by comparing the case of Latin America with that of Romania, another country economically dependent on Western Europe, in order to probe the particular ways in which liberal economic ideas were diffused, accepted, or rejected in different ''neocolonial'' regions. Moving beyond mechanical interpretations, then, contributors to the volume have made the complexity of liberal ideals, and of their implementation as policy, the centerpiece of the analysis.

As the organizer of the conference that gave rise to this book and as a historian involved in tracing the dynamic of the critiques of liberal policy in the twentieth century, Joseph Love is interested in contrasting the trajectory of liberal ideas in Latin America with those in Eastern Europe, specifically Romania. He shows in his essay that the process by which ideas were generated, debated, and accepted in the nineteenth century was very different in the two regions. While an academic tradition, participation in the Marxist-populist debate and the concomitant importance of a university-trained intelligentsia developed early in Romania, in Latin America intellectuals were not specialists but *pensadores* or essayists who generally did not criticize their countries' integration into the world system. Initially, moreover, liberal economic policy was more successful in Latin America, at least in some countries. This combination of factors, argues Love, made the relatively uncritical acceptance of liberalism possible in Latin America and impossible in Romania.

In contrast to Love, who looks back at the nineteenth century from the vantage point of the 1930s and 1940s, Paul Gootenberg and Frank Safford begin from the wars of independence and move through the 1850s. The question they ask is not why liberalism persisted so long, but why and how it took so long to get going. Indeed, in both Peru and Colombia, as the authors show, liberal policy was not hegemonic until around midcentury.

In his study of Colombia, Safford periodizes the gradual hardening of liberal ideas among the country's economic, political, and intellectual elites. Against a backdrop of disadvantage provided by Colombia's difficult topography and problematic integration into export production, debates over the advisability of free trade versus protectionism went on at various points in the first three decades after independence. Periods of moderate liberalism were interspersed with more protectionist times, until dogmatic free trade liberalism became dominant in the 1850s. With only one short period of crisis in the 1880s, Safford argues, the hegemony of liberal ideas endured in Colombia through the 1940s. In a sense, he implies that post–1850 liberal hegemony was ultimately responsible for projecting back a similar—and perhaps false—hegemony for liberalism in the previous period. Yet at the same time, he seems to be saying that, in whatever form, liberalism actually was predominant in Colombia from 1820 on. "If Colombia was not born liberal . . . in the same manner as Buenos Aires," Safford argues, "it was baptized liberal in the independence era and reaffirmed that commitment in still stronger terms at midcentury" (see Chapter 2 in this volume).

Gootenberg's analysis of Peru shares none of Safford's ambivalence. Until the mid–1840s, the very process through which liberal ideas were introduced doomed them to failure in Peru. Initially pushed by Bolivarian foreigners, later championed by an especially unpalatable group of merchants from the United States, free trade liberalism became the whipping boy of most caudillo coalitions coming to power in the two conflictual decades after independence. The balkanization of the economy and weakness of the central state, moreover, militated against any effective implementation of policy, resulting sometimes in de facto protectionism. It was only around 1845–50, Gootenberg concludes, that the situation changed. The increasing availability of guano revenues combined with changes in the political landscape (the disenchantment of protectionist merchants with conservative governments, the liberals taking on the more popular banners of regional autonomy and export promotion) to facilitate the triumph and long-term dominance of free trade policy.

Chronologically, the essay by Tulio Halperín Donghi spans the middle period between the Gootenberg/Safford vision of the earlier nineteenth century and Nils Jacobsen's and Steven Topik's discussions of late nineteenth- and early twentieth-century case studies. Interested in understanding the paradoxes and underlying contradictions in the Argentine elite's dominant vision of a country born liberal, Halperín traces the political coming of age of the so-called Young Generation (late 1830s and 1840s), some of whose members would point the way for the nation-building generation of 1880. Focusing on Bartolomé Mitre and Domingo F. Sarmiento as opposing poles within this common yet internally fragmented vision, Halperín unravels the elements that went into fashioning the hegemonic perspective of the 1880s. Most Argentine intellectuals of this generation believed, first of all, that Argentina's lack of a feudal past (being a frontier society through-out the colonial period) made it uniquely qualified to enter the modern world untainted by the original sin of Iberian colonialism. In direct contrast to other countries that, to borrow Safford's phrasing, needed to be "baptized liberal," Argentina was simply born that way. As Halperín notes, of course, such a vision of Argentina presupposed a certain selection of "the Argentina that really counted"—which by the nineteenth century was the littoral, the coastal provinces that benefited from the trade of Buenos Aires. Thus this vision of Argentina's uniqueness was the banner of the new Argentina, a littoral Argentina, in its conquest of hegemony over Argentina as a whole.

But in addition to this dramatic contradiction between the littoral and *tierra adentro*, literally the remote "inside" lands that contained both a stronger feudal heritage from the Peruvian viceroyalty and the populations most resistant to liberal state making, Halperín also probes a more hidden contradiction in the ideology of the liberal generation of 1880. As especially dramatized in 1856 by the short-lived and regionally specific "agrarian reform" of Chivilcoy, the free market liberalism that was to become so successful in the Argentina of the 1860s and beyond was in direct contradiction to the dream of a socially conscious liberalism, of agrarian egalitarianism, with which some intellectuals (most no-tably Sarmiento) sometimes toyed. Indeed, the greatest irony of Argentina's liberal birth would be that its economic success, as manifested in free trade growth, would be predicated on its social failure—the creation of a highly stratified agrarian class structure where the great estates and rudimentary tech-niques often associated with feudalism would instead be wrought by a world capitalist system.

Examining specific cases of liberal policy discussions and implementation for the 1890–1930 period, Jacobsen and Topik reemphasize some of the general methodological themes of the collection. Jacobsen focuses on Peru, a country (as he and Gootenberg both point out) considered by many to be a classic example of a free trade open economy. Topik compares Brazil and Mexico, comparatively stable polities engaged, as of the late nineteenth century, in dynamic forms of export production guided by liberal principles. A common conclusion reached by both authors is that, whether one considers actual state policy or the economic ideas circulating more broadly at the time, no rigid concept of liberalism as imported from Europe seems to fit. Instead, intellectuals and policy makers were eclectic, flexibly combining principles and measures from both free trade and protectionist doctrine. In all three countries, the actual mix varied by region and time period, depending on local conditions and on the existing social, political, and economic balance of forces.

In order to understand the influence of local conditions, class interests, and clientelistic networking on the formulation of national policy, Jacobsen undertakes a regionally based analysis of Peru's southern highlands. He shows how elites in southern Peru developed a free trade orientation from the particular way they experienced the conditions their region faced in the 1895–1930 period. Not only did its connection to foreign markets (especially Bolivia and England) predispose the south in a free trade direction, but the specific forms taken by protectionism—which usually gave priority to more efficient coastal and northern industry and agriculture—proved noxious to local economies. Ultimately, therefore, debates over free trade were embedded in an intensely conflictual political discussion between regional constituencies in Peru, a discussion involving a wide spectrum of reactions to the post–1895 process of state making and political centralization. The free trade orientation of the Peruvian state, Jacobsen concludes, was less the result of pressure from a cohesive national oligarchy and more a fragile compromise achieved through the balancing of diverse regional interests, represented by loosely conformed and internally fragmented power groups.

Basing his study on national-level statistics, Topik compares the extent to which Brazilian and Mexican states implemented liberal principles in the period 1888–1910. In contrast to the widely held images of the Porfirian state in Mexico as a strong centralized authoritarian structure and the Brazilian state in the Old Republic as a decentralizing, noninterventionist one, Topik finds that the former was less interventionist or active in the economy than the latter. The Brazilian state spent more, had a larger debt, repeatedly failed to balance the budget, and invested directly in state enterprises. The Mexican, by contrast—with the exception of land and labor policies—was much more laissez-faire, spending less and balancing the budget. The explanation for these unexpected results, Topik argues, is complex and involves an understanding of previous history in each country as well as an analysis of the differing role of foreign investment in each case. In Brazil, the state had been historically stronger, in part because of the smooth transition to independence, yet the economy was weaker and more dependent on one export product. At the same time, however, the export sector was nationally owned, and the Brazilian national bourgeoisie was stronger. Under such conditions, state intervention in favor of national export production could be more successful. In Mexico, on the other hand, the state was historically extremely weak in the postindependence period, while the economy was more diversified and subject to greater direct foreign investment. The national bourgeoisie was weaker, and the state tended to respond more directly to the

pressure of foreign investors, applying liberal policy by the book, while facili-
tating accumulation through its land and labor policies. Ultimately, therefore,
the implementation of policy depended in each country on previous processes
of class and state formation, class conflict, and on the role previously taken by
foreign capital.

Taken together, the essays in this book definitively put to rest the notion that
the dominance of liberalism in nineteenth-century Latin America was inevitable
and uncomplicated. Not fully accepted in many countries until midcentury, free
trade policy continued to be negotiated and modified in political conflict and
debate between classes and regions. Even states formally committed to liberal
principles applied them selectively and eclectically. In many cases liberal thought
itself was internally contradictory or fragmented, and the dominance of one
strand over another depended on local struggles. In the end, despite the very
real importance and influence of economic liberalism, it is no longer possible
to lay the blame for Latin American underdevelopment exclusively on free trade
policy. If indeed it is true, as Topik says, that "economic liberalism has been
seen as the ideological blueprint for the construction of neocolonial economies"
(see Chapter 5 in this volume), then somewhere along the way the blueprint got
misfiled.

Where does this leave us? Having gotten rid of two sets of false determinisms,
we are left with the much more complicated task of constructing a new approach.
This quest has barely begun and will certainly continue for quite a while. Yet
here as well, the present collection of essays provides us with some very important
initial clues.

One intriguing one is that, in a number of different countries, 1845–50 constituted an important watershed period in the acceptance or increased prestige
of liberal policy. As Gootenberg, Safford, and Halperín all make clear, it was
only during these years that liberalism established a hegemonic presence in Peru,
Colombia, and Argentina, in all three cases after some violence. With only minor
modifications one could add Chile and Mexico to the list, since in both countries
the 1850s were a particularly conflictual decade in which dominant class factions
violently contested the nature of state policy. By the 1860s, liberalism of a
relatively laissez-faire variety had triumphed in both.[9]

A second important generalization has to do with the internal conflicts and
historical dynamism of liberal thought and policy. Gootenberg makes clear in
his essay, for example, that the specific policies associated with liberalism
changed radically from the 1820s to the 1840s. If Peruvian liberalism was initially
foreign dominated, centralist, and elitist, by midcentury it had taken on the
nationalist banners of regional autonomy and export promotion. In Argentina,
too, as Halperín so carefully documents, economic and social liberalisms fought
with each other, sometimes within the thought of a single intellectual. Still in
1856, while the first blush of victory against Juan Manuel de Rosas had not
faded, it was possible in Chivilcoy to raise the land question, that is, the social
cost to the gauchos and other rural folk of the great estate's expansion. By the

1880s, the very triumph of economic liberalism doomed the dream of an egalitarian agrarian order.

Other cases not treated in this book lend additional credence to the point. In Chile, as Maurice Zeitlin has recently shown, the 1850s dream of a more egalitarian society with a diversified economy was stopped short by the end of the century. Instead of agrarian reform and state support for industry, economic liberalism became an open door to foreign capital. Rather than the broad participation by artisans, peasants, and workers envisioned at midcentury, political liberalism fossilized into a limited parliamentary democracy with congressional control of the executive branch.[10] And in Mexico, the radical liberalism that inspired the 1855 revolution and garnered support from peasants interested in a more just agrarian order stumbled on the realities of social control and race war. By the 1870s, support for foreign investment and authoritarian suppression of ongoing democratic rumblings became the order of the day.[11]

In the final analysis, what the cases treated here suggest is that, given the specific conditions under which liberalism was debated and adopted in nineteenth-century Latin America, both its character and ultimate effect varied greatly by case and time period. The role of social conflict—as it mediated between stubborn colonial legacies and visionary attempts at transformation—was central. In recognizing this, we are forced to move beyond a separation of economic and political liberalisms. For as Gootenberg and Safford suggest for Peru and Colombia, the timing and nature of liberal hegemony owed as much to existing forms of class struggle as it did to the content of free trade policy itself. In both countries, liberalism finally reigned supreme after intense confrontations between the dominant classes and militant, protectionist artisans. In these two cases at least, what united free traders politically was a threat from below, and the final triumph of liberal economic policy was, from the very start, intimately intertwined with social control and political centralization.[12]

In contrast to Europe, then, where liberalism arose in the context of a bourgeois challenge to the centralism and economic monopolies of absolutist states, liberalism in Latin America was discussed in the context of state making and of stubbornly precapitalist social and economic relations. From Guatemala to Chile, from Argentina to Colombia, debates over liberal policy combined economic growth concerns with the need for political stabilization and labor control. The results were different from case to case, depending on the specific independence processes and preexisting social, economic, and cultural relations. But overall, rather than decentralizing or demilitarizing the state, political liberalism in Latin America tended toward the authoritarian, centralist, and militarist realities of social control. Given the colonial heritage of racial, social, and economic inequality, economic liberalism broke monopolies and protectionisms only to further concentrate wealth. In the last analysis, the liberal free market vision much preceded the socioeconomic reality it needed to come to fruition, subordinating liberalism to the dominant classes' need to centralize political control and dooming its egalitarian implications.[13]

Yet the social or egalitarian strands of liberalism were stillborn in Latin America not because of some overarching, conspiratorial oligarchic plan, but because of the particular struggles of identifiable social forces, struggles not decided a priori but in the very heat of the conflict itself. And it is here that we have barely begun to understand the impact of liberalism. Economically, we still need to uncover what effects liberal policy actually had at the local level. What economic relations and structures existed before liberalism arose in each region, and how did these affect the application of policy? Case by case, how did liberal policy change local relations, laws, structures, and customs?[14] We also need to know much more about how one proceeds from the existence of ideas to their acquiring prestige or political prominence. Here as well, there are political, social, and economic struggles involved, and ideas are negotiated, modified, and intermingled as a result.

The final challenge lies in combining this new focus on the empirical case with what is still valuable from previous perspectives. Here, the careful attention to political detail and ideology of the pre-*dependentista* writers should be rescued. Equally important, in our eagerness to make each case complex, variegated, and unique, we must not lose sight of the *dependentistas*' positive insights. For even as we note the specificities of local struggles, we must also remember that the adoption of free trade policy (as Safford points out) became easier in Latin America after the abolition of the British Corn Laws and that social conservatism combined more naturally with economic liberalism after 1848, wherever one happened to live. And no matter how academically objective we can become, it is perhaps also important to remember that the initial impulse to criticize economic liberalism came not from the academy, but from the strife-ridden sphere of politics and policy making. This sense of dialogue between present and past, therefore, which originally gave dependency theory its great dynamism, is also a positive legacy. What the dialogue has to tell us may be less definite or optimistic about the future than it was in the 1960s, inhabiting as we presently do (to borrow Halperín's words) "the somber landscape" of the late 1980s. Yet we have little choice but to continue it, since embedded within this dialogue are our hopes of a further understanding, whether of our own century or of the conflictually liberal century that preceded it.

NOTES

1. A complete listing of the earlier *dependentista* scholars is beyond the scope of this essay. Any list, however, would have to include Cardoso and Faletto, *Dependencia y desarrollo*; Frank, *Capitalism and Underdevelopment* and *Latin America: Underdevelopment or Revolution*; Furtado, *Formação econômica do Brasil* and *Formação econômica de América Latina*; and Prado, Jr., *História econômica do Brasil*. For particularly interesting discussions of dependency theory in Latin America—its implications, limitations, and revisions—as well as some additional bibliographical suggestions, see Cardoso, "Consumption of Dependency Theory"; Halperín Donghi, " 'Dependency Theory' "; and Stern, "Feudalism, Capitalism, and the World-System."

2. The continued influence of nineteenth-century liberal historians and the nature of their ideology is the subject of Burns, "Ideology." For a discussion of the failures to communicate between Latin American and U.S. scholars on the issue of dependency, see Stern, "Feudalism, Capitalism, and the World-System."

3. This is what Halperín argues in " 'Dependency Theory.' " Works he does not cite but that would support his argument include Hale, *Mexican Liberalism*; da Costa, *Da senzala a colônia*; and his own *Historia contemporánea*.

4. See, for example, Blakemore, *British Nitrates*; and Platt, *Latin America*, and *Business Imperialism*.

5. Some especially dramatic examples of this perspective are Bonilla and Spalding, "La independencia"; Bonilla, *Guano y burguesía*; Yepes, *Perú*; and Burns, *Latin America* and *The Poverty of Progress*.

6. On Carrera, see especially Burns, *The Poverty of Progress*, pp. 96–106; and Miceli, "Rafael Carrera." On Paraguay, see White, *Paraguay's Autonomous Revolution*; Whigham, "The Iron Works of Ibycui"; and Williams, "Paraguay's Nineteenth Century Estancias" and "Foreign Técnicos."

7. This conspiratorial tone is part of what Gootenberg objects to in the dependency-influenced literature. In addition to the sources in notes 1 and 5, see Frank, *Lumpen-burguesía y lumpendesarrollo*.

8. Some of the works in this new tendency are Brown, *Socioeconomic History*; Mallon, *Defense of Community*; Wasserman, *Capitalists, Caciques, and Revolution*; and Weinstein, *Amazon Rubber Boom*.

9. For analyses emphasizing the social conflict that underlay the triumph of liberalism in Chile and Mexico, see respectively Zeitlin, *Civil Wars*, and Mallon, "Peasants and State Formation."

10. Zeitlin, *Civil Wars*.

11. Mallon, "Peasants and State Formation."

12. Recent work on Chilean artisans suggests a similar dynamic there, as well. In addition to Zeitlin, see Luis Romero, "Sociedad de la Igualdad."

13. In addition to the sources already cited, see Szlajfer, "Against Dependent Capitalist Development"; Reinhardt, "The Consolidation"; and McCreery, " 'Odious Feudalism.' "

14. In "Communal and Private Control of Land," Mayer specifically addresses the problem of local applications of liberal policy and ideology. He makes clear that the results are never given, and are modified by local interests and struggles even at the village level.

SELECTED BIBLIOGRAPHY

Abel, Christopher, and Colin Lewis, eds. *Latin America, Economic Imperialism and the State: The Political Economy of the External Connection from Independence to the Present*. London: Athlone Press, 1985.

Academia de Ştiinţe Sociale şi Politice. "Titu Maiorescu." In *Istoria filozofiei romanesti*. Vol. 1, pp. 353–396. Bucureşti: Academia, 1972.

Anderson, Perry. *Considerations on Western Marxism*. London: NLB, 1976.

Anna, Timothy E. *The Fall of the Royal Government in Peru*. Lincoln: University of Nebraska Press, 1979.

Appleby, Gordon. "Exportation and Its Aftermath, The Spatio-Economic Evolution of the Regional Marketing System in Highland Puno, Peru." Ph.D. diss., Stanford University, 1978.

"The Argentine Industrial Exhibition." *Review of the River Plate*, Dec. 1933: 11–17.

Aricó, José. *Marx y América Latina*. 2d ed. México: Alianza Editorial Mexicana, 1982.

Arnaud, Pascual. *Estado y capitalismo en América Latina: Casos de México y Argentina*. México: Siglo XXI, 1981.

Aurelian, P[etru] S. *Viitorul nostru economic*. Bucuresti: Vointa Naţională, 1890.

Baca Tupayachi, Epifanio. *Cusco: Sistemas viales, articulación y desarrollo regional*. Cuadernos para el debate regional, no. 10. Cuzco: Centro de Estudios Regionales "Bartolomé de las Casas," 1983.

Baltes, Peter. "José María Pando: colaborador de Gamarra." Tesis de Bachiller, Pontificia Universidad Católica del Perú, 1968.

Bartra, Roger, et al. *Modos de producción en América Latina*. Lima: Delva, 1976.

Basadre, Jorge. *Historia de la República del Perú*. 6th ed. 12 vols. Lima: Universitaria, 1968.

———. *La multitud, la ciudad y el campo en la historia del Perú*. Lima: A. J. Rivas, 1929.

Bauer, Arnold J. "Rural Spanish America, 1870–1930." In *Cambridge History of Latin America*, edited by Leslie Bethell. Vol. 4, pp. 151–186. Cambridge: Cambridge University Press, 1986.

Bauer, Arnold J., and Ann Hagerman Johnson. "Land and Labour in Rural Chile, 1850–1935." In *Land and Labour in Latin America*, edited by Kenneth Duncan and Ian Rutledge. Pp. 83–102. Cambridge: Cambridge University Press, 1977.

Bazant, Jan. *Historia de la deuda exterior de México, 1823–1946*. México: El Colegio de México, 1968.

Bedoya, Guillermo. *Estadística de exportación de la región sur del Perú por la via de Mollendo*. Arequipa, 1923–38 [annual].

Bejarano, Jesús Antonio. "Aníbal Galindo—Economista." Introduction to *Estudios económicos y fiscales*, by Aníbal Galindo. Bogotá: ANIF-COLCULTURA, 1978.

Belaúnde, Víctor Andrés. *Memorias*. Vol. 1, *Arequipa de mi infancia*. Lima: Lumen, 1960.

———. *La realidad nacional*. 2d ed. Lima: "Mercurio Peruano," 1945. [Originally published in 1931.]

Berend, Ivan T., and Gyorgy Ranki. *The European Periphery and Industrialization: 1780–1914*. Cambridge: Cambridge University Press, 1982.

Berg, Ronald, and Frederick S. Weaver. "Toward a Reinterpretation of Political Change in Peru During the First Century of Independence." *Journal of Inter-American Studies and World Affairs*, 20 (Feb. 1978): 69–84.

Bergquist, Charles W. *Coffee and Conflict in Colombia, 1886–1910*. Durham, N. C.: Duke University Press, 1978.

Bertram, Geoff. "Modernización y cambio en la industria lanera en el sur del Perú, 1919–1930: Un caso de desarrollo frustrado." *Apuntes*, 3, no. 6 (1977): 3–22.

Blair, Calvin S. "Nacional Financiera: Entrepreneurship in a Mixed Economy." In *Public Policy and Private Enterprise in Mexico*, edited by Raymond Vernon. pp. 191–240. Cambridge, Mass.: Harvard University Press, 1964.

Blakemore, Harold. *British Nitrates and Chilean Politics, 1886–1896: Balmaceda and North*. London: Athlone Press, 1974.

Bloch, Marc. *Feudal Society*. Translated by L. A. Manyon. 2 vols. Chicago: University of Chicago Press, 1961.

Bollinger, William S. "The Bourgeois Revolution in Peru: A Conception of Peruvian History." *Latin American Perspectives* 4 (Summer 1977): 18–57.

———. "The Evolution of Dependence: U.S.-Peruvian Trade, 1824–1923." MS. University of California, Los Angeles, 1973.

Boloña, Carlos. "Tariff Policies in Peru, 1880–1980." D.Phil. Diss. Oxford University, 1981.

Bonilla, Heraclio. "La emergencia del control norteamericano sobre la economía peruana, 1850–1930." *Estudios Sociales Centroamericanos* 5 (1976): 97–122.

———. *Gran Bretaña y el Perú: los mecanismos de un control económico*. Lima: IEP, 1977.

———. *Guano y burguesía en el Perú*. Lima: IEP, 1974.

———. *Un siglo a la deriva: ensayos sobre el Perú, Bolivia y la guerra*. Lima: IEP, 1980.

————. "El Perú entre la independencia y la guerra con Chile." In *Historia del Perú*, edited by Juan Mejía Baca. Pp. 395–473. Lima: Mejía Baca, 1980.

————, comp. *Gran Bretaña y el Perú, 1826–1919: Informes de los consules británicos.* 5 vols. Lima: IEP, 1977.

Bonilla, Heraclio, Lía del Río, and Pilar Ortiz de Zevallos. "Comercio libre y crisis de la economía andina: el caso del Cuzco." *Histórica* 2 (July 1978): 1–25.

Bonilla, Heraclio, and Karen Spalding. "La Independencia en el Perú: las palabras y los hechos." In *La Independencia en el Perú*, edited by Heraclio Bonilla and Pierre Chaunu. Pp. 15–65. Lima: IEP, 1972.

Bonilla, Heraclio and Pierre Chaunu, eds. *La independencia en el Perú*. Lima: IEP, 1972.

Brazil. Banco do Brasil. *Relatório, 1924*. Rio de Janeiro, 1924.

Brazil. Contadoria Geral da República. *Resumo do orçamento da receita e despeza para o exercício de 1893*. Rio de Janeiro: Imprensa Nacional, 1893.

————. *Tabela explicativa do orçamento para o exercício de 1912*. Rio de Janeiro, n. d.

Brazil. Diretoria Geral de Estatística (DGE). *Anuário estatístico, 1908/1912*. Vol. 2. Rio de Janeiro: Departamento de Estatística, 1927.

————. *Anuário estatístico, 1939/1940*. Rio de Janeiro: Impr. Nacional, 1940.

Brazil. Ministério da Fazenda. *Contas do exercício financeiro de 1925 e relatório da Contadoria da República*. Rio de Janeiro: Imprensa Nacional, 1926.

————. *Relatório apresentado ao Presidente da República dos Estados Unidos do Brasil no ano de 1899*. Rio de Janeiro: Imprensa Nacional, n. d.

————. *Relatório apresentado ao Presidente da República dos Estados Unidos do Brasil no ano 1905*. Rio: Imprensa Nacional, 1905.

Brown, Jonathan C. *A Socio-Economic History of Argentina, 1776–1860*. Cambridge: Cambridge University Press, 1979.

Buescu, Mircea. *Brasil, disparidades de renda no passado*. Rio de Janeiro: APEC, 1979.

Bulnes, Francisco. *The Whole Truth about Mexico*. Detroit: Blaine, Ethridge, 1972. [Originally published in 1916.]

Bunge, Alejandro. *La economía argentina*. 4 vols. Buenos Aires: Impr. Argentina, 1928–30.

Burga, Manuel, and Alberto Flores Galindo. *Apogeo y crisis de la República Aristocrática*. Lima: "Rikchay Perú", 1979.

Burga, Manuel, and Wilson Reátegui. *Lanas y capital mercantil en el sur del Perú. La Casa Ricketts, 1895–1935*. Lima: IEP, 1981.

Burns, E. Bradford. "Ideology in Nineteenth-Century Latin American Historiography." *Hispanic American Historical Review* 58:3 (1978): 409–31.

————. *Latin America: A Concise Interpretive History*. 2nd ed. Englewood Cliffs, N.J.: Prentice-Hall, 1977.

————. *The Poverty of Progress: Latin America in the Nineteenth Century*. Berkeley: University of California Press, 1980.

Bushnell, David. *The Santander Regime in Gran Colombia*. Newark, Del.: University of Delaware Press, 1954.

Bustamante Roldán, Darío. "Efectos económicos del papel moneda durante la Regeneración." *Cuadernos Colombianos* 4 (1974): 559–660.

Camacho Roldán, Salvador. *Escritos varios*. 3 vols. Bogotá: Lib. Colombiana, 1892–95.

Camprubi Alcázar, Carlos. *Historia de los bancos en el Perú (1860–79)*. Lima: Lumen, 1957.

Caravedo Molinari, Baltazar. "Economía, producción y trabajo (Perú, siglo XX)." In *Historia del Perú*, edited by Juan Mejía Baca. Vol. 8, pp. 191–361. Lima: Mejía Baca, 1980.

———. "Poder central y descentralización: Perú, 1931." *Apuntes* 5, no. 9 (1979): 111–29.

Cardoso, Fernando Henrique. "The Consumption of Dependency Theory in the United States." *Latin American Research Review* 12, no. 3 (1977): 7–24.

——— and Enzo Faletto. *Dependency and Development in Latin America*. Translated by Marjory Urquidi. Berkeley: University of California Press, 1979. [Originally published in Spanish in 1969.]

Carone, Edgard, ed. *O pensamento industrial no Brasil (1880–1945)*. Rio de Janeiro: DIFEL, 1977.

Carpio, Juan. "Rebeliones arequipeñas del siglo XIX y configuraciones de la oligarquía 'nacional.' " *Análisis* 11 (May-August 1982): 33–45.

Carreira, Liberto de Castro. *História financeira e orcamentária do Império no Brasil*. Rio de Janeiro: Fundação Casa Rui Barbosa, 1980. [Originally published in 1889.]

Cartas y mensajes de Santander. Edited by Roberto Cortázar. 10 vols. Bogotá: Academia Colombiana de Historia, 1953–56.

Casasús, Joaquín. *Las reformas de la ley de instituciones de crédito*. México: Oficina Impresora de Estampillas, 1908.

Chiaramonte, José Carlos. *Nacionalismo y liberalismo económicos en la Argentina, 1860–1880*. Buenos Aires: Solar-Hachette, 1971.

Chirinos Pacheco, Benjamín. *El imperialismo yanqui y la dictadura bolchevique*. Arequipa, 1929.

Chirot, Daniel. *Social Change in a Peripheral Society: The Creation of a Balkan Colony*. New York: Academic Press, 1976.

Clayton, Lawrence. "Private Matters: The Origins and Nature of U.S.-Peruvian Relations, 1820–50." *The Americas*, 62 (April 1986): 377–419.

Coatsworth, John H. "Obstacles to Economic Growth in Nineteenth-Century Mexico." *American Historical Review*, 83 (February 1978): 80–100.

———. "The State and the External Sector." Paper delivered at the Latin American Studies Association Meeting, Mexico City, September 1983.

Colegio de México. *Estadísticas económicas del Porfiriato: Comercio exterior de México, 1877–1911*. México: El Colegio de México, 1960.

Colegio de México. *Estadísticas económicas del Porfiriato: Fuerza de trabajo e actividad económica por sectores*. México: El Colegio de México, [1965 ?].

Colmenares, Germán. "La nación y la historia regional en los paises andinos, 1870–1930." *Revista Andina* 3, no. 2 (1985): 311–30.

El Comercio del Plata. Montevideo, March 19, 1846. Reprinted in *Rosas y sus opositores*, by Florencio Varela. Buenos Aires: Gleizer, 1929.

Conant, Charles A. *The Banking System of Mexico*. In Senate Documents of the U.S. Congress. 61st Cong., 2nd sess., 1909–10. Vol. 19. Washington D.C.: Government Printing Office, 1910.

Concha, Malaquias. "Balanza de Comercio," *Revista Económica* [Santiago] 2, 23 (Mar. 1889): 305–33.

———. *La lucha económica*. Santiago: Impr. Nacional, 1910.

Conferencia económica del Sur. Arequipa: "El Deber," 1932.

Congreso de Cúcuta [1821]. *Libro de Actas*. Bogotá: Banco de la República, 1971.

Congresso Brasileiro da Indústria. *Anais*. Vol. 1. São Paulo; 1945.

Contador, Cláudio, and Cláudio Haddad. "Produção real, moeda e preços: A experiência brasileira no período 1861–1970." *Revista Brasileira de Estatística* 36 (1975): 407–40.

Cornejo, Mariano H. *Discursos políticos*. Lima: Impr. del Estado, 1913.

Cortés Conde, Roberto, and Shane J. Hunt, eds. *The Latin American Economies: Growth and the Export Sector, 1880–1930*. New York: Holmes and Meier, 1985.

Cortés Conde, Roberto, and Stanley J. Stein, eds. *Latin America: A Guide to Economic History 1830–1930*. Berkeley: University of California Press, 1977.

Cosío Villegas, Daniel. *La cuestión arancelaria en México*. 5 vols. México: A. Mijares, [1932 ?].

Cotler, Julio. *Clases, estado y nación en el Perú*. Lima: IEP, 1978.

da Costa, Emília Viotti. *Da senzala á colônia*. São Paulo: Difusão Européia do Livro, 1966.

Dancuart, Pedro Emilio, ed. *Anales de la hacienda pública del Perú: Historia y legislación fiscal de la República*. 24 vols. Lima: Gil, 1902–26.

Davies, Thomas M. *Indian Integration in Peru. A Half Century of Experience, 1900–1948*. Lincoln: University of Nebraska Press, 1974.

Dávila, Tomás. *Medios que se proponen al actual Congreso Constitucional del Perú, y al Gobierno Supremo, para salvar de su total destrucción la casi-arruinada agricultura de la importante Provincia de Moquegua*. Arequipa: Francisco Ibáñez y Hermano, 1853.

Dean, Warren. "The Brazilian Economy, 1870–1930." In *Cambridge History of Latin America*, edited by Leslie Bethell. Vol. 5, pp. 685–724. Cambridge: Cambridge University Press, 1986.

———. *The Industrialization of São Paulo, 1880–1945*. Austin: University of Texas Press, 1969.

Deane, Phyllis, and Cole, W. A. *British Economic Growth, 1688–1969*. Cambridge: Cambridge University Press, 1969.

Delpar, Helen. *Red Against Blue. The Liberal Party in Colombian Politics, 1863–1899*. University, Ala.: University of Alabama Press, 1981.

Demetrescu, Eugen. "Liberalismul Economic." In *Enciclopedia României*. Vol. 3, pp. 261–74. Bucureşti: n. d.

Deustua, José, and José Luis Rénique. *Intelectuales, indigenismo y descentralismo en el Perú. 1897–1931*. Debates Andinos, no. 4. Cuzco: Centro de Estudios Rurales Andinos "Bartolomé de las Casas," 1984.

Díaz-Alejandro, Carlos F. *Essays on the Economic History of the Argentine Republic*. New Haven, Conn.: Yale University Press, 1970.

———. "Stories of the 1930's for the 1980's." National Bureau for Economic Research: Conference Paper No. 130. Mimeo, 1981.

Díaz Dufoó, Carlos. *Limantour*. México: Eusebio Gómez de la Puente, 1910.

Diniz, Eli, and Renato Raúl Boschi. *Empresariado nacional e estado no Brasil*. Rio de Janeiro: Forense, 1978.

Dobrogeanu-Gherea, Constantin. "Un mic răspuns la o mică recenzie." In *Opere Complete*, by Constantin Dobrogeanu-Gherea. Vol. 3, pp. 454–56. Bucureşti: Editura Politică, 1977. [Originally published in 1907.]

————. *Neoiobagia: Studiu economico-sociologic al problemei noastre agrare*. Vol. 4 of *Opere Complete*, by Constantin Dobrogeanu-Gherea. Bucureşti: Editura Politică, 1977. [Originally published in 1910.]

————. "Post-scriptum sau cuvinte uitate." pp. 476–504. In *Opere Complete*, by Constantin Dobrogeanu-Gherea. Vol. 3. Bucureşti: Editura Politică, 1977. [Originally published in 1908.]

————. *Socialismul in Ţările Inapoiate*. Bucureşti: Editura Partidului Social-Democrat, 1945. [Originally published in 1912.]

Domínguez, Jorge I. *Cuba, Order and Revolution*. Cambridge, Mass.: Belknap Press, 1978.

Doyle, Michael W. *Empires*. Ithaca: Cornell University Press, 1986.

Drapognie, J. E. *La verdad en la cuestión indígena (apuntes)*. Arequipa: Quiroz, 1922.

Duncan, Julian. *Public and Private Operation of Railways in Brazil*. New York: Columbia University Press, 1932.

Duncan, Kenneth, and Ian Rutledge, eds. *Land and Labour in Latin America: Essays on the Development of Agrarian Capitalism in the Nineteenth and Twentieth Centuries*. Cambridge: Cambridge University Press, 1977.

Dunn, W.E. *Peru. A Commercial and Industrial Handbook*. U.S. Department of Commerce. Bureau of Foreign and Domestic Commerce. Trade Promotion Series, no. 25. Washington, D.C. Government Printing Office, 1925.

Eidelberg, Philip Gabriel. *The Great Rumanian Peasant Revolt of 1907: Origins of a Modern Jacquerie*. Leiden: E.J. Brill, 1974.

Escritos de dos economistas coloniales: Don Antonio de Narváez y la Torre y Don José Ignacio de Pombo. Edited by Sergio Elías Ortiz. Bogotá: Banco de la República, 1965.

Estrada de Ferro Central do Brasil. *Relatório, 1893*. Rio de Janeiro: Imprensa Nacional, 1893.

Estrada, Víctor Emilio. *Ensayo sobre la balanza económica del Ecuador*. Guayaquil, 1922.

El Exilio Español en México: 1939–1982. México: Fondo de Cultura Económica, 1982.

Faoro, Raymundo. *Os donos do poder: Formação do patronato político brasileiro*. 2nd ed. 2 vols. São Paulo: Globo/USP, 1975.

Flores Galindo, Alberto. *Arequipa y el sur andino: Siglos XVII–XX*. Lima: Horizonte, 1977.

————. "El militarismo y la dominación británica (1825–1845)." In *Nueva historia general del Perú*. edited by Carlos Araníbar and Heraclio Bonilla. Pp. 107–123. Lima: Mosca Azul, 1979.

Flores Galindo, Alberto, Orlando Plaza, and Teresa Oré. "Oligarquía y capital comercial en el sur peruano (1870–1930)." *Debates en Sociología* 3 (1978): 53–75.

Frank, Andre Gunder. *Capitalism and Underdevelopment in Latin America: Historical Studies of Chile and Brazil*. New York: Monthly Review Press, 1967.

————. *Latin America: Underdevelopment or Revolution: Essays on the Development of Underdevelopment and the Immediate Enemy*. New York: Monthly Review Press, 1970.

————. *Lumpenburgesía y lumpendesarrollo: Dependencia, clase y política en Latinoamérica*. Santiago: Prensa Latinoamericana, 1970. [Published in English as *Lumpenbourgeoisie and Lumpendevelopment: Dependency, Class, and Politics in Latin America*. New York: Monthly Review Press, 1972.]

Friedman, Douglas. *The State and Underdevelopment in Spanish America: The Political Roots of Dependency in Peru and Argentina*. Boulder, Colo.: Westview Press, 1984.

[Frisancho, José.] *Algunas vistas fiscales concernientes al problema indígena del Agente Fiscal de Azángaro, Dr. D. José Frisancho*. Lima: El Progreso Editorial, [1916].

Fuentes, Hildebrando. *Cuzco y sus ruínas: Apuntes geográficos, históricos, estadísticos y sociales*. Lima: Imprenta del Estado, 1905.

Furtado, Celso. *The Economic Growth of Brazil*. Translated by Ricardo de Aguiar and Eric Drysdale. Berkeley: University of California Press, 1965. [Originally published in Portuguese as *Formação econômica do Brasil*. Rio de Janeiro: Fondo de Cultura, 1959.]

———. *Formação econômica da América Latina*. Rio de Janeiro: Lia, 1969.

Galindo, Aníbal. *Estudios económicos y fiscales*. Bogotá: ANIF-COLCULTURA, 1978.

Gamarra, Manuel Jesús. *Orientación y organización: Población y descentralización, programa de reconstrucción nacional*. Cuzco: Rozas, 1926.

García Calderón, Francisco. *Le Pérou contemporaine, étude sociale*. Paris: Dujarrie, 1907.

Gerschenkron, Alexander. *Bread and Democracy in Germany*. Berkeley: University of California Press, 1943.

———. "Economic Development in Russian Intellectual History of the Nineteenth Century." In *Economic Backwardness in Historical Persective*, by Alexander Gerschenkron. Pp. 152–97. Cambridge, Mass.: Belknap Press, 1966.

Glade, William P. "Latin America and The International Economy, 1870–1914." In *Cambridge History of Latin America*, edited by Leslie Bethell. Vol. 4, pp. 1–56. Cambridge: Cambridge University Press, 1986.

Glave, Luis Miguel. "Trajines. Un capítulo en la formación del mercado interno colonial." *Revista Andina*, 1, no. 1 (1983): 9–67.

González Navarro, Moisés. *Estadísticas sociales del porfiriato*. México: Secretaría de Educación, Dirección General de Estadística, 1956.

González Roa, Fernando. *El problema ferrocarrilero y la compañía de los ferrocarriles nacionales de México*. México: Liga de Economistas Revolucionarios de la República Mexicana, 1975. [Originally published in 1915.]

Gootenberg, Paul. "Artisans and Merchants: The Making of an Open Economy in Lima, Peru, 1830 to 1860." M.Phil. thesis, University of Oxford, 1981.

———. *Between Silver and Guano: Protectionist Elites to a Liberal State in Peru, 1820–1850*. Princeton University Press, forthcoming.

———. "Merchants, Foreigners and the State: The Origins of Trade Policies in Post-Independence Peru." Ph.D. diss., University of Chicago, 1985.

———. "The Patterns of Economic Institutional Change in Nineteenth-Century Peru." B. A. thesis, University of Chicago, 1978.

———. "The Social Origins of Protectionism and Free Trade in Nineteenth-Century Lima." *Journal of Latin American Studies* 14 (Nov. 1982): 329–58.

Gorman, Stephen. "The State, Elite and Export in Nineteenth Century Peru." *Journal of Interamerican Studies and World Affairs* 21, no. 3 (Aug. 1979): 395–418.

Graham, Richard. *Britain and the Onset of Modernization in Brazil: 1850–1914*. Cambridge: Cambridge University Press, 1968.

———. *Independence in Latin America: A Comparative Approach*. New York: Knopf, 1972.

Gurza, Jaime. *Nuestros bancos de emisión*. México: Imprenta Central, 1905.

Haddad, Cláudio L. S. *Crescimento do produto real no Brasil, 1900–1947*. Rio de Janeiro: Fundação Getúlio Vargas, 1978.

Hale, Charles A. *Mexican Liberalism in the Age of Mora, 1821–1853*. New Haven, Conn.: Yale University Press, 1968.

———. "Political and Social Ideas in Latin America, 1870–1930." In *Cambridge History of Latin America*, edited by Leslie Bethell. Vol. 4, pp. 367–441. Cambridge: Cambridge University Press, 1986.

Halperín Donghi, Tulio. " 'Dependency Theory' and Latin American Historiography." *Latin American Research Review* 17, no. 1 (1982): 115–30.

———. "Economy and Society in Post-Independence Latin America." In *Cambridge History of Latin America*, edited by Leslie Bethell. Vol. 3, Pp. 299–345. Cambridge: Cambridge University Press, 1985.

———. *Guerra y finanzas en los orígenes del estado argentino (1791–1850)*. Buenos Aires: Belgrano, 1982.

———. *Historia contemporánea de América Latina*. Madrid: Alianza Editorial, 1969.

Hartz, Louis. "A Theory of the Development of the New Societies." In *The Founding of New Societies: Studies in the History of the United States, Latin America, South Africa, Canada, and Australia*, Edited by Louis Hartz. Pp. 1–65. New York: Harcourt, Brace and World, 1964.

Hazen, Dan C. "The Awakening of Puno: Government Policy and the Indian Problem in Southern Peru, 1900–1955." Ph.D. diss. Yale University, 1974.

Helguera, Joseph Léon. "The First Mosquera Administration in New Granada, 1845–1849." Ph.D. diss. University of North Carolina, 1958.

Hennessy, Alistair. "Latin America." In *Populism: Its Meaning and National Characteristics*, edited by Ghiţa Ionesco and Ernest Gellner. Pp. 28–61. London: Weidenfeld and Nicholson, 1969.

Hernández y Sánchez-Barba, Mario. "Ciclos Kondratieff y modelos de frustración económica ibero-americana (siglo XIX)." *Revista da la Universidad de Madrid* 20, no. 78 (1971): 203–36.

Herrera Alarcón, Dante. *Rebeliones que intentaron desmembrar el sur del Perú*. Callao: Colegio Militar Prado, 1961.

Herzen, Alexander. *My Past and Thoughts*. Berkeley: University of California Press, 1982.

Hicks, John. *A Theory of Economic History*. Oxford: Oxford University Press, 1969.

Hirschman, Albert O. *The Passions and the Interests: Political Arguments for Capitalism before Its Triumph*. Princeton, N.J.: Princeton University Press, 1977.

———. "Rival Views of Market Society." In *Rival Views of Market Society and Other Essays* by Albert O. Hirschman. Pp. 105–41. New York: Viking, 1986.

Hobsbawm, Eric J. "La Convención, Peru: A Case of Neo-Feudalism." *Journal of Latin American Studies*, 1, no. 1 (1969): 31–50.

Holloway, Thomas. *Immigrants on the Land. Coffee and Society in São Paulo, 1886–1934*. Chapel Hill: University of North Carolina Press, 1980.

Humphreys, R. A., comp. *British Consular Reports on the Trade and Politics of Latin America: 1824–1826*. Camden Third Series. Vol. 63. London: Royal Historical Society, 1940.

Hunt, Shane J. "Growth and Guano in Nineteenth Century Peru." Discussion Paper 34, RPED, Woodrow Wilson School, Princeton University, 1973.

————. "Growth and Guano in Nineteenth Century Peru." Pp. 255–319. In *The Latin American Economies: Growth and the Export Sector, 1880–1930*, edited by Roberto Cortés Conde and Shane J. Hunt. New York: Holmes and Meier, 1985.

Hunt, Shane J., and Pablo Macera. "Interpretive Essay." In *Latin America: A Guide to Economic History, 1830–1930*, edited by Roberto Cortés Conde and Stanley J. Stein. Pp. 547–71. Berkeley: University of California Press, 1977.

"Ideas conservadoras de buena ley." *Los Debates* (Buenos Aires ?), July 24, 1857.

Internacional Comunista. *VI Congreso*. Vol. 2: *Informes y Discusiones*. México: Pasado y Presente, 1978. [The congress took place in 1928.]

Ionescu, Ghiţa. "Eastern Europe." In *Populism: Its Meaning and National Characteristics*, edited by Ghiţa Ionescu and Ernest Gellner. Pp. 97–121. London: Weidenfeld and Nicholson, 1969.

Izquierdo, Rafael. "Protectionism in Mexico." In *Public Policy and Private Enterprise in Mexico*, edited by Raymond Vernon. Pp. 241–89. Cambridge, Mass.: Harvard University Press, 1964.

Jacobsen, Nils. "Cycles and Booms in Latin American Export Agriculture: The Example of Southern Peru's Livestock Economy, 1855–1920," *Review* [of the Fernand Braudel Center] 7, no. 3 (1984): 443–507.

————. "Landtenure and Society in the Peruvian Altiplano: Azángaro Province, 1770–1920." Ph.D. diss., University of California, Berkeley, 1982.

————. "The Wool Export Economy of Peru's Altiplano and the Region's Livestock Haciendas: Expansion Without Change." MS, University of California, Berkeley 1979.

Jaramillo, Juan Diego. *Bolívar y Canning, 1822–1827*. Bogotá: Banco de la República, 1983.

Johnson, David Church. "Social and Economic Change in Nineteenth-Century Santander, Colombia." Ph.D. diss., University of California, Berkeley, 1975.

"Junimea." *Dicţionar Enciclopedic Romîn* 2 (Bucureşti: Editura Politică, 1964).

Katz, Friedrich. "Labor Conditions on Haciendas in Porfirian Mexico." *Hispanic American Historical Review* 54, no. 1 (1974): 1–47.

Kay, Cristóbal. *El sistema señorial europeo y la hacienda latinoamericana*. Translated by Roberto Gómez Ciriza. México: Era, 1980.

Keen, Benjamin, and Wasserman, Mark. *A Short History of Latin America*. Boston: Houghton Mifflin, 1980.

Kerig, Dorothy. "The Colorado River Land Company." Ph.D. diss., University of California, Irvine. Forthcoming.

Kindleberger, Charles P. "The Rise of Free Trade in Western Europe: 1820–1875." *Journal of Economic History* 35 (March 1975): 20–56.

Kitching, Gavin. *Development and Underdevelopment in Historical Perspective: Populism, Nationalism and Industrialization*. London: Methuen, 1982.

Kroeber, Clifton B. *Man, Land and Water: Mexico's Farmlands Irrigation Policies, 1885–1911*. Berkeley: University of California Press, 1983.

Laclau, Ernesto. "Modos de producción, sistemas económicos y población excedente: Aproximación histórica a los casos argentino y chileno." *Revista Latinoamericana de Sociología* 5, no. 2 (1969): 276–316.

Langer, Erick. "Espacios coloniales y economías nacionales: Bolivia y el Norte argentino, 1810–1930." *Siglo XIX: Revista de Historia* 2, no.4 (July-Dec. 1987): 135–60.

Ledos, Carlos. *Consideraciones sobre la agricultura*. Lima: José Masías, 1847.

Leff, Nathaniel H. *Underdevelopment and Development in Brazil*. 2 vols. London: George Allen & Unwin, 1982.

Leguía, Jorge Guillermo. "Las ideas de 1848 en el Perú." In *Estudios históricos*, by Jorge Guillermo Leguíta. Pp. 113–44. Santiago: Ercilla, 1939.

Lenin, V[ladimir] I. *The Development of Capitalism in Russia: The Process of the Formation of a Home Market for Large-scale Industry*. 2d ed. Moscow: Foreign Languages Publishing House, 1956. [Originally published in Russian in 1899.]

Levin, Jonathan V. *The Export Economies. Their Pattern of Development in Historical Perspective*. Cambridge, Mass.: Harvard University Press, 1960.

Liévano Aguirre, Indalecio. *Rafael Núñez*. Bogotá: Organización Continental de los Festivales del Libro, 1960. [Originally published in 1944.]

Liss, Peggy K. *Atlantic Empires: The Network of Trade and Revolution, 1713–1826*. Baltimore: Johns Hopkins University Press, 1983.

Lizares Quiñones, José Angelino. *Carta política del Sr. Coronel J. A. Lizares Quiñones a los electores de la provincia de Azángaro, cuya representación ha ejercido ante la Cámara nacional de Diputados*. Lima: "La Nueva Unión" de F. Peters, n.d.[1924].

————. *Los problemas de la federación del Perú y la confederación mundial*. 2d ed. Lima: "La Opinión Nacional," 1919.

López J., Sinecio. "El estado oligárquico en el Perú: un ensayo de interpretación." *Revista Mexicana de Sociología* 40, no. 3 (1978): 991–1007.

López Más, Julio. "La gran industria capitalista y el mercado interno." *Allpanchis* 13 (1979): 144–88.

Louis, William R., ed. *Imperialism: The Robinson and Gallagher Controversy*. New York: New Viewpoints, 1976.

Love, Joseph L. "Manoilescu, Prebisch, and the Thesis of Unequal Exchange." *Rumanian Studies* 5 (1980–86): 125–33.

————"Raúl Prebisch and the Origins of Doctrine of Unequal Exchange." *Latin American Research Review* 15, no. 3 (1980): 45–72.

————. *São Paulo in the Brazilian Federation, 1889–1937*. Stanford: Stanford University Press, 1980.

Lovón Zavala, Gerardo. *Investigación sobre desarrollo regional, Cusco 1950–1980*. Informe: *Sector Industria*. Cuzco: Centro de Estudios Rurales Andinos "Bartolomé de las Casas," 1981.

Ludwig, Armin K. *Brazil: A Handbook of Historical Statistics*. Boston: G. K. Hall, 1985.

Lynch, Nicolás. *El pensamiento social sobre la comunidad indígena en el Perú a principios del siglo XX*. Cuzco: Centro de Estudios Rurales Andinos "Bartolomé de las Casas," 1979.

McCreery, David. " 'An Odious Feudalism': *Mandamiento* Labor and Commercial Agriculture in Guatemala, 1858–1920." *Latin American Perspectives* 13, no. 1 (1986): 99–118.

Macera, Pablo. "Algodón y comercio exterior peruano en el siglo XIX." In *Trabajos de historia*, by Pablo Macera. Vol. 3, pp. 275–96. Lima: Instituto Nacional de Cultura, 1977.

McGreevy, William P. *An Economic History of Colombia, 1845–1930*. Cambridge: Cambridge University Press, 1971.

Madalengoitia, Laura. "El estado oligárquico y la transición hacia una nueva forma de

estado en el Perú." In *Burguesía y estado liberal*, by Marcial Rubio, Enrique Bernales, and Laura Madalengoitia. Pp. 275–346. Lima: DESCO, 1979.

Madgearu, Virgil. *Imperialismul Economic şi Liga Naţiunelor*. [Bucureşti]: Cultura Naţională, n. d.

Mallon, Florencia E. *The Defense of Community in Peru's Central Highlands: Peasant Struggle and Capitalist Transition, 1860–1940*. Princeton, N. J.: Princeton University Press, 1983.

———. "Peasants and State Formation in Nineteenth Century Mexico: Morelos, 1848–1958." In *Political Power and Social Theory*. Forthcoming.

———. Review of *The Poverty of Progress* by E. Bradford Burns. *The Americas* 41, no. 3 (1985): 118–20.

Manoilescu [Manoilesco], Mihail. "Curs de Economie Politică şi Raţionalizare." Bucureşti: Editura Politechnicei, 1940. Mimeo.

———. "Productividad del trabajo y comercio exterior." Translated by Edgar Mahn Hecker. *Economía* 8, nos. 22–23 (Sept. 1947): 50–77.

———. *Le siècle du corporatisme: Doctrine du corporatisme intégral et pur*. Paris: Félix Alcan, 1934.

———. "Teoria schimburilor internaţionale şi a protectionismului." Unpub. and rev. ed. of *Théorie du Protectionnisme*, by Mihail Manoilescu.[1940] Typescript.

———. *Théorie du protectionnisme et de l'échange international*. Paris: Marcel Giard, 1929.

Marchant, Anyda. *Viscount Mauá and the Empire of Brazil: A Biography of Irineu Evangelista de Sousa*. Berkeley: University of California Press, 1965.

Mariátegui, José Carlos. "Point de vue anti-imperialiste." In *Le Marxisme en Amérique Latine de 1909 à nos jours: Anthologie*, edited by Michael Lowy. Pp. 112–16. Paris: Maspero, 1980. [Originally published in 1929.]

Marx, Karl. *Capital*. Translated by Samuel Moore and Edward Aveling from 3d German ed. Vol. 1. Moscow: Foreign Languages Publishing House, 1961. [Originally published in German in 1867.]

Mathew, W. M. "The First Anglo-Peruvian Debt and its Settlement, 1822–1849." *Journal of Latin American Studies* 2 (December 1968): 562–86.

———. "The Imperialism of Free Trade: Peru, 1820–1870." *Economic History Review*, 2d ser. 21 (December 1968): 562–86.

Mayer, Enrique. "Communal and Private Control of Land in an Andean Village in the Twentieth Century." Paper presented at conference, The Apogee and Decline of Economic Liberalism in Latin America, Urbana, Illinois, April 10–11, 1987.

Melzer, John T. S. "Kingdom to Republic in Peru: The 'Consulado de Comercio' of Lima and the Independence of Peru." Ph.D. diss., Tulane University, 1978.

Memoria que la Junta Nacional de la Industria Lanar presenta por el año 1942. Lima, 1943.

Mexican Investor, 1906.

México. Comisión Monetaria. *Actas de las juntas generales y documentos a ellas anexos*. México: Oficina Impresora de Estampillas, 1904.

———. *Datos para el estudio de la cuestión monetaria en México*. México: Oficina Impresora de Estampillas, 1903.

México. Secretaria de Fomento. *Anuario estadístico de la República Mexicana, 1906*. Mexico: Oficina Tip. de la Secretaría de Fomento, 1907.

——— *Cuadro sinóptico y estadístico de la República Mexicana, año de 1900.* México: Secretaría de Formento, 1901.

Mexico. Secretaría de Hacienda y Crédito Público. *La hacienda através los informes presidenciales a partir de la independencia hasta 1950.* México, 1951.

——— *Memoria, 1909–1910.* Vol. I. México.

———. *Memoria de hacienda y crédito público . . . de 1 de julio de 1899 a 30 de junio de 1900.* Mexico: Oficina Impr. de Estampillas, 1903.

Miceli, Keith L. "Rafael Carrera: Defender and Promoter of Peasant Interests in Guatemala." *The Americas* 31, no. 1 (1974): 72–95.

Miller, Rory. "The Coastal Elite and Peruvian Politics, 1895–1919." *Journal of Latin American Studies* 14, no. 1 (May 1982): 97–120.

Miroshevski, V. M. "El 'populismo' en el Perú: Papel de Mariátegui en la historia del pensamiento social latinoamericano." In *Mariátegui y los orígenes del marxismo latinoamericano*, edited by José Aricó. Pp. 55–70. México: Pasado y Presente, 1980. [Originally published in Russian in 1941.]

Molina, Gerardo. *Las ideas liberales en Colombia, 1849–1914.* 2nd ed. Bogotá: Tercer Mundo, 1971.

[Molina, Wenceslao.] *Discurso académico de apertura del año universitario de 1902 pronunciado por el Dr. Wenceslao Molina, catedrático de zootécnica de la Facultad de Ciencias.* Lima: San Pedro, 1902.

Molina Enríquez, Andrés. *Los grandes problemas nacionales.* México: Carranza, 1909.

More, Federico. *Zoocracia y canibalismo.* Lima: La Llamarada, 1933.

Mörner, Magnus. "The Extent and Limitation of Change: Cuzco, Peru, 1895–1920." MS, Göteborgs Universitet, 1987.

———. "Latin American 'Landlords' and 'Peasants' and the Outer World During the National Period." In *Land and Labour in Latin America: Essays on the Development of Agrarian Capitalism in the Nineteenth and Twentieth Centuries* edited by Kenneth Duncan and Ian Rutledge. Pp. 455–82. Cambridge: Cambridge University Press, 1977.

———. *Notas sobre el comercio y los comerciantes del Cusco desde fines de la colonia hasta 1930.* Lima: IEP, 1979.

Mouzelis, Nicos. *Politics in the Semi-Periphery: Early Parliamentarism and Late Industrialization in the Balkans and Latin America.* London: Macmillan, 1986.

Nacional Financiera. *Statistics on the Mexican Economy.* México, 1956.

Navarrete R., Alfredo. "The Financing of Economic Development." In *Mexico's Recent Economic Growth: The Mexican View*, by Enrique Pérez López, et al. Pp. 105–30. Translated by Marjory Urquidi. Austin: University of Texas Press, 1967.

Nery, M. F. J. de Santa-Anna. *Le Brésil en 1889.* Paris: Charles Delagrave, 1889.

Nolan, Louis Clinton. "The Diplomatic and Commerical Relations of the United States and Peru, 1826–1875." Ph.D. diss., Duke University, 1935.

Norbeta Casanova, Juan. *Ensayo económico-político sobre el porvenir de la industria algodonera fabril del Perú.* Lima: José Masías, 1849.

North, Douglass C., and Robert P. Thomas. *The Rise of the Western World: A New Economic History.* Cambridge: Cambridge University Press, 1976.

Nueva Granada. Ministerio de Hacienda y Crédito Público. *Informe 1833.* Bogotá, 1833.

Ohlin, Bertil. "Protection and Non-competing Groups." *Weltwirtschaftliches Archiv* 33 (1931) 1: 33–45.

Olivera, Eduardo. *Miscelánea: Escritos económicos, administrativos, ecónomorurales, agrícolas, ganaderas, exposiciones, discursos inaugurales y parlamentarios, viajes, correspondencia, historia y legislación*. Buenos Aires: Sudamericana de Billetes de Banco, 1910.

Orlove, Benjamin. *Alpacas, Sheep and Men*. New York: Academic Press, 1977.

Ospina Vásquez, Luis. *Industria y protección en Colombia, 1810–1930*. Medellín: Santa Fé, 1955.

Page, Barbara Butler. "Legitimacy and Revolution: The Cases of Mexico and Brazil." Ph.D. diss. University of California, Los Angeles, 1973.

Palacios Moreyra, Carlos. *La deuda anglo-peruana, 1822–1890*. Lima: Studium, 1983.

Palma, José Gabriel. "Growth and Structure of Chilean Manufacturing Industry from 1830 to 1935: Origins and Development of a Process of Industrialization in an Export Economy." D.Phil. thesis, University of Oxford, 1979.

Pan American Union. *Bulletin*. 1905. Washington, D.C.

Paris, Robert. *La formación ideológica de José Carlos Mariátegui*. Translated by Oscar Terán. México: Siglo XXI, 1981.

Park, James William. *Rafael Núñez and the Politics of Colombian Regionalism, 1863–1886*. Baton Rouge: Louisiana State University Press, 1985.

Patria: El florecimiento de México. April 2, 1906. México: Bouligny & Schmidt, 1906.

Paz-Soldán, Mateo. *Geografía del Perú*. 2 vols. Paris: Fermin Didot, 1862–63.

Peralta Vásquez, Antero. *La faz oculta de Arequipa*. Arequipa: Coop. Ed. Universitaria, 1977.

Phelps, D. M. "Industrial Expansion in Temperate South America." *American Economic Review* 25 (1935): 273–81.

Piel, Jean. "The Place of the Peasantry in the National Life of Peru in the Nineteenth Century." *Past and Present* 46 (Feb. 1970): 108–33.

Pike, Fredrick B. *The Modern History of Peru*. New York: Praeger, 1967.

Platt, D. C. M. "The Imperialism of Free Trade: Some Reservations." *Economic History Review*, 2d ser. 21 (Aug. 1968): 296–306.

———. *Latin America and British Trade, 1806–1914*. New York: Harper and Row, 1973.

———, ed. *Business Imperialism, 1840–1930: An Inquiry Based on British Experience in Latin America*. Oxford: Clarendon Press, 1977.

Polanyi, Karl. *The Great Transformation*. Boston: Beacon Press, 1957.

Polar, Jorge. *Arequipa: Descripción y estudio social*. 2d ed. Arequipa: Rojas y Franco, 1922. [Originally published in 1891.]

Ponce, Fernando Agustín. "The Social Structure of Arequipa, 1840–1879." Ph.D. diss. University of Texas at Austin, 1980.

Portocarrero, Gonzalo. *Ideologías, funciones del estado y políticas económicas: Perú, 1900–1980*. Lima: Pontificia Universidad Católica del Perú, Programa Académico de Ciencias Sociales, 1982.

Prado, Caio, Jr. *História econômica do Brasil*. 5th ed. São Paulo: Brasiliense, 1959.

———. "O Programa da Aliança Nacional Libertadora." *Nova Escrita/Ensaio* 4, no. 10 [1983?]: 121–36. [Originally published in 1935.]

Prebisch, Raúl. See under United Nations.

Presidente da la República [de Chile, Pedro Aguirre Cerda]. *Mensaje . . . en la apertura de las sesiones ordinarias del Congreso Nacional: 21 de mayo de 1940*. Santiago: Imprenta Nacional, [1940].

Los Programas del conservatismo. Bogotá: Directorio Nacional de Unidad Conservadora, 1967.

Pupo Nogueira, Otávio. *Em torno da tarifa aduaneira*. São Paulo, 1931.

Quiroga, Manuel A. *La evolución jurídica de la propiedad rural en Puno*. Thesis, Universidad de Arequipa. Arequipa: Quiróz Perea, 1915.

Quiroz Norris, Alfonso W. "La consolidación de la deuda interna peruana, 1850–58: los efectos sociales de una medida financiera estatal." Tesis de Bachiller, Pontificia Universidad Católica del Perú, 1980.

Racovski, C[ristian]. "Chestia agrară: Probleme şi soluţii," *Viitorul Social*, no. 1 (Aug. 1907): 27–43.

———. *La Roumanie des Boyards (Contribution a l'histoire d'une oligarchie)*. Bucureşti: Cercul de Editura Socialistă, 1909.

Randall, Laura. *A Comparative Economic History of Latin America, 1500–1914*. 4 vols. Ann Arbor, Mich.: University Microfilms International, 1977.

Ratzer, José. *Los Marxistas del 90*. Córdoba: Pasado y Presente, 1969.

———. *El movimiento socialista en Argentina*. Buenos Aires: Agora, 1981.

Rector, John L. "Merchants, Trade and Commercial Policy in Chile, 1810–1840." Ph.D. diss., Indiana University, 1976.

Reinhardt, Nola. "The Consolidation of the Import-Export Economy in Nineteenth Century Colombia: A Political-Economic Analysis." *Latin American Perspectives* 13, no. 1 (1986): 75–98.

Relaciones de mando de los virreyes de la Nueva Granada: Memorias económicas. Edited by Gabriel Giraldo Jaramillo. Bogotá: Banco de la República, 1954.

Restrepo, José Manuel, *Diario político y militar*. 4 vols. Bogotá: Imprenta Nacional, 1954.

Revilla, Julio. "Industrialización temprana y lucha ideológica en el Perú, 1890–1910," *Estudios Andinos* 17/18 (1981): 3–40.

Rey de Castro, Carlos. *Antagonismos económicos: Protección y librecambio; tratado de comercio entre el Perú y el Brasil*. Barcelona: Vda. de Luis Tasso, 1913.

Ricardo, David. *On the Principles of Political Economy and Taxation*. In *The Works and Correspondence of David Ricardo*, edited by Piero Sraffa. Cambridge: Cambridge University Press, 1962. [Originally published in 1817.]

Rivas, Medardo. *Los trabajadores de tierra caliente*. Bogotá: Ministerio de Educación de Colombia, 1946.

Rivero, Francisco de. *Memoria o sean apuntamientos sobre la industria agrícola del Perú y sobre algunos medios que pudieran adoptarse para remediar su decadencia*. Lima: Monterola, 1845.

Robinson, Ronald. "Non-European Foundations of European Imperialism: Sketch for a Theory of Collaboration." In *Studies in the Theory of Imperialism*, edited by Roger Owen and Bob Sutcliffe. Pp. 117–43. London: Longman, 1972.

Roca, J. Gerardo. *Estudio económico de la Provincia del Cuzco*. Thesis, Universidad del Cuzco. Cuzco: "El Comercio," 1921.

Rodríguez, Gustavo Humberto. *Ezequiel Rojas y la primera república liberal*. Bogotá: Universidad Externado de Colombia, 1984.

Rodríguez O., Jaime E. *Down from Colonialism*. Los Angeles: UCLA Chicano Studies Research Center, 1983.

Romero, Emilio. *Historia económica del Perú*. Buenos Aires: Ed. Sudamericano, 1949.

Romero, Emilio, and César Levano. *Regionalismo y centralismo: Presencia y proyección de los 7 ensayos*. Lima: Amauta, 1969.

Romero, José Luis. *El desarrollo de las ideas en la sociedad argentina del siglo XX*. 2d ed. Buenos Aires: Solar, 1983.

———. *El pensamiento político de la derecha latinoamericana*. Buenos Aires: Paidos, 1970.

Romero, Luis Alberto. *La Sociedad de la Igualdad: los artesanos de Santiago de Chile y sus primeras experiencias políticas*. Buenos Aires: Instituto Torcuato DiTella, 1978.

———. "La Sociedad de la Igualdad: liberales y artesanos en la vida política de Santiago de Chile." *Siglo XIX: Revista de Historia*, 2, no. 3 (1987): 15–36.

Sáenz Leme, Marisa. *A ideologia dos industriais brasileiros (1919–1945)*. Petrópolis [Brazil]: Vozes, 1978.

Safford, Frank Robinson. "Commerce and Enterprise in Central Colombia, 1821–1870." Ph.D. diss. Columbia University, 1965.

———. "Politics, Ideology and Society in Post-Independence Spanish America." In *The Cambridge History of Latin America*, edited by Leslie Bethell. Vol. 3, pp. 347–421. Cambridge: Cambridge University Press, 1985.

Samper, Miguel. *Escritos político-económicos*. 4 vols. Bogotá: Cromos, 1925–27.

San Juan Victoria, Carlos, and Salvador Velázques Ramírez. "El estado y las políticas económicas en el Porfiriato." Edited by Ciro Cardoso. Pp. 65–96. In *México en el siglo XIX: historia económica y de la estructura social*, México: Nueva Imagen, 1980.

Sarmiento, Domingo Faustino. *Epistolario entre Sarmiento y Posse, 1845–1888*. 2 vols. Buenos Aires: Museo Histórico Sarmiento, 1946–47.

———. *Facundo: Civilización y barbarie*. Edited by Alberto Palcos. Buenos Aires: 1961. [Originally published in 1845.]

———. *Obras completas*. 55 vols. Buenos Aires: Luz del Día, 1948–56.

Schwartz, Roberto. "As ideias fora do lugar." *Estudos CEBRAP*, no. 3 (1973).

Semmel, Bernard. *The Rise of Free Trade Imperialism: Classical Political Economy and the Empire of Free Trade and Imperialism, 1750–1850*. Cambridge: Cambridge University Press, 1970.

Servín G., Armando. "Nuestra política tributaria de 1869 a 1911." *El Trimestre Económico* 7 (1940):425–62.

Siciliano, Alexandre, Jr. *Agricultura, comércio e indústria no Brasil (em face do regime aduaneiro)*. São Paulo: Centro das Indústrias do Estado de São Paulo, 1931.

Simonsen, Roberto. *Crises, Finances and Industry*. São Paulo: São Paulo Editora, n.d.

Simonsen, Roberto, and Eugênio Gudin. *A controvérsia do planejamento na economia brasileira*. Rio de Janeiro: IPEA/INPES, 1977.

Sinkin, Richard. *The Mexican Reform, 1855–1876: A Study in Liberal Nation-Building*. Austin: University of Texas Press, 1979.

Skidmore, Thomas E., and Peter H. Smith. *Modern Latin America*. New York: Oxford University Press, 1984.

Skopcol, Theda, Peter B. Evans, and Dietrich Rueschemeyer, eds. *Bringing the State Back In*. Cambridge: Cambridge University Press, 1985.

Slatta, Richard W. *Gauchos and the Vanishing Frontier*. Lincoln: University of Nebraska Press, 1983.

Smith, Adam. *An Inquiry into the Nature and Causes of the Wealth of Nations*. 2d ed. [sic] Oxford: Clarendon Press, 1880.

Smith, Peter H. *Politics and Beef in Argentina, Patterns of Conflict and Change*. New York: Columbia University Press, 1969.

Sociedad Ganadera del Departamento de Puno. *Memorial presentado al Supremo Gobierno*. Arequipa: Córdova, 1921.

Spiegel, Henry William. *The Growth of Economic Thought*. Durham, N. C.: Duke University Press, 1983.

Stein, Stanley J. *Vassouras: A Brazilian Coffee County, 1850–1900*. Cambridge, Mass.: Harvard University Press, 1957.

Stein, Stanley J., and Barbara H. Stein. *The Colonial Heritage of Latin America: Essays on Economic Dependence in Perspective*. New York: Oxford University Press, 1970.

Stere, C[onstantin]. "Socialdemocratism sau poporanism?" *Viaţa românească*, anul 2, no. 8 (Aug. 1907): 170–193, no. 9 (Sept.): 313–41, no. 10 (Oct.): 15–48 [sic], no. 11 (Nov.): 173–208; and anul 3, no. 1 (Jan. 1908): 49–75, no. 4 (Apr.): 59–80.

Stern, Steve J. "Feudalism, Capitalism and the World-System in the Perspective of Latin America and the Caribbean." *American Historical Review*. Forthcoming.

Szlajfer, Henryk. "Against Dependent Capitalist Development in Nineteenth-Century Latin America: The Case of Haiti and Paraguay." *Latin American Perspectives* 13, no. 1 (1986): 45–74.

Tamayo Herrera, José. *Historia del indigenismo cuzqueño, siglos XVI–XX*. Lima: Instituto Nacional de Cultura, 1980.

Tamayo Herrera, José. *Historia social del Cusco republicano*. 2d ed. Lima: Universo, 1981.

Tantaleán Arbulu, Javier. *Política económico-financiera y la formación del estado: siglo XIX*. Lima: CEDEP, 1983.

Taylor, Arthur J. *Laissez-faire and State Intervention in Nineteenth-Century Britain*. London: Macmillan, 1972.

Taylor, George Rogers. *The Transportation Revolution*. New York: Holt, Rinehart and Winston, 1951.

Temperley, Harold. *The Foreign Policy of Canning, 1822–27: The Neo-Holy Alliance and the New World*. 2d ed. London: Archon Books, 1966.

Tenenbaum, Barbara. "Planning for Mexican Industrial Development: The Liberal Nation State, Tariff Policy, and Nationalism, 1867–1910." Paper presented at American Historical Association meeting, San Francisco, December 28, 1983.

———. *The Politics of Penury, Debts and Taxes in Mexico, 1821–1856*. Albuquerque: University of New Mexico Press, 1986.

Thery, Edmond. *La situation économique et financière de la Roumanie*. Paris: Economiste Européen, 1904.

Thorp, Rosemary. "Latin America and the International Economy from the First World War to the World Depression." In *Cambridge History of Latin America*, edited by Leslie Bethell. Vol. 4, pp. 57–81. Cambridge: Cambridge University Press, 1986.

———, ed. *Latin America in the 1930's: The Role of the Periphery in the World Crisis*. London: Macmillan, 1984.

Thorp, Rosemary, and Geoffrey Bertram. *Peru 1890–1977: Growth and Policy in an Open Economy*. New York: Columbia University Press, 1978.

Topik, Steven. "The Domination of Capitals: Mexico City and Rio de Janeiro, 1888–1911." In *Proceedings of the Seventh Congress of Mexican and North American Historians*, edited by Eric Van Young. México: UNAM, forthcoming.

———. *The Political Economy of the Brazilian State, 1889–1930*. Austin: University of Texas Press, 1987.

———. "State and Economy: Brazil under the Empire and Republic." Office for Public Sector Studies. Institute of Latin American Studies, Technical Papers Series no. 47. Austin: University of Texas, 1985.

———. "State Interventionism in a Liberal Regime: Brazil, 1889–1930." *Hispanic American Historical Review* 60, no. 4 (Nov. 1980): 593–616.

Tristán, Flora. *Peregrinaciones de un paria*. Translated by Emilia Romero. Lima: Cultura Antártica, 1946. [Originally published in 1836].

Turner, John Kenneth. *Barbarous Mexico*. Austin: University of Texas Press, 1969. [Originally published in 1911.]

United Nations: Economic Commission for Latin America. *The Economic Development of Latin America and Its Principal Problems*. Lake Success, N.Y.: United Nations, 1950. [Originally published in Spanish in 1949.]

U.S. Department of Commerce. *Historical Statistics of the United States: Colonial Times to 1957*. Washington, D.C.: Government Printing Office, 1961.

U.S. Federal Trade Commission. *Report on Trade and Tariffs in Brazil, Uruguay, Argentina, Chile, Bolivia and Peru*. Washington, D.C.: Government Printing Office, 1916.

Urquiaga, José Sebastián. *Sublevaciones de indígenas en el departamento de Puno*. Arequipa: Franklin, 1916.

Urrutia, Miguel. "El sector externo y la distribución de ingresos en Colombia en el siglo XIX." *Revista del Banco de la República* 541 (November 1972): 1974–87.

Valcárcel, Luis. "La cuestión agraria en el Cuzco." *Revista Universitaria* [Cuzco] 3, no. 9 (1914): 16–38.

———. *Memorias*. Edited by José Matos Mar, José Deustua, and José Luis Rénique. Lima: IEP, 1981.

Vargas, Getúlio. *A nova política do Brasil*. Vol. 1. Rio de Janeiro: José Olympio, 1938.

Vargas, Pedro Fermín de. *Pensamientos políticos y memorias sobre la población del Nuevo Reino de Granada*. Bogotá: Banco de la República, 1953.

Vaughn, Mary Kay. *Estado, clases sociales y educacion en México*. Vol 1. México: SEP/Fondo de Cultura Económica, 1982.

Véliz, Claudio. *The Centralist Tradition in Latin America*. Princeton, N. J.: Princeton University Press, 1980.

Venturi, Franco. *Roots of Revolution: A History of Populism and Socialist Movements in Nineteenth Century Russia*. Translated by Francis Haskell. New York: Knopf, 1960.

Vernon, Raymond, ed. *Public Policy and Private Enterprise in Mexico*. Cambridge, Mass.: Harvard University Press, 1964.

Vieira, Evaldo. *Autoritarismo e corporativismo no Brasil (Oliveira Vianna e Companhia)*. 2d ed. São Paulo: Cortez, 1981.

Villanueva, Javier. "Economic Development." In *Prologue to Perón: Argentina in*

Depression and War 1930–1943, edited by Mark Falcoff and Ronald H. Dolkhart. Pp. 57–82.Berkeley: University of California Press, 1975.

Villareal, René. *El desequilibrio externo en la industrialización de México (1929–1975): Un enfoque estructuralista.* México: Fondo de Cultura Económica, 1976.

Villela, Annibal, and Wilson Suzigan. *Política do governo e crescimento da economia brasileira, 1889–1930.* Rio de Janeiro: IPEA/INPES, 1973.

Villena, Francisco. "La sociedad arequipeña y el Partido Liberal, 1885–1920." *Análisis* 8–9 (May-Dec. 1979): 82–108.

Villers, M. G. *La hacienda pública de los estados.* 2 vols. México: Oficina Impr. de Estampillas, 1903.

Viner, Jacob. *International Trade and Economic Development.* Glencoe, Ill.: Free Press, 1952. [A series of lectures delivered in Rio de Janeiro in 1950.]

————. Review of *Théorie du protectionnisme et de l'échange international*, by Mihail Manoilescu. *Journal of Political Economy* 40 (1932): 121–25.

Walicki, A[ndrzej] *The Controversy over Capitalism: Studies in the Social Philosophy of the Russian Populists.* Oxford: Clarendon Press, 1969.

Wasserman, Mark. *Capitalists, Caciques, and Revolution.* Chapel Hill: University of North Carolina Press, 1984.

Weaver, Frederick S. *Class, State and Industrial Structure: The Historical Process of South American Industrial Growth.* Westport, Conn.: Greenwood Press, 1980.

Weinstein, Barbara. *The Amazon Rubber Boom, 1850–1920.* Stanford: Stanford University Press, 1983.

Wells, Allen. *Yucatan's Golden Age: Haciendas, Henequen and International Harvester.* Albuquerque,: University of New Mexico Press, 1985.

Whigham, Thomas L. "The Iron Works of Ibycui: Paraguayan Industrial Development in the Mid-Nineteenth Century." *The Americas* 35, no. 2 (1978): 201–18.

White, Richard Alan. *Paraguay's Autonomous Revolution, 1810–1840.* Albuquerque: University of New Mexico Press, 1978.

Wibel, John Frederick. "The Evolution of a Regional Community within the Spanish Empire and Peruvian Nation: Arequipa, 1780–1845." Ph.D. diss., Stanford University, 1975.

Wileman, J. F., ed. *The Brazilian Yearbook, 1909.* Rio de Janeiro: Brazilian Yearbook, 1909.

Williams, John Hoyt. "Foreign Técnicos and the Modernization of Paraguay, 1840–1870." *Journal of Interamerican Studies and World Affairs* 19, no. 2 (1977): 233–57.

————. "Paraguay's Nineteenth Century Estancias de la República." *Agricultural History* 47, no. 3 (1973): 206–16.

Wills, Guillermo. *Observaciones sobre el comercio de la Nueva Granada, con un apéndice relativo al de Bogotá.* Bogotá: Banco de la República, 1952. [Originally published in 1831.]

Wright, Marie Robinson. *The Old and the New Peru. A Story of the Ancient Inheritance and the Modern Growth and Enterprise of a Great Nation.* Philadelphia: George Barric & Sons, 1908.

Yepes del Castillo, Ernesto. "Los inicios de la expansión mercantil capitalista en el Perú (1890–1930)." In *Historia del Perú*, edited by Juan Mejía Baca. Vol. 7, pp. 305–403. Lima: Mejía Baca, 1980.

————. *Perú 1820–1920: Un siglo de desarrollo capitalista*. Lima: IEP-Campodónico, 1972.

Zea, Leopoldo. *The Latin-American Mind*. Translated by James H. Abbott and Lowell Dunham. Norman: University of Oklahoma Press, 1963.

Zeitlin, Maurice. *The Civil Wars in Chile (or the Bourgeois Revolutions That Never Were)*. Princeton, N.J.: Princeton University Press, 1984.

Zeletin, Ştefan [pseud. for Ştefan Motas]. *Burghezia română: Origina şi rolul ei istoric*. Bucureşti: Cultura Naţională, 1925.

INDEX

administrative overhead: in Mexico and Brazil, 131–32

agrarian conflict in Argentina, 115

agricultural technology, 6

agriculture: expanding in Argentine pampas, 106–107

agriculture and manufacturing: reciprocal relations, 49

Alamán, Lucas, 10

Alberdi, Juan Batista, 99

alcabala, 43

Amaral, Azevedo, 25

Añales de la Sociedad Rural Argentina, 110

Anderson, Perry, 20

Andrada e Silva, José Bonifácio, 10

arbitristas, 38

Arequipa: immigrant merchants important in, 150; importance of, 149–50, 152; industrialization in, 150–51; liberalism in, 76; liberals calling for industrial protection, 156; population growth in, 163; as regional liberal center, 78

Argentina: absence of local peasantry in pampas, 103; agricultural expansion in pampas, 106–107; army as penal institution, 110–11; army recruitment problems, 110, 111; British cotton imports to, 104; collective negotiations for tenancy contracts, 114; colonial past influencing, 99–100; conflict in Chivilcoy, 107, 108–109; conscription of rural population, 111, 112; diverging from Spanish American norm, 100–102; economic growth in, 3; economic liberalism preventing egalitarian agrarian order, 183–84; economy expanded by exports, 2–3; effect of stock-raising on economy, 105; export economy in, 106; export reduction following Great Depression, 7; free market liberalism in, 181; *Grundherrschaft* rural society in, 5; increasing dependency on immigrant labor, 113–14; industrialization increasing in, 7; isolation of interior provinces, 103–104; Italian tenant farmers in, 4; labor and tenancy systems in wheat regions, 4; latifundium

ABOUT THE EDITORS AND CONTRIBUTORS

JOSEPH L. LOVE is Professor of History at the University of Illinois, Urbana-Champaign. He is the author of *Rio Grande do Sul and Brazilian Regionalism* and *São Paulo in the Brazilian Federation*. His current project concerns the economic ideas and ideologies in Latin America and Romania in this century.

NILS JACOBSEN is Assistant Professor of History at the University of Illinois, Urbana-Champaign, and has previously taught at the Universität Bielefeld in West Germany. He edited (together with Hans-Jürgen Puhle) *The Economies of Mexico and Peru During the Late Colonial Period, 1760–1810* and is currently completing a regional study on the Peruvian Altiplano between 1770 and 1930.

PAUL E. GOOTENBERG is Assistant Professor of History at Brandeis University in Waltham, Massachusetts. His study *Between Silver and Guano: Protectionist Elites to a Liberal State in Peru, 1820–1850* will be published shortly by Princeton University Press. Presently he is engaged in a comparative study of trade policies and state formation in a number of Latin American countries during the mid-nineteenth century.

TULIO HALPERÍN DONGHI is Professor of History at the University of California at Berkeley. Author of the classic *Historia contemporánea de América Latina*, he has written many books on nineteenth- and twentieth-century Argentina.

FLORENCIA E. MALLON is Associate Professor of History at the University of Wisconsin, Madison. She is the author of *The Defense of Community in Peru's Central Highlands: Peasant Struggle and Capitalist Transition, 1860–1940* and is presently studying peasant movements in Mexico during the 1860s.

FRANK R. SAFFORD is Professor and Chairman of the Department of History at Northwestern University in Evanston, Illinois. He is the author of *The Ideal of The Practical* and other studies on society and politics in Colombia and Latin America in general during the nineteenth century. His history of Colombia, authored jointly with Marco Palacios for the Oxford Latin American National Histories series, will appear shortly.

STEVEN C. TOPIK is Associate Professor of History at the University of California at Irvine. His book *The Political Economy of the Brazilian State, 1889–1930* appeared in 1987. He is now engaged in a study comparing the economic role of the state in Mexico and Brazil during the early twentieth century.